Better Homes and Gardens

ENCYCLOPEDIA
of
COOKING

Volume 15

Entice both family and guests with flavorful Veal Scallopine
served over hot, buttered noodles. Garnish with a generous
sprinkling of snipped parsley, if desired.

On the cover: Elegant is the word for this light Turkey
Soufflé. A creamy, subtly seasoned dill-mushroom sauce complements the soufflé's delicate turkey flavor.

BETTER HOMES AND GARDENS BOOKS®
NEW YORK • DES MOINES

©Meredith Corporation, 1971. All Rights Reserved.
Printed in the United States of America.
First Printing.
Library of Congress Catalog Card Number: 73-129265
SBN 696-02015-7

SCALLOPINE, SCALLOPINI (*skä' luh pē' nē, skal' uh*)

—An Italian dish that contains thin, boneless pieces of meat, most commonly veal, called scallopine. The thin veal pieces sometimes are pounded even thinner before they are browned and cooked in a sauce, usually containing wine or tomatoes. In the United States, veal steaks or cutlets are used in recipes calling for the scallopine cut.

Veal Scallopine

Elegant enough for company—

>   1 tablespoon all-purpose flour
> $\frac{1}{2}$ teaspoon salt
>   Dash pepper
>   4 veal cutlets (about 1 pound)
> $\frac{1}{4}$ cup salad oil
> $\frac{1}{2}$ medium onion, thinly sliced
>   1 16-ounce can tomatoes, cut up
>   1 3-ounce can sliced mushrooms, undrained
>   1 tablespoon snipped parsley
>   1 tablespoon capers, drained
> $\frac{1}{4}$ teaspoon garlic salt
> $\frac{1}{4}$ teaspoon dried oregano leaves, crushed
>
>   • • •
>
>   6 cups water
> $1\frac{1}{2}$ teaspoons salt
>   1 teaspoon salad oil
>   4 ounces noodles
>   1 tablespoon butter or margarine

In shallow bowl combine all-purpose flour, $\frac{1}{2}$ teaspoon salt, and pepper; coat veal cutlets lightly with flour mixture. In medium skillet brown veal slowly in $\frac{1}{4}$ cup hot oil. Remove meat from skillet. Add sliced onion to skillet; cook till tender but not brown.

Add cooked veal cutlets, cut-up tomatoes, sliced mushrooms with liquid, snipped parsley, drained capers, garlic salt, and crushed oregano to skillet. Cover and simmer till veal is tender, about 20 to 25 minutes.

To cook noodles, combine water, $1\frac{1}{2}$ teaspoons salt, and 1 teaspoon salad oil in large saucepan; bring to vigorous boil. Add noodles; cook till tender, but still firm. Drain. Add butter; toss together. Arrange veal on hot buttered noodles; top with sauce. Serves 4.

Veal Scallopine with Wine

> $1\frac{1}{2}$ pounds veal cutlets, cut $\frac{1}{4}$ inch thick
> $\frac{1}{3}$ cup all-purpose flour
> $\frac{1}{4}$ cup butter or margarine
>   1 tablespoon lemon juice
>   1 chicken bouillon cube
> $\frac{1}{4}$ cup dry white wine
>   1 3-ounce can sliced mushrooms, drained
>   2 tablespoons sliced ripe olives
>   2 tablespoons snipped parsley

Coat veal cutlets with flour. In large skillet, brown cutlets in hot butter or margarine, a few at a time. Place all browned cutlets in skillet. Add $\frac{1}{2}$ cup water, lemon juice, chicken bouillon cube, and $\frac{1}{8}$ teaspoon pepper. Simmer, covered, till tender, about 30 minutes. Remove cutlets to warm platter. Add dry white wine, drained mushrooms, sliced ripe olives, and snipped parsley to skillet. Heat just to boiling. Pour sauce over cutlets. Serves 6.

SCAMORZE (*ska môrd' dzē*)

—A fairly mild, yellowish white, Italian fresh cheese originally made of buffalo's milk but now often made of cow's or goat's milk. Scamorze is similar in flavor and appearance to another Italian cheese Mozzarella.

The manufacture of scamorze involves one unusual step—stretching the cheese until it is elastic. Afterward, it is molded into an oval the size of a large lemon, soaked in brine, and finally air dried.

In Italy, scamorze is particularly popular when toasted or fried and served with toast or fried eggs. (See also *Cheese.*)

SCAMPI (*skam' pē*)

—The Italian name of a shellfish of the Adriatic sea that is closely related to shrimp and prawns. The name is often mistakenly used to refer to any large variety of shrimp. It is also misused in the name of various shrimp dishes. On restaurant menus, although the listing "shrimp scampi" is redundant, it is understood to mean shrimp cooked in the Italian-style for scampi, that is, by broiling the whole shrimp including the tail and serving it with a sauce containing garlic and frequently olive oil.

SCANDINAVIAN COOKERY

A look at the foods and food preparation of Denmark, Sweden, Norway, and Finland.

The great peninsula that extends from above the Arctic Circle to the North and Baltic seas encompasses three of the four countries that make up Scandinavia—Sweden, Finland, and Norway. The fourth country—Denmark—juts out from the European continent. Geography accounts for both similarities and differences in the basic foods of the four countries. For example, all of these countries have extensive seacoasts, and, as would be expected, fish and shellfish play an important part in the diet. However, mountainous Norway has little land available for growing food, while Sweden and Denmark have a long history of agricultural abundance. Finland, a land of lakes and forests, has a plentiful supply of game and wild foods, but little agricultural production.

The Scandinavians always have used a lot of seafood, particularly herring, which is still one of the most common dishes. Foods from the forests are also popular. This pattern has existed from the time of the Vikings, those hardy warlike people who roamed Scandinavia from the eighth to the tenth century. They gathered berries and nuts and hunted for elk and deer in the forests, and fished for herring, oysters, and mussels in the sea and inland fjords and lakes. Besides relying to a great extent on hunting and fishing for food,

Scandinavian fare

‹—A Decorated Ham, Stuffed Celery, Quick Swedish Meatballs, and Swedish Brown Beans are part of a Swedish smorgasbord.

the Vikings also raised chickens and geese and, at least to some extent, cultivated vegetables such as onions and cabbage.

From the Viking period through the successive years that resulted in the gradual development of four independent countries, all of Scandinavia was at some time a part of Sweden. The result is a thread of similarity that runs through the basic cuisine of the Scandinavian countries. This is particularly noticeable when you compare the foods of Denmark, Sweden, and Norway. Although the Swedish influence on the food pattern of Finland is still evident, it is somewhat overshadowed by the strong Russian influence that resulted from Finland's role as part of the Russian Empire for about 100 years—from the early 1800s to 1917.

Fish

Since all the Scandinavian countries have seacoast as part of their border, quite naturally the Scandinavians make use of the fish and seafood easily available. Fish is especially important in Norway and Finland, where little land is available for agricultural production. In fact, fish of one type or another is often eaten as many as six times a week. Because of this, you might assume that the Norwegians and Finns have a large collection of special fish recipes. But, this is not the case, since Norwegian and Finnish cooks generally use simple preparation methods such as grilling, steaming, and poaching.

This lack of fish recipes does not reflect on the imaginativeness of the natives at all. Rather it is proof that these people are

convinced that the best flavor fish can have is a fresh flavor. Since many kinds of fish are continually available, this fresh flavor is easily captured by serving fish that were caught only a few hours earlier.

The two fish that rank highest in importance in the Scandinavian countries are cod and herring. Even though these two fish have been abundant in Scandinavian waters for centuries, they never would have become a staple food and important export if the Scandinavians hadn't learned long ago how to preserve them.

Although some cod and herring are dried, pickled, or preserved in some other way, salting is the processing method most commonly used. When salting was first used, it was the only way the Scandinavians had of preserving their large catches. In fact, salted cod and herring kept so well that they could be shipped throughout Europe. They also became popular as food for lengthy journeys, particularly sea voyages. Today, however, more modern methods of preservation such as canning and freezing make salting no longer necessary as a preservative. Even so, the taste of salted fish is so appealing that thousands of salted cod and herring are produced each year for consumption in the Scandinavian countries as well as for shipment all over the world. In fact, almost all large United States supermarkets carry a selection of preserved fish products that are imported from the Scandinavian countries.

Besides salting, the Scandinavians have several distinctive ways of preserving and serving fish. For example, today's Norwegians retain an unusual fish dish from their ancestors, *lutefisk*. Codfish is soaked in a lye solution until it becomes a rather soft, somewhat jellylike mass. This is sometimes made at home, but more often bought ready to cook.

As with some dishes in the cuisine of almost any country, *lutefisk* is best-liked by people who acquired a taste for it during childhood and it is slow to gain favor with others. A second noteworthy Norwegian fish dish is fish pudding. This combination of fish, bread crumbs, and a thick sauce is served in most Norwegian homes about once a week.

Both the Swedes and the Norwegians continue to use age-old recipes to make fermented fish. The Swedes use herring to make their *surstromming*, while the Norwegians ferment trout. Although their preparation methods differ, both *surstromming* and fermented trout are potent concoctions that share with *lutefisk* the distinction of seeming peculiar to the majority of non-Scandinavians.

Lutefisk Special

Cook 8 small peeled potatoes in boiling, salted water till tender, about 25 to 35 minutes. Meanwhile, in saucepan bring 2 cups water and 1 teaspoon salt to boiling. Add 1 pound lutefisk, cut in serving-sized pieces. Cover and simmer till fish is tender, 15 minutes.

Melt 3 tablespoons butter or margarine in saucepan. Blend in 2 tablespoons all-purpose flour, ½ teaspoon salt, and ½ teaspoon dry mustard. Add 1¼ cups milk. Cook quickly, stirring constantly, till thickened and bubbly. Melt ½ cup butter or margarine. Serve mustard sauce over potatoes and melted butter or margarine with lutefisk. Makes 4 servings.

Horseradish-Sauced Steamed Fish

Use 1 pound fresh or frozen fish fillets or steaks, or one 3-pound dressed fish. Thaw frozen fish. Bring 2 cups water to boiling in 10-inch skillet or fish poacher with tight-fitting cover. Sprinkle fish with 1 teaspoon salt. Place fish on a greased rack in pan so that fish does not touch water. Cover pan tightly and steam till fish flakes easily when tested with a fork—fillets, 3 to 4 minutes; steaks, 6 to 8 minutes; dressed, 20 to 25 minutes. Carefully remove fish. Serve with chilled Horseradish Sauce.

Horseradish Sauce: In small mixing bowl combine 1 cup dairy sour cream, 3 tablespoons drained prepared horseradish, ¼ teaspoon salt, and dash paprika. Chill thoroughly.

Swedish bread

←Celebrate the holidays by serving festive Lucia Braid decorated with walnut halves and red and green candied cherries.

Meat

Despite the abundance of fish that is available, Scandinavians also eat meats—pork, lamb, beef, poultry, and other meats. In fact, Denmark exports a large amount of pork and beef to the rest of Europe and to the British Isles.

In Denmark, pork is the favorite meat. Roasted pork, sometimes stuffed with fruit such as apples and figs, is one of the favorite pork dishes. However, it is by no means the only way pork is served. Pork chops, bacon, ham, pork loins, and other pork cuts are all used as main dishes. Pork pieces are used as stew meat or in casseroles, and ground pork is incorporated in casseroles and the popular meatballs or patties, called *frikadeller*.

Norway is a rugged mountainous land that will not support much domestic farming but is ideal for sheep raising. Norwegians seem to have inherited a love of mutton and wild game from their Viking ancestors. One Norwegian specialty is the dried, salted, and smoked leg of mutton, served in paper thin slices.

Beef, veal, pork, lamb, and poultry all have many uses in Swedish cookery. However, Swedish meatballs are probably the best-known Swedish meat dish. Characterized by their light texture which is achieved by adding mashed potatoes or milk-soaked bread to the meat mixture, these meatballs are a must at a smorgasbord and are also served at other meals.

Since much of Finland is covered with trees, the Finns have learned to appreciate the foods found in the deep forests. Game is plentiful and popular, and the Finnish cooks prepare it well. The Finns love of the wild taste is even carried to the cooking of domestic meats by using juniper berries to give forest flavor to poultry, or serving wild lingonberry preserves with many kinds of roasted meats.

Throughout Scandinavia, food is treated with respect, and thrift demands that none be wasted. To achieve this, the Scandinavians make many dishes that use variety meats. For example, a Danish meat dish called mock turtle is made from a calves head, and one of Finland's national favorites is a baked liver and rice dish.

Baked Liver and Rice (Finland)

An unusual, yet delicious casserole—

  2 cups water
  1 cup uncooked long-grain rice
  3 cups milk
  ¼ cup chopped onion
  1 tablespoon butter or margarine
  1½ pounds beef liver, ground
      (2½ cups)
  ¼ pound ground pork
  ½ cup raisins
  3 tablespoons dark corn syrup
  2 teaspoons salt
  1½ teaspoons dried marjoram leaves,
      crushed
    Dash pepper
    Canned cranberry sauce

In saucepan combine water and uncooked long-grain rice; bring to boiling, stirring once or twice. Simmer, uncovered, till water is absorbed, about 10 minutes. Add milk; cook over low heat, stirring occasionally, till the rice is tender, about 10 to 15 minutes. Meanwhile, cook chopped onion in butter or margarine till tender but not brown.

In mixing bowl combine cooked rice, cooked onion, ground liver, ground pork, raisins, dark corn syrup, salt, crushed marjoram, and pepper. Pour meat mixture into a well-greased 13x9x2-inch baking dish. Bake at 400° for 40 to 45 minutes. Serve hot accompanied by canned cranberry sauce. Makes 12 servings.

Glazed Yule Ham (Sweden)

  1 10- to 14-pound fully cooked
      ham
    Orange marmalade
  1 8-ounce package cream cheese,
      softened
    Cooked whole prunes (optional)
    Poached apple halves (optional)

Bake ham at 325° for 3½ to 4 hours; 30 minutes before end of baking time, brush with orange marmalade. Cool ham. Put cream cheese into a pastry bag with a large decorator tip or into a syringe-type decorator. Press cheese out into desired piping atop ham. Garnish with prunes and apples, if desired.

Swedish Meatballs

¾ pound lean ground beef
½ pound ground veal
¼ pound ground pork
1½ cups soft bread crumbs
1 cup light cream
½ cup chopped onion
3 tablespoons butter or margarine
1 egg
¼ cup finely snipped parsley
1¼ teaspoons salt
Dash pepper
Dash ground ginger
Dash ground nutmeg
Gravy

Grind meats together twice. Soak bread in cream about 5 minutes. Cook onion in *1 tablespoon* of the butter till tender. Mix meats, crumb mixture, onion, egg, parsley, and seasonings. Beat 5 minutes at medium speed on electric mixer, or mix by hand till well combined. Chill. Shape into 1½-inch balls; brown in remaining butter. Remove from skillet. Make Gravy; add meat. Cover; cook 30 minutes, basting occasionally. Makes 30 meatballs.

Gravy: Melt 2 tablespoons butter in skillet with drippings. Stir in 2 tablespoons all-purpose flour. Add 1 beef bouillon cube dissolved in 1¼ cups boiling water and ½ teaspoon instant coffee powder. Cook, stirring constantly, till gravy is thickened and bubbly.

Serve guests a selection of Norwegian cookies and sweet breads including decoratively shaped Stag's Antlers, sugar dusted Fattigman (see *Fattigman* for recipe), and Cardamom Braid.

Baked goods and desserts

Scandinavian cooks are exceptionally fine bakers. Flavorful white bread, hearty rye bread, crisp cookies, flaky pastries, and many-layered cakes are all turned out in volume by the Scandinavians.

Two ingredients—cardamom and almonds—are used so extensively in Scandinavian baked goods that they are considered typically Scandinavian. The pleasant flavor of cardamom enhances cookies, cakes, and pastries. In fact, this spice is so popular that it often is sprinkled lightly on top of baked goods as well as being used in them. Almonds—sliced, chopped, ground, and in the form of almond paste— are widely used in Scandinavian cookies, cakes, sweet breads, and pastries.

Scandinavians traditionally keep more than one kind of cookie on hand to serve both invited and unexpected company. Since this requires frequent baking, the Scandinavians have become adept at making all kinds of cookies. Most of these cookies are characterized by a delightful crispness. Once this crispness was due to the use of salt of hartshorn as a leavening agent. Today, however, many Scandinavians use baking powder for leavening and rely on the buttery richness of the dough to produce the delicate crispness.

Borrow from Sweden and serve this delicious main dish, Swedish Meatballs. The gravy which accompanies the meatballs is subtly flavored with beef bouillon and instant coffee powder.

Although cooks from all four Scandinavian countries share the distinction of being good bakers, the baked goods they make differ from country to country. Denmark, Sweden, Norway, and Finland each have specialties of their own.

Danish baking is typified by the generous use of butter and cream. Fillings rich with cream are used between as many as six to eight layers of cake or pastry for elegant desserts, while butter adds richness to cakes, cookies, pastries, and many other delectable baked goods.

By far the best-known Danish specialty, and probably the best-known Scandinavian baked food, is Danish pastry. The rich, flaky breads and rolls that are known in other countries as typical Danish pastry are called *wienerbrod* (Vienna bread) or *dansk kage* (Danish cake) in Denmark. The popularity of Danish pastry is quickly apparent when you see the mammoth displays of pastries in shop windows along the streets of Danish cities. In fact, the Danes feel that a cup of coffee is lost without a Danish pastry, and so the hundreds of pastry shops ensure that there are enough of the pastries for everyone.

The multiple, flaky layers characteristic of Danish pastry are achieved by rolling butter into the yeast dough, folding, and then chilling the dough. From this basic dough, various pastries are made by varying the shape and/or filling.

Other Danish favorites include light textured *aebleskiver* (Danish doughnuts), baked in a special pan on top of the range, and the buttery, rich *sandkage*, which resembles an American pound cake.

The baking of Sweden, though not as rich in butter and cream as that of Denmark, is also delicious. Shades of color and flavor for rye bread loaves go from cakelike *limpa*, flavored with orange peel or caraway, to deep brown, hearty caraway rye. Sour milk bread that can be stacked in drawers is popular in northern Sweden. The thin, round rye disk with a hole in the middle is the flat bread preferred in the south. Swedish white flour baking centers on luscious coffee cakes and rolls with fruit or almond fillings, saffron and cardamom Christmas breads, thin and dainty pancakes (*plattar*), and waffles.

The Swedes also make dozens of types of cookies, some molded or cut into fancy shapes, some shaped with a cookie press, some sweet, and others richly spiced.

Norwegian cooks make especially good bread. Their sturdy rye bread loaves are round and slightly flattened. Flat bread is made of barley, rye, and oats, and buttered and sugared potato bread (*lefse*) is a holiday treat. However, Norwegians also turn out some fancier dishes. Their coffee cakes and tea rings are beautiful and delicious. Cookie baking keeps Norwegian cooks busy, especially before Christmas, turning out *kringle,* sand tarts (*sandbakkels*), and cardamom cookies.

Reflecting the characteristic heartiness of the typical Finnish diet, breads are especially important in Finland. Several grains (for example, wheat, oats, barley, and rye) are popularly used to make Finnish breads. Rye bread, ranging from moist, thick loaves to flat, hard loaves, is particularly favored. Other Finnish favorites, such as black bread and buckwheat pancakes, reflect the Russian influence on the Finnish cuisine.

Although sweet breads, cakes, and cookies often serve as dessert, the Scandinavians also enjoy other desserts, including puddings and fruit soups, although favorites vary from country to country.

The Danes are known for their love of food and to them, dessert is an essential part of the meal. Fresh fruits, puddings, fruit soups, and pancakes wrapped around a sweet filling all are enjoyed. And to perk up any dessert, the Danes just add some thick rich cream, often whipped.

In Norway, one of the national favorites is a hot sour cream porridge called *rommegrot*. This dessert is considered essential for holidays and other special occasions. Fruit soups and a red berry pudding called *rodgrot* are other Norwegian favorites.

In Sweden and Finland, berries are particularly plentiful and so are frequently used in desserts. Raspberries, strawberries, blueberries, and lingonberries are popularly used in puddings, tarts, and fruit soups. The Swedes especially enjoy thin pancakes filled or topped with lightly sweetened berries, and a special Finnish dessert is a whipped berry pudding.

Danish Pastry

Serve these extra-flaky pastries warm—

1½ cups butter
3½ to 4 cups sifted all-purpose
    flour
  2 packages active dry yeast
1¼ cups milk
¼ cup sugar
  1 teaspoon salt
  1 egg
      . . .
    Almond Filling
    Confectioners' Icing

Cream butter with ⅓ *cup* of the flour; pat or roll between 2 sheets of waxed paper to form a 12x6-inch rectangle. Chill thoroughly.

In large mixer bowl combine yeast and 1½ *cups* of the flour. Heat milk, sugar, and salt just till warm. Add to dry mixture in mixer bowl; add egg. Beat at low speed with electric mixer for ½ minute, scraping sides constantly. Beat 3 minutes at high speed. By hand, stir in enough remaining flour to make soft dough.

Turn out and knead on lightly floured surface until smooth and satiny, about 5 minutes. Let rest 10 minutes. Roll dough in a 14-inch square on lightly floured surface. Place the thoroughly chilled butter mixture on half the dough. Fold over other half of dough, pinching edges to seal. Roll dough on lightly floured surface into a 20x12-inch rectangle. Fold in thirds. (If butter softens, chill after each rolling.) Roll again into a 20x12-inch rectangle. Repeat the folding and rolling 2 more times. Chill at least 1 hour after last rolling.

Working on floured surface, shape dough into almond fans, twists, or bunting rolls. Place rolls on *ungreased* baking sheet. Let rise in warm place till almost double, 45 to 60 minutes. Bake at 425° for 8 to 10 minutes. If desired, brush tops immediately with Confectioners' Icing. Serve warm. Makes about 36.

Almond Filling: Thoroughly cream together ¼ cup butter or margarine and ¼ cup sugar. Add ¼ cup ground, blanched almonds and 1 to 2 drops almond flavoring; mix thoroughly.

Confectioners' Icing: Add sufficient light cream to 2 cups sifted confectioners' sugar to make of spreading consistency (about 2 tablespoons cream). Add 1 teaspoon vanilla and dash salt. Mix until smooth.

Shapes for Danish Pastry

Almond fans: Roll ⅓ of Danish Pastry dough into 12x9-inch rectangle. Cut in 4x2-inch pieces. Place 1 level teaspoon Almond Filling in center of each; fold lengthwise. Seal edges tightly; curve slightly. Snip side opposite sealed edge at 1-inch intervals.

Twists: Roll ⅓ of dough into 12x8-inch rectangle. Cut in 6x¾-inch strips. Hold ends of strip; twist in opposite directions. Form into circle, knot, figure-8, or snail shape.

Bunting rolls: Roll ⅓ of dough into 12x9-inch rectangle. Cut into 3-inch squares. Place 1 teaspoon Almond Filling in center of each. Fold opposite corners to center; overlap. Seal.

Cardamom Braid (Norway)

  1 package active dry yeast
2¾ to 3 cups sifted all-purpose
    flour
  ¾ teaspoon ground cardamom
  ¾ cup milk
  ¼ cup butter or margarine
  ⅓ cup sugar
  ½ teaspoon salt
  1 egg

In large mixer bowl combine yeast, ¾ *cup* of the flour, and cardamom. Heat together milk, butter or margarine, sugar, and salt till warm, stirring occasionally to melt butter. Add to dry mixture in mixer bowl; add egg. Beat at low speed with electric mixer for ½ minute, scraping sides of bowl constantly. Beat 3 minutes at high speed. By hand, stir in enough of the remaining flour to make a moderately soft dough. Turn out onto lightly floured surface; knead till smooth and elastic, 5 to 8 minutes. Place in lightly greased bowl, turning once to grease surface. Cover; let rise till almost double, about 1¼ hours. Punch down.

Turn out onto lightly floured surface and divide dough in thirds; form into balls. Let rest 10 minutes. Roll each ball to a 16-inch long rope. Line up the 3 ropes, 1 inch apart, on greased baking sheet. Braid loosely, beginning in the middle and working toward ends. Pinch ends together and tuck under. Cover; let rise till almost double, 40 minutes. Brush with milk and sprinkle with sugar, if desired. Bake at 375° for 20 to 25 minutes.

Rum Pudding (Denmark)

In mixing bowl add ¼ teaspoon salt to 3 egg yolks; beat till thick and lemon-colored. Gradually beat in 6 tablespoons sugar. In saucepan soften 1 envelope unflavored gelatin in ⅔ cup milk; heat till gelatin dissolves. Cool slightly. Add milk mixture gradually to egg yolk mixture, beating constantly. Add 3 tablespoons rum. Chill till partially set. Whip 1 cup whipping cream; fold into gelatin mixture. Turn into 6 individual molds. Chill till set. Unmold and serve with Raspberry Sauce. Makes 6 servings.

Raspberry Sauce: Combine ¼ cup sugar and 1 tablespoon cornstarch; stir in one 10-ounce package frozen raspberries, thawed, and ⅓ cup cold water. Cook and stir till thickened and bubbly; boil 2 minutes. Sieve; chill.

Grandmother's Jelly Cookies (Sweden)

Pretty as well as good-tasting—

>   1 cup butter or margarine
>   ¾ cup sugar
>   1 egg
>   3 cups sifted all-purpose flour
>   ½ teaspoon salt
>   2 slightly beaten egg whites
>   ½ cup finely chopped, blanched
>   almonds
>   ¼ to ⅓ cup sugar
>   ¼ to ½ cup currant jelly

Cream together butter or margarine and the ¾ cup sugar till light and fluffy. Beat in egg. Sift together flour and salt; add to creamed mixture. Mix thoroughly.

Divide dough in half; roll one half to ⅛-inch thickness on a lightly floured board. Cut into 2½-inch circles. Roll out remaining half of dough to ⅛-inch thickness; cut with 2-inch scalloped cookie cutter. Using a very small cutter or thimble, cut a 1-inch circle out of center of smaller rounds. Brush tops of smaller rounds with egg whites; sprinkle with almonds and remaining sugar.

Place cookies on *ungreased* cookie sheets; bake at 375° for 8 to 10 minutes. Cool. Place small amount of jelly in center of larger cookies. Top with smaller cookies; press together. Makes about 3 dozen cookies.

An unusual shape coupled with a delicious spicy flavor make Finnish Viipuri Twist an extra-special yeast bread worth making.

Uppakrakakor (Sweden)

>   1 cup butter or margarine
>   ½ cup sifted confectioners' sugar
>   1¾ cups sifted all-purpose flour
>   ⅔ cup cornstarch
>   1 slightly beaten egg
>   ½ cup chopped, blanched almonds
>   2 teaspoons granulated sugar

Cream together butter and confectioners' sugar till light and fluffy. Sift together flour and cornstarch; add to creamed mixture, blending thoroughly. Chill 30 minutes. (Dough should remain chilled while working, so remove only 1 quarter from refrigerator at a time.) Roll out to ⅛-inch thickness on floured surface; cut into 2-inch circles. Place on *ungreased* cookie sheets. Fold each cookie almost in half so edges do not quite meet. Brush tops with beaten egg; sprinkle with almonds and granulated sugar. Bake at 350° till cookies are light, golden yellow, about 10 minutes. Makes about 4½ dozen.

Swedish cookies include Brandy Rings (see *Brandy* for recipe), Uppakrakakor, Rye Cookies, and Grandmother's Jelly Cookies.

Aebleskiver (Danish Doughnuts)

Especially good with coffee—

In mixing bowl sift together 1 cup sifted all-purpose flour, 1 teaspoon sugar, ½ teaspoon baking soda, ¼ teaspoon salt, and ¼ teaspoon ground cardamom. Combine 1¼ cups buttermilk, 2 well-beaten egg yolks, and ½ teaspoon vanilla. Stir half buttermilk mixture into dry ingredients in mixing bowl; mix just till smooth. Stir in remaining liquid. Fold 2 stiffly beaten egg whites into batter.

To cook doughnuts heat aebleskiver pan* (a special pan with a small cup for each doughnut) over low heat; oil each cup lightly. Spoon 2 tablespoons batter into each cup. Cook till bubbles form and edges appear dry, about 2 to 3 minutes. Gently turn with 2 wooden picks. Cook till second side is golden brown, about 2 to 3 minutes. Repeat with remaining batter. Dust with confectioners' sugar and serve hot with applesauce or jelly. Makes 20.

*Batter can also be cooked on lightly greased griddle, using 2 tablespoons per pancake.

Lucia Braid (Sweden)

Serve this delicious bread as a Christmas treat—

      2 packages active dry yeast
      5 to 5⅓ cups sifted all-purpose
         flour
      ½ teaspoon ground cardamom
    1⅓ cups milk
      ½ cup shortening
      ½ cup sugar
    1½ teaspoons salt
      2 eggs
           • • •
      Confectioners' Sugar Glaze
      Walnut halves
      Red and green candied cherries

In large mixer bowl combine active dry yeast, *2½ cups* of the all-purpose flour, and cardamom. In saucepan heat milk, shortening, sugar, and salt just till warm, stirring occasionally to melt shortening. Add to dry mixture in mixer bowl; add eggs. Beat at low speed with electric mixer for ½ minute, scraping sides of bowl constantly. Beat 3 minutes at high speed. By hand, stir in enough of the remaining all-purpose flour to make a soft dough.

Turn dough out onto well-floured surface. Knead till smooth and elastic, about 8 to 10 minutes. Place dough in lightly greased bowl; turn once to grease surface. Cover; let rise in warm place till double, about 2 hours. Punch down. Divide dough in half; cover and let rest 10 minutes. Divide one half of the dough into 4 parts. Roll 3 parts of dough into 20-inch strands; braid. Carefully place braid around greased 6-ounce juice can on greased baking sheet. Seal ends together to form continuous braid. Divide fourth part of dough in half. Shape into two 20-inch strands and twist together. Place twist on top of braid. Repeat with remaining half of dough.

Let dough rise in warm place till double, about 1 hour. Bake at 350° till bread is golden, about 25 minutes. Carefully remove the juice can. While wreaths are still warm, brush with Confectioners' Sugar Glaze. Decorate tops with walnut halves and red and green candied cherries. Makes 2 wreaths.

Confectioners' Sugar Glaze: Add enough milk *or* light cream to 2 cups sifted confectioners' sugar to make of spreading consistency. Add 1 teaspoon vanilla and dash salt; mix well.

Finnish Viipuri Twist

In large mixer bowl combine 2 packages active dry yeast, 2½ cups sifted all-purpose flour, ½ teaspoon ground cardamom, and ½ teaspoon ground nutmeg. Heat together 2 cups milk, ¼ cup butter or margarine, ¾ cup sugar, and 1 teaspoon salt just till warm, stirring occasionally to melt butter. Add to dry ingredients in mixer bowl; beat ½ minute on low speed of electric mixer, scraping bowl constantly. Beat 3 minutes at high speed. By hand, beat in enough of 3 to 3¼ cups all-purpose flour to make a moderately stiff dough. Turn out onto lightly floured surface. Knead till smooth and elastic, about 5 to 8 minutes.

Place in greased bowl, turning once to grease surface. Cover and let rise till double, 1 to 1½ hours. Punch down; divide into 3 parts and let rest for about 10 minutes.

On floured surface, shape 1 part of the dough into a roll 36 inches long. Cross ends of dough to form a circle, having each end extend about 6 inches. Holding ends of dough toward center of circle, twist together twice. Press ends together and tuck under center of top of circle, forming a pretzel-shaped roll. Place on greased baking sheet. Repeat with 2 remaining parts of dough. Let rise again till almost double, about 45 minutes. Bake at 375° for about 20 minutes. Stir together 1 slightly beaten egg and 1 tablespoon water; brush on hot breads. Makes 3 loaves.

Stag's Antlers (Norway)

Delicately cardamom flavored—

In mixing bowl cream ½ cup butter or margarine and ¾ cup sugar till light and fluffy. Beat in 2 egg yolks and 1 whole egg. Add ¼ cup milk and ½ teaspoon ground cardamom. Sift together 2¼ cups sifted all-purpose flour, ½ cup cornstarch, 1 teaspoon baking soda, and ½ teaspoon salt. Add to egg mixture; blend thoroughly. Chill dough thoroughly.

Roll dough out on lightly floured surface to ¼-inch thickness. Cut into 2x1-inch strips. Transfer to *ungreased* cookie sheets. Cut 2 slits in each strip, ¾ inch from each end and cutting across a little more than half the width of the strip. Curve to open slits. Bake at 350° till golden, 10 to 12 minutes. Sprinkle with sugar. Cool. Store in airtight container. Makes 72.

Rye Cookies (Sweden)

- **½ cup butter or margarine**
- **⅓ cup sugar**
- **½ cup rye flour**
- **½ cup whole wheat flour**
- **½ cup sifted all-purpose flour**
- **¼ teaspoon baking powder**

Cream together butter and sugar till light and fluffy. Stir in rye flour and whole wheat flour. Sift together all-purpose flour, baking powder, and ¼ teaspoon salt; stir into creamed mixture. Gradually add 2 to 3 tablespoons cold water, mixing just till moistened. Shape into a ball. Roll cookie dough out on lightly floured surface to ⅛-inch thickness.

Cut into 2½-inch rounds. Using a thimble, cut a ½-inch circle, just off-center, from each cookie. Prick surface with fork, if desired. Place on *ungreased* cookie sheet. Bake at 375° till lightly browned, about 10 to 12 minutes. Cool slightly before removing from cookie sheet. Makes 4 to 5 dozen.

Sandbakkels (Norway)

- **1 cup butter or margarine**
- **1 cup sugar**
- **1 egg**
- **1 teaspoon almond extract**
- **3 cups sifted all-purpose flour**
- **1 cup apricot preserves**
- **2 teaspoons lemon juice**
- **¼ cup chopped red candied cherries**
- **¼ cup toasted, sliced almonds**

Thoroughly cream butter or margarine and sugar. Add egg and almond extract; beat well. Stir in sifted flour. Pinch off small ball of dough and place in center of 2½-inch sandbakkel mold*; with your thumb, press dough evenly and as thinly as possible over bottom and sides. Place molds on cookie sheet.

Bake at 350° till lightly browned, 12 to 14 minutes. Cool. To remove, invert mold; tap lightly. (Clean molds with dry cloth.)

Just before serving, combine preserves, lemon juice, and cherries. Place 1 teaspoon of mixture in each cookie tart. Stir in almonds or sprinkle over. Makes about 3½ dozen.

*They look like tiny, fluted, tart pans. If not available, use tiny foilware pans instead.

Smorgasbord

Mention of Scandinavian cookery almost invariably brings to mind the smorgasbord. In fact, an adaptation of this lavish meal is found in all the Scandinavian countries. For example, the special buffet meal called *voileinpapoyta* is the Finn's form of the smorgasbord. However, the true smorgasbord (literally bread and butter table) belongs to Sweden.

The traditional smorgasbord, which actually only dates back to the late 1800s, consists of dozens of dishes spread out on a large table. Considering the huge amount of food, it is not at all surprising that as the diner approaches the smorgasbord, he is often overwhelmed. A second look, however, shows that the typical smorgasbord selections can be broken down into four groups—herring dishes (such as pickled, smoked, marinated, and fried herring); other fish dishes and/or cold egg dishes (for example, smoked eel, jellied salmon, stuffed eggs, and fried salmon fins); cold meats and salads (including ham, roast beef, tongue, pickled onions, beets, and cucumbers), and hot dishes (Swedish meatballs, rice pudding, omelets, fried kidneys, stuffed onions, and fried mushrooms).

During the course of a smorgasbord, you should use four plates—one for each group of dishes. Although you will soon find that it's virtually an impossible task to sample every dish on the smorgasbord, you can easily taste a representative sample if, from the start, you will just remember to save room for the dishes yet to come.

Stuffed Celery

> Cream cheese, softened
> Blue cheese, crumbled
> Celery sticks
> Capers
> Canned pimiento, cut into
>   tiny diamonds

Beat together cream cheese and blue cheese (add to suit your taste) till fluffy. Stuff celery with cheese. Dot filled celery with capers and pimiento. Stand celery up around inverted tumbler. Hide glass with celery leaves.

Decorated Ham

> Canned ham, chilled
> Unpeeled cucumber
> Canned asparagus spears, chilled
> Canned pimiento strip
> Wedge of bread (about ⅓ of an
>   unsliced loaf)
> Lettuce
> Curly endive
> Radish roses
> Bright red apple
> Lettuce *or* individual vegetable
>   salads

Place chilled ham on large platter. Run tines of fork down cucumber, notching skin all around. Cut cucumber in ¼-inch slices, then cut slices in half. Stand these half-circles on edge, overlapping them, to make 2 parallel rows along top of ham at side edges.

Between cucumber rows center a bundle of 3 or 4 asparagus spears tied with pimiento. For a Yuletide touch, wrap 2 asparagus spears in 2 thin ham slices and stand on end to resemble a candle at center of each side of ham; hold in place with wooden picks.

For the backdrop, stand the wedge of bread on its smallest side with the long slope toward one end of the ham. Completely cover bread with lettuce and endive, tacking with wooden picks. Dot with radish roses, also held by wooden picks. Nestle bright red apple between greenery and ham. Garnish platter with lettuce or individual vegetable salads.

Swedish Brown Beans

> 1 pound Swedish brown beans
> 3 inches stick cinnamon
> ⅓ cup brown sugar
> ¼ cup vinegar
> 2 tablespoons dark corn syrup

Rinse beans; drain. Add 6 cups cold water; cover and let stand overnight. (Or bring water and beans slowly to boiling; simmer 2 minutes. Cover; let stand 1 hour.) Add cinnamon and 1½ teaspoons salt. Cover; simmer till beans are about tender, 1½ to 2 hours. Add sugar and vinegar. Cook, uncovered, till beans are tender and liquid is desired consistency, 30 minutes; stir occasionally. Add syrup. Serves 6.

Quick Swedish Meatballs

Thoroughly combine 2 pounds ground beef, 2 cups soft bread crumbs, two 3-ounce packages cream cheese, ¼ cup *dry* onion soup mix, ½ teaspoon salt, ½ teaspoon ground nutmeg, and ½ cup milk. Shape into 40 small balls.

Brown in large skillet, shaking skillet to keep balls round. Cover and cook 20 to 25 minutes. Remove meatballs. Drain off fat, leaving ¼ cup fat in skillet; blend in 2 tablespoons all-purpose flour. Stir in 2 cups milk all at once. Cook and stir till thickened and bubbly. Return meatballs to skillet; cover and cook till heated through. Serves 10 to 12.

Individual characteristics

Even though Denmark, Norway, Sweden, and Finland are generally lumped together as Scandinavia, each of these four countries still retains a character of its own. This individuality shows up in cookery where there are particular foods and techniques that are typical only of one or the other of the Scandinavian countries.

For example, the Danes are known for their extensive use of the butter, cream, and eggs that are so plentiful there. In fact, they put their own stamp on breads, pastries, cookies, soups, and almost every other dish by adding butter or cream.

One of the characteristics of Norwegian cooking is the generous use of sour cream. Much as the Danes use butter and sweet cream, the Norwegians use sour cream in soups, sauces, salads, porridge, waffles, and meat and vegetable dishes.

Swedish cooks are artists in using subtle touches to individualize the foods they prepare. They add a touch of beet juice to the cream used to dress herring or a bit of sugar to give just the right finishing touch to a creamy sauce. They also put a little cream in their meat croquettes and cold mashed potatoes in meatballs to give the finished product a light texture. Sauces are important dress-ups also, especially for vegetables, poultry, meat, or fish.

Finland's forests yield many foods, including mushrooms, which the Finns particularly enjoy. From spring to autumn, the Finns gather large quantities of mushrooms from the over fifty edible varieties that are found in the Finnish countryside. These tasty delicacies are often pickled, fried, or used in soups, sauces, salads, stews, and main dishes. (See *Danish Cookery, Norwegian Cookery, Swedish Cookery* for additional information.)

SCHAUM TORTE *(shoum' tôrt')* – A dessert made of layers of crushed fruit and meringue shells. (See also *Torte*.)

SCHAV *(shchäv)* – A pale green soup, Russian and Magyar in origin, which is now primarily associated with Jewish cookery. It is made of water, sorrel (sour grass) leaves, lemon juice, a well-beaten egg, and seasonings. Served either hot or cold, schav is popularly garnished with a dollop of sour cream, sliced hard-cooked egg, lemon or lime slices, or snipped parsley. (See also *Jewish Cookery*.)

SCHMALTZ, SCHMALZ *(shmälts, shmôlts)* – The Jewish word for rendered fat of meat animals or poultry. It usually refers to rendered chicken fat, and is of two types— one simply salted for use in cake baking and one flavored with onion. The former is made by melting small bits of chicken fat over very low heat. As melted fat accumulates, it is poured off and strained. The fat for flavored schmaltz is melted over low heat with chopped onion (and garlic if desired) and bits of chopped chicken skin. It is used to add piquancy to meat or vegetables dishes. Schmaltz should be kept tightly covered and refrigerated. (See also *Jewish Cookery*.)

SCHNECKEN *(shnek' uhn)* – Fruit- or nut-filled sweet rolls, shaped like snails.

SCHNITZ *(shnits)* – The Pennsylvania Dutch name for dried sliced apples. (See also *Pennsylvania Dutch Cookery*.)

SCHNITZ AND KNEPP *(shnits' uhn kuh nep', -knep')* – A Pennsylvania Dutch main dish prepared with dried apple slices called *schnitz*, dumplings called *knepp*, and ham or pork. The dish is also sometimes made without the meat. (See also *Pennsylvania Dutch Cookery*.)

SCHNITZEL (*s̪hnit′ suhl*) — The German and Austrian word for a cutlet, usually veal, that has been dipped in egg, then in bread crumbs, and finally sautéed or fried in fat before it is seasoned and garnished.

An American version of schnitzel includs a filled ham slice coated and fried in shortening. (See also *Wiener Schnitzel*.)

Filled Ham Schnitzel

Mushrooms and parsley make up the filling—

        1 6-ounce can chopped mushrooms,
            drained and finely chopped
        3 tablespoons butter or margarine
        2 tablespoons snipped parsley
        1 tablespoon all-purpose flour
        8 slices boiled ham
        1 slightly beaten egg
        ½ cup all-purpose flour
        ½ cup fine dry bread crumbs
        3 tablespoons shortening

Brown mushrooms in butter with parsley. Add 1 tablespoon flour; cook and stir for 2 minutes. Cool. Spread mixture on one half of each slice of ham. Fold other half over; press to secure. Dip schnitzel in egg, then in ½ cup flour, back into egg, and then in crumbs. Brown on both sides in hot shortening. Makes 4 servings.

SCONE — A plain or sweet biscuitlike tea cake made of baking powder dough that is enriched with eggs and milk or cream. A Scottish food, scones originally were made with oatmeal and baked on a griddle.

Prepare scones for baking in the oven or on a griddle by first rolling the dough to an even thickness. Then, cut the dough into any one of a number of shapes—circles, diamonds, or wedges.

For soft sides, allow the sides of the scones to touch during baking and split them apart after baking. For crisp sides, bake the scones separately without letting the sides touch. In either case, brush the top of the scones before baking with a beaten egg or milk. This gives them a rich, golden color. Turn scones that are baked on a griddle so as to allow them to cook through completely.

Score meats by slashing through the fat layer on the edge just to but not through the meat. This prevents curling during cooking.

Tea Scones

        2 cups sifted all-purpose flour
        2 tablespoons sugar
        3 teaspoons baking powder
        6 tablespoons butter
        1 slightly beaten egg
        ½ cup milk

Sift together dry ingredients and ½ teaspoon salt. Cut in butter till mixture resembles coarse crumbs. Add egg and milk, stirring till dough follows fork around bowl. Knead on floured surface 15 times; cut in half. Shape each half into ball; pat to circle ½ inch thick and 6 inches in diameter; cut in 8 wedges.

Place the wedges on an *ungreased* baking sheet, without allowing sides to touch. Brush with egg, if desired. Bake at 425° till deep golden brown, 12 to 15 minutes. Makes 16.

SCOOP — **1.** A shovel- or ladle-type utensil made of plastic, metal, or wood and designed for dipping food from one container to another. Examples include ice cream scoops and scoops for coffee, sugar, flour, and other ground or powdered ingredients. **2.** To dip or hollow out.

When filling fruits or vegetables, such as baked potatoes, tomatoes, oranges, or green peppers with seasoned food mixtures, use a spoon to scoop out the insides of foods first. (See also *Utensil*.)

Run tines of fork lengthwise down unpeeled cucumber, all around, breaking through skin. Slice scored cucumber in thin slices.

SCORE—To make shallow slits or slashes partway through the outer surface of food for functional or decorative purposes.

Scoring the fat layer of meat allows fat drainage and crisping of the meat during cooking. To score steaks, chops, or ham slices, use a sharp knife to slash through the fat layer on the edge just to the meat. This prevents the meat from curling and folding as it cooks.

When scoring less tender cuts of meat such as beef flank steak or round steak, cut slashes in the long, fibrous surface in an overall diamond pattern. This shortens the long meat fibers, making the meat more tender and easier to chew. Scoring the surface of meat enables a marinade to better penetrate the meat, making it more flavorful and tender.

Many homemakers score foods to make their meals more appetizing. To give a ham a decorative appearance, cut an overall pattern of squares or diamonds through the outside fat layer. It is also quite easy to decorate fruits and vegetables by scoring them lengthwise. Simply use the tines of a fork to break through the skins of the fruit or vegetables, then run the fork down the fruit. Slice and use the fruit or vegetable in salads, as a garnish, or as a relish.

SCOTCH BROTH—A thin soup of Scottish origin made of mutton or lamb, barley, and/or mixed vegetables. (See also *Soup.*)

Scotch Broth

Combine and simmer lamb or mutton, barley, and mixed vegetables to make this hearty soup—

> 1 pound boneless lamb, cut in 2-inch cubes
> 4 cups water
> 1 teaspoon salt
> 1 bay leaf, crushed
> 2 whole cloves
> 3 sprigs parsley
> ½ cup chopped onion
>
> • • •
>
> ¼ cup pearl barley
> ½ cup diced carrots
> ¼ cup diced celery
> ¼ cup diced turnip

In 3-quart saucepan combine lamb, water, salt, bay leaf, cloves, parsley, and ¼ *cup* of the chopped onion. Bring mixture to boiling; reduce heat and simmer, covered, till meat is tender, about 2 hours. Remove meat from soup; cut into small pieces. Set the meat aside.

Strain stock; add barley. Simmer mixture for 30 minutes. Add carrots, celery, turnip, and remaining chopped onion. Cook till vegetables are tender, about 30 minutes longer. Add meat; heat through. Makes 4 or 5 servings.

SCOTCH HAM—A cook-before-eating style of ham that is cured but not smoked. The ham is marketed as a regional specialty by New England processors. Because it is processed with a sweet pickle brine, it also known as sweet pickle ham.

Scotch ham has a delicate, pink color and a mild flavor. It is occasionally used to prepare the familiar boiled dinner with potatoes and carrots. (See also *Ham.*)

SCOTCH WHISKY—A Scottish-made whiskey based on malt barley. The distinctive, smoky flavor of Scotch whisky is developed by drying the barley over open peat fires. Before bottling, Scotch whisky imported by United States markets is aged in wooden casks for at least four years.

Scotch whisky of the past differed profoundly from what most people recognize as Scotch whisky today. Originally, the whisky was distilled solely from germinated or malted barley and produced an intense-flavored liquor. This is still made and sold in Scotland. Now, however, Scotch whisky, also called Scotch, is most often a milder blend of malt and grain whiskies, which appeals to more palates.

These two forms of Scotch whisky are well accepted today, but in years past there was considerable contention in Scotland over just what whisky was. The Scots of the Highlands, originators of Scotch whisky, have always distilled the malt whisky. Although its potency was well liked by Highlanders, more sophisticated individuals in Great Britain were not fond of the strong flavor. With the development of patent stills, which enabled distillation of grain blends, milder Scotch whiskies were produced, much to the dismay of the Highlanders. In the 1905 court decision of the "What is whisky" case, however, the patent distillers won a long-fought battle. Ninety-nine percent of all Scotch that is exported today consists of this grain-blended type.

Half the Scotch produced is consumed by people of the United States. Popular drinks include Scotch and soda, Scotch on the rocks, Rob Roy, Scotch mist, and rusty nail. (See also *Whiskey*.)

Season Scrambled Eggs with Tomatoes with dried oregano leaves and parsley flakes for a new and interesting breakfast idea.

Cook scrambled eggs over low heat. Lift and turn eggs with a wide spatula so uncooked mixture goes to the bottom of the skillet.

SCRAMBLE — 1. A preparation method in which ingredients are stirred together while cooking. **2.** A cereal snack that gets its name from items that are tossed together.

The term is most commonly associated with stirring beaten eggs with milk and seasonings while cooking in butter. The cooked dish is called scrambled eggs.

Preparation methods for scrambled eggs vary a great deal. For creamy, golden-yellow scrambled eggs, beat the eggs with the liquid, usually milk or light cream, before cooking. For a flecked yellow and white appearance, break the eggs in a skillet and stir while cooking.

For either method, the eggs are usually cooked in a skillet. However, for softer, less rich scrambled eggs, omit the butter and cook the egg mixture in the top of a double boiler. This method takes about twice as long. Calorie watchers can scramble eggs in nonstick pans without butter.

If the family seems to lose interest in your scrambled eggs, vary the flavor by tossing in herbs and seasonings such as parsley, chives, or thyme. Vegetables such as tomato wedges, green pepper strips, or sliced mushrooms also add flavor and color. Add a delectable flavor by cooking scrambled eggs in bacon drippings. For hearty brunches add diced, cooked meats such as chicken or ham. Or dribble melted cheese over the scrambled eggs. (See *Cereal, Egg* for additional information.)

Scrambled Eggs with Tomatoes

      6 eggs
 ¼ cup milk
 ½ teaspoon salt
 ¼ teaspoon dried oregano leaves,
      crushed
 ¼ teaspoon dried parsley flakes
      Dash pepper
      2 tablespoons butter or margarine
      1 8-ounce can tomatoes, drained
      and cut up

Combine eggs, milk, salt, crushed oregano, parsley flakes, and pepper. Beat with fork till mixture is smooth and yellow. Melt butter in skillet over medium heat. Add egg mixture and cook, lifting mixture gently from bottom of pan with spatula. When eggs are nearly done, lightly fold in tomato pieces; turn out immediately onto heated platter. Makes 4 servings.

Chicken Scramble

      8 beaten eggs
      2 ounces *natural* Cheddar cheese,
      shredded (½ cup)
 ¼ cup milk
 ½ teaspoon salt
      Dash pepper
      3 tablespoons butter or margarine
      1 cup cooked chicken, cut in
      julienne strips
      1 tablespoon snipped chives

In bowl combine first 5 ingredients. Set electric skillet at 320°; melt butter in skillet. Add chicken and chives; cook and stir 3 minutes. Add egg-cheese mixture. Cook, stirring occasionally, till eggs are set. Makes 6 servings.

SCRAPE—To rub over food with a sharp or moderately blunt instrument to remove the outer coating. Scraping skins off new potatoes or carrots are examples.

SCRAPER—A long-handled, rubber-bladed instrument, firm but flexible, used to scrape food from containers without scratching them. Often called rubber spatula, a scraper is also good for folding in beaten egg whites and for folding omelets.

SCRAPPLE—A cooked meat product originated by thrifty Pennsylvania Dutch farmers to use up the small bits of pork left after butchering. The liver, tongue, meaty bones, and all scraps left from butchering are thoroughly boiled, producing a broth. Seasoning the mixture is an individual part of the preparation. Formerly, the Germans used buckwheat flour to thicken scrapple, although the Pennsylvania Dutch preferred a combination of buckwheat and cornmeal. Now, cornmeal is usually used.

After the scrapple has been boiled to a mushlike stage, it is packed into loaf pans to set, then chilled. At serving time, it is sliced and sautéed or fried. Sometimes, the slices are dipped in eggs and a crumb mixture before frying. Although scrapple is usually served with hot maple or brown sugar syrup, some people prefer it with catsup or hot fruit.

Scrapple is bought ready to fry, canned or packaged, as Philadelphia scrapple. (See also *Pennsylvania Dutch Cookery*.)

Sausage Scrapple

      2 pounds bulk pork sausage
      1 14½-ounce can evaporated milk
      (1⅔ cups)
      3 cups water
 1½ cups yellow cornmeal
 ½ teaspoon salt
      All-purpose flour *or* cornflake
      crumbs
      2 beaten eggs
      3 to 4 tablespoons shortening
      Syrup

Brown sausage slowly, breaking it up into small pieces; drain off excess fat. Combine milk and water. Add 4 cups of the milk mixture to sausage. Reserve remaining milk mixture. Heat sausage mixture to boiling; slowly stir in cornmeal and salt. Cook 5 minutes, stirring constantly. Pour into greased 9x5x3-inch loaf pan. Chill the mixture till firm.

Unmold and cut into ¼-inch slices. Dip in flour *or* cornflake crumbs. Combine eggs and remaining milk mixture. Dip slices in egg mixture, then in flour or crumbs again. In skillet brown in hot shortening on both sides. Serve hot with warm syrup. Serves 10 to 12.

SCRIPTURE CAKE—A rich cake made entirely from ingredients that are mentioned in the *Holy Bible,* such as raisins and nuts. Old-fashioned recipes for this cake carried the verse recipes as well as, or often in place of, the ingredient listings.

Scripture Cake

          ½ cup Judges 5:25
          ¾ cup Jeremiah 6:20
        2¼ cups I Kings 4:22
          1 teaspoon Amos 4:5
            Dash Leviticus 2:13
            II Chronicles 9:9
          3 Jeremiah 17:11
          ½ cup Judges 4:19
          ⅓ cup I Samuel 14:25
          1 cup I Samuel 30:12
          1 cup Nahum 3:12
          ½ cup Numbers 17:8

In large mixer bowl cream Judges 5:25 (butter or margarine); blend in Jeremiah 6:20 (molasses). Sift together I Kings 4:22 (sifted all-purpose flour); Amos 4:5 (baking powder); Leviticus 2:13 (salt); and II Chronicles 9:9 (½ teaspoon ground cinnamon, ¼ teaspoon ground cloves, and ⅛ teaspoon ground ginger). Combine Jeremiah 17:11 (beaten eggs); Judges 4:19 (sour milk *or* buttermilk); and I Samuel 14:25 (honey). Stir to combine.

Add the egg mixture and the sifted dry ingredients alternately to creamed mixture. Mix well. Stir in I Samuel 30:12 (raisins); Nahum 3:12 (chopped figs); and Numbers 17:8 (chopped almonds). Turn mixture into greased and lightly floured 9x5x3-inch loaf pan. Bake at 325° for 1¼ to 1½ hours. Let cool in pan 10 minutes; turn out. When the cake has cooled completely, wrap and store overnight.

SCROD *(skrod)*—A young cod or haddock. This term describes the market size rather than a species. The young fish averages in weight from 1½ to 2½ pounds.

The meat is tender, white, and flaky. Delicate scrod flavor combines well with seasonings such as curry and is delicious baked, broiled, or used in chowders. Scrod is popular in Europe and on the east coast of the United States. (See also *Cod.*)

Curried Scrod

    1½ pounds fresh or frozen scrod
          fillets (young haddock or cod)
    ½ cup chopped onion
    2 tablespoons butter or margarine
    1 to 1½ teaspoons curry powder
    2 tablespoons all-purpose flour
    ¾ teaspoon salt
    1 cup milk
    2 tablespoons chopped, canned
          pimiento
    3 cups hot cooked rice

Thaw frozen fillets. Cut into 4 or 5 portions. Place fillets in an 11¾x7½x1¾-inch baking dish. Cook onion in butter till tender but not brown. Stir in curry powder; heat 1 minute. Blend in flour and salt. Add milk all at once. Cook and stir till thickened and bubbly. Stir in pimiento. Pour over fish. Bake, uncovered, at 350° till fish flakes easily when tested with a fork, about 25 minutes. Spoon sauce over fish once or twice during baking. Serve with hot rice. Makes 4 or 5 servings.

SCUP *(skup)*—A type of porgy, a fish of the eastern United States. (See also *Porgy.*)

SCUPPERNONG *(skup′ uhr nong′, -nong′)*—
1. A sweet, thick-skinned, greenish yellow grape of the muscadine variety that grows well in the southern United States. The fruit is excellent for use in grape jams. 2. A sweet, rich, white wine made from scuppernong grapes. (See also *Grape.*)

SEA BASS—A saltwater fish found along the east and west coasts of North America. The sea bass, also called blackfish, is a lean fish with firm, sweet, white flesh. It ranges in size from ½ to 4 pounds.

There are two other types of sea bass— the white sea bass, which weighs up to 50 pounds, and the black sea bass, which weighs from 50 to 600 pounds.

Although popular as a game fish, sea bass also are caught commercially and sold whole, or cut in fillets or steaks.

This fish can be boiled, fried, or steamed. With butter added, it also may be baked or broiled. A 3½-ounce uncooked portion contains 96 calories. (See also *Bass.*)

Barbecued Bass Steaks

    2 pounds fresh or frozen bass
        steaks
  ⅓ cup salad oil
    1 tablespoon sesame seed, toasted
    1 tablespoon lemon juice
    1 tablespoon wine vinegar
    1 tablespoon soy sauce
  ½ teaspoon salt

If using frozen fish, thaw. Cut into 6 portions. Place in single layer in shallow dish. Combine remaining ingredients. Pour over fish. Marinate 30 minutes at room temperature; turn once. Remove fish; reserve marinade.

    Place fish in *well-greased*, wire broiler basket. Grill over *medium-hot* coals for 10 minutes. Turn and baste with marinade. Grill till fish flakes easily when tested with a fork, 5 to 8 minutes longer. Makes 6 servings.

Broiled Bass Steaks

    2 pounds fresh or frozen bass steaks
      or other fish steaks
  ½ cup catsup
  ¼ cup salad oil
  ¼ cup lemon juice
    1 teaspoon instant minced onion
    1 teaspoon Worcestershire sauce
    1 teaspoon prepared mustard
  ½ teaspoon garlic salt
  ¼ teaspoon salt

Thaw frozen steaks. Cut into 6 portions. Place fish in a single layer in shallow dish. Combine remaining ingredients. Pour sauce over fish; let stand 1 hour at room temperature, turning once or twice. Remove fish; reserve sauce.

    Place fish in a single layer on greased rack of broiler pan. Broil about 4 inches from heat till fish flakes easily when tested with a fork, about 10 to 15 minutes. Baste with reserved sauce several times during broiling. Serves 6.

SEA FOAM—A divinity-type candy made of brown sugar syrup and beaten egg whites, sometimes with nuts added. The flavor of sea foam candy has been adapted to cake frosting by using brown sugar in Seven Minute Frosting. (See also *Candy*.)

Sea Foam

Have a friend help you make this candy—

      Butter or margarine
  1¾ cups light brown sugar
   ¾ cup granulated sugar
   ¼ cup light corn syrup
   ¼ teaspoon salt
   ½ cup water
    2 egg whites
    1 teaspoon vanilla
   ½ cup broken pecans (optional)

Butter sides of heavy 1½-quart saucepan. In it combine light brown sugar, granulated sugar, light corn syrup, salt, and water. Cook, stirring constantly, till sugars dissolve and mixture comes to boiling. Cook to hard-ball stage (260°) without stirring. Remove from heat.

    Immediately beat egg whites till stiff peaks form. Pour hot syrup in a thin stream over beaten egg whites, beating constantly at high speed on electric mixer. Add vanilla.

    Continue beating till mixture forms soft peaks and begins to lose gloss, 10 minutes. Stir in broken pecans, if desired. Let stand about 2 minutes; drop by rounded teaspoons onto waxed paper. Makes 2 to 3 dozen pieces.

Sea Foam Frosting

Top your best cake with this candylike frosting—

    2 unbeaten egg whites
  1½ cups brown sugar
    2 teaspoons light corn syrup *or*
      ¼ teaspoon cream of tartar
  ⅓ cup cold water
     Dash salt
    1 teaspoon vanilla

Place all ingredients *except* vanilla in top of double boiler (not over heat); beat 1 minute with electric or rotary beater. Place over, but not touching, boiling water and cook, beating constantly, till frosting forms stiff peaks, about 7 minutes (don't overcook).

    Remove from boiling water. Pour into mixing bowl, if desired. Add vanilla and beat till of spreading consistency, about 2 minutes. Frosts tops and sides of two 8- or 9-inch layers, top of 13x9-inch cake, or 2 dozen cupcakes.

SEAFOOD—Saltwater fish or shellfish eaten as food. The term seafood in menus and cookery refers mainly to shellfish. Snails, turtles, frogs, octopuses, and squid are sometimes included in this broad category of seafood because they are prepared like fish and shellfish. (See *Fish, Shellfish* for additional information.)

Clam-Haddock Chowder

¼ cup all-purpose flour
¼ cup shortening, melted
1 teaspoon curry powder
4 cups clam juice
3 cups fish stock *or* water
½ cup chili sauce
¼ cup tomato purée
. . .
½ cup diced celery
½ cup chopped onions
1 teaspoon salt
Dash pepper
⅛ teaspoon saffron
⅛ teaspoon dried thyme leaves, crushed
⅛ teaspoon dried rosemary leaves, crushed
½ pound haddock, diced
½ cup peeled, diced potatoes
¼ cup diced leeks
. . .
1½ cups minced clams
1 cup cooked tomatoes
¾ cup diced green pepper
1 clove garlic, minced
1 teaspoon snipped parsley
⅓ cup Madeira *or* sherry wine
12 soft-shell clams, cooked

Blend all-purpose flour, melted shortening, and curry powder in a deep saucepan; cook 2 minutes, stirring constantly. Gradually add clam juice, fish stock or water, chili sauce, and tomato purée. Cook mixture until thickened and bubbly, stirring constantly.

Add celery, onions, salt, pepper, saffron, thyme, and rosemary. Simmer 15 minutes. Add haddock, potatoes, and leeks; cook 15 minutes. Add minced clams, tomatoes, green pepper, and garlic; cook 15 minutes. Remove mixture from heat; add snipped parsley, Madeira or sherry, and cooked clams. Makes 6 to 8 servings.

Shore Dinner

Partially cook frozen lobster tails by simmering in salted water 10 minutes. With scissors, snip each lobster shell open, remove the meat, and cut in thirds. Peel and devein the shrimp, leaving last section of the shell and tail intact. String the following on rotating skewers: lobster chunks, shrimp, scallops, cherry tomatoes, and stuffed green olives.

Brush with lemon-butter (1 part lemon juice to 2 parts melted butter). Sprinkle with salt. Place rotating skewers on grill. Broil till the seafood is done, about 8 to 10 minutes, brushing frequently with lemon-butter. Before serving the food, sprinkle it with snipped parsley. Serve this dish piping hot with Tartar Sauce (see *Tartar Sauce* for recipe).

SEAFOOD SEASONING—A ground blend of ingredients used to flavor fish, shellfish, chowders, and sauces. Some of the ingredients included in commercial blends are salt, celery seed, mustard, thyme, ginger, peppers, allspice, and bay leaves.

Sprinkle this seasoning over fish and shellfish either before broiling, baking, and grilling or before serving. Enhance the flavor of dishes made with or served with fish and shellfish by adding seafood seasoning. Soups, chowders, stuffings, tartar sauce, Newburg sauce, and lemon-butter sauce can be flavored to taste.

Another spicy blend called shrimp boil or crab boil can be added to the water used to cook seafood, mainly shellfish.

SEAR—To brown food quickly. Searing, once used extensively, is done by cooking the food for a short time in a very hot oven or on top of the range at high heat. This forms a brown crust that has a good caramelized flavor. However, it has been found that meats roasted in a slow oven without searing retain their juices, shrink little, and have a browned, flavorful surface.

The first step in braising meats is not the same as searing. In braising, meats are browned *slowly* in a little fat.

SEASON—To add herbs and spices to enhance the basic character of a dish. Food should be seasoned carefully to develop a harmonious blend. Seasoning should enhance the dish's flavor, yet must not overpower the flavor of the main ingredient.

The recipe direction, "season to taste," means to add the herb or spice till the desired flavor is achieved. Begin with ¼ teaspoon for each 4 servings, 1 pound of meat, or 2 cups of sauce or vegetables. Then, if not enough, increase the amount gradually. When the desired level is reached, note total amount on recipe.

If a recipe calls for a seasoning, but no herbs or spices are specified, season with salt and pepper. Other seasonings also can be added according to the type of food and personal taste.

When to add seasonings

For full flavor, add seasonings during cooking rather than waiting until just before serving. If the food requires long cooking, add seasonings during the last half hour.

SEASONED PEPPER—A commercial blend of black pepper, sweet pepper, sugar, and spices. The ingredients and proportions vary from manufacturer to manufacturer. Some types of seasoned pepper have one predominant seasoning, for example, lemon pepper. Use it in place of black pepper for extra flavor. (See also *Pepper*.)

SEASONED SALT—A mixture of salt, spices, herbs, and various ingredients. Each manufacturer's blend differs, but sugar, onion, garlic, cornstarch, spices, and herbs are usually included in the formula.

Seasoned salt adds zip to vegetables, main dishes, and salads. The extra flavor quite often transforms an ordinary dish into an intriguing food.

If you like, make your own seasoned salt and vary the level of seasoning as desired. Homemade seasoning makes a very nice gift. Save empty spice bottles and shaker tops and fill with seasoned salt. Tie a ribbon around the neck and enclose a recipe for the salt or for a special way to use it. (See also *Salt*.)

Seasoned Salt

½ teaspoon dried marjoram leaves
½ teaspoon dried thyme leaves
⅛ teaspoon dillseed
⅓ cup salt
2 teaspoons paprika
1 teaspoon dry mustard
½ teaspoon curry powder
½ teaspoon garlic salt
½ teaspoon celery salt
¼ teaspoon onion powder

Place marjoram, thyme, and dillseed in blender container; crush by turning blender on and off. Add remaining ingredients and blend.

Or crush marjoram, thyme, and dillseed by hand; combine all ingredients in screw-top jar and shake till well combined. Makes ⅓ cup.

Country Potato Salad

1 pound small new potatoes (8 to 10), cooked and peeled
3 cups torn lettuce
2 hard-cooked eggs, diced
3 tablespoons thinly sliced green onion
6 slices bacon
¼ cup vinegar
1 teaspoon seasoned salt
¼ teaspoon celery seed

Leave very small potatoes whole; halve or quarter larger ones. In bowl, combine potatoes, lettuce, eggs, and onion. In skillet, cook bacon till crisp; drain, reserving ¼ cup drippings. Crumble bacon; add to salad.

To reserved drippings in skillet, add vinegar, seasoned salt, celery seed, and ⅛ teaspoon pepper. Heat mixture to boiling. Then, pour over potato mixture. Toss quickly; serve immediately. Makes 4 to 6 servings.

SEASONING—A small amount of spices, herbs, and condiments added to improve the taste, aroma, and feel of a food. Feel refers to temperature and consistency of the food. For instance, chili powder makes a dish hot and filé gives a slippery texture to foods. (See *Flavoring, Herb, Spice* for additional information.)

SEA TROUT—A lean, saltwater fish found chiefly in the Atlantic and Gulf coasts. They are also called weakfish.

There are several types of sea trout available on the market. The gray, spotted, and white sea trout are marketed both whole and filleted. The whole ones average about one or two pounds. All are white fleshed, tender, and delicate. The flavor varies from type to type.

Sea trout can be boiled, steamed, or fried. To bake or broil sea trout, brush the fish with butter or shortening before cooking. (See also *Fish*.)

SEAWEED—A collective term for a number of sea plants used in various capacities involving food and food preparation. Examples include carrageen or Irish moss and dulse. Seaweed is high in iodine and this is its most important nutritive contribution. Seaweed can be eaten as a relish or cooked and served as a vegetable. Sometimes it is used as a thickening agent in foods such as pudding.

SEC (*sek*)—The French word for dry which means unsweet when applied to still wines, and indicates that a small amount of sugar is present when used in connection with sparkling wines.

SECKEL PEAR (*sek' uhl, sik'-*)—A small, yellowish-brown variety of pear which originated near Philadelphia during the eighteenth century. This delectable pear is named after the Pennsylvania farmer who developed it. The sweet, spicy flavor and very firm texture of the Seckel pear make it particularly suitable for pickling and preserves. (See also *Pear*.)

SEEDCAKE—A sweet, butter cake or cookie of Irish and Scottish origin that contains caraway seed, sesame seed, or poppy seed. These seeds are mixed into the rich cake batter before baking.

SELF-RISING FLOUR—A commercial flour product to which leavening and salt have been added during processing. Self-rising flour can be used for quick breads (except popovers), pastry, cookies, and cakes (except sponge cakes). Because homemakers in the South bake more quick breads, this type of flour is more commonly found in that area. (See also *Flour*.)

SELTZER WATER—1. A naturally effervescent mineral water containing uncombined carbon dioxide from Nieder Seltzers of the Wiesbaden, Germany, district. 2. Artificially carbonated effervescent water used in making soft drinks and in mixing alcoholic drinks. Seltzer water is often called carbonated water or soda water.

SEMISWEET CHOCOLATE—A type of chocolate suitable for cooking and eating that contains a small amount of sugar. Available packaged in bars, squares, or pieces, this chocolate is processed the same way as sweet chocolate save that less sweetening is added. Sometimes it is mint-flavored.

Semisweet chocolate melts easily during range-top cooking, yet holds its shape during baking at moderate oven temperatures. This is best illustrated by the intact pieces found in baked chocolate chip cookies and cakes. Melted semisweet chocolate squares are used for the chocolate coating on candies or for flavoring other types of candy. (See also *Chocolate*.)

Cake Mix Pronto Cookies

Full of chocolate pieces and nuts—

1 package 2-layer-size yellow
    cake mix
¼ cup butter or margarine,
    softened
⅓ cup milk
1 egg
½ teaspoon maple flavoring
   . . .
1 6-ounce package semisweet
    chocolate pieces (1 cup)
½ cup chopped walnuts

Combine cake mix, butter or margarine, milk, egg, and maple flavoring; beat until smooth. Stir in semisweet chocolate pieces and chopped walnuts. Drop from teaspoon onto greased cookie sheet. Bake at 375° for about 12 minutes. Let stand a few seconds before removing from sheet. Makes about 4½ dozen cookies.

Mocha-Frosted Drops

½ cup shortening
2 1-ounce squares unsweetened chocolate
1 cup brown sugar
1 egg
1 teaspoon vanilla
½ cup buttermilk *or* sour milk
1½ cups sifted all-purpose flour
½ teaspoon baking powder
½ teaspoon baking soda
¼ teaspoon salt
½ cup chopped walnuts
1 6-ounce package semisweet chocolate pieces (1 cup)
Mocha Frosting
Walnut halves

Melt shortening and unsweetened chocolate together in a saucepan. Cool mixture for 10 minutes. Stir in the brown sugar. Beat in the egg, vanilla, and buttermilk *or* sour milk.

Sift together dry ingredients and add to chocolate mixture. Stir in nuts and chocolate pieces. Drop from teaspoon on greased cookie sheet. Bake at 375° about 10 minutes. Remove from pan and cool. Frost with Mocha Frosting. Top with walnut half, if desired. Makes 42.

Mocha Frosting: Cream ¼ cup butter, 2 tablespoons unsweetened cocoa powder, 2 teaspoons instant coffee powder, and dash salt. Beat in 2½ cups confectioners' sugar, 1½ teaspoons vanilla, and enough milk until the frosting is of spreading consistency.

Chocolate Chip Cake

Chopped chocolate is layered in batter—

1 package 2-layer-size white cake mix
1 6-ounce package semisweet chocolate pieces (1 cup)
Sea Foam Frosting (See *Sea Foam*)

Prepare cake mix according to package directions. Reserving 3 tablespoons, chop remaining chocolate pieces. In 2 greased and lightly floured 8x1½- or 9x1½-inch round pans, alternate layers of batter with chopped chocolate. Bake as directed on package. Cool; frost with Seafoam Frosting. Dot with reserved chocolate.

Chocolate-Orange Rolls

Combine 1 package active dry yeast and 1½ cups sifted all-purpose flour. Heat together ½ cup milk, ¼ cup sugar, 2 tablespoons butter or margarine, and ½ teaspoon salt *just till warm*, stirring to melt butter. Add to dry mixture; add 2 eggs. Beat at low speed with electric mixer for ½ minute, scraping sides of bowl constantly. Beat 3 minutes at high speed. By hand, stir in ¾ to 1 cup sifted all-purpose flour, just enough to make a moderately soft dough.

Turn dough out onto lightly floured surface. Knead till smooth and elastic, about 4 to 5 minutes. Place dough in greased bowl; turn once to grease surface. Cover; let rise in warm place till double, about 1 hour. Punch down; turn out onto lightly floured surface. Cover; let dough rest for 10 minutes. Mix together ¼ cup sugar and 1 tablespoon shredded orange peel.

Roll dough to 15x10-inch rectangle. Spread with 2 tablespoons *softened* butter; sprinkle with the sugar mixture, then with ½ cup semisweet chocolate pieces. Roll up jelly-roll fashion, starting with the long side. Then, cut roll into 18 slices; place slices, cut side down, in two 9x9x2-inch baking pans (9 rolls in each pan). Let dough rise till nearly double, about 25 to 30 minutes. Bake at 375° till golden brown, about 12 to 15 minutes. Makes 18.

Chip-Cherry Fruitcake

3 eggs
1 cup sugar
1½ cups sifted all-purpose flour
1½ teaspoons baking powder
¼ teaspoon salt
1 6-ounce package semisweet chocolate pieces (1 cup)
2 cups chopped pecans
1 8-ounce package dates, coarsely snipped (1⅓ cups)
1 cup halved candied cherries

Beat eggs; stir in sugar. Sift together flour, baking powder, and salt; combine with chocolate pieces, pecans, dates, and candied cherries. Fold in egg-sugar mixture. Turn into greased and paper-lined 9x5x3-inch loaf pan. Place pan of water on bottom oven rack while baking. Bake on top rack at 325° for 1 hour. Cool slightly. Remove from pan; cool on rack.

SEMOLINA *(sem' uh lē' nuh)* — A coarse granulation of the durum wheat endosperm. It is made by grinding and bolting (sifting) durum wheat, separating the bran and germ to produce a granular product of not more than three percent flour. The term semolina comes from the Latin word *simila* which means finely ground wheat flour.

Semolina is used as the gluten in making high-quality pasta products. It is also used in making cereals, puddings, and soups. (See also *Durum Wheat.*)

SENEGALESE *(sen' uh go lēz', -les', -guh-)* — A term used as part of a recipe title which indicates that curry is an ingredient.

SESAME SEED *(ses' uh mē)* — A tiny, pale honey-colored seed with a mild, sweet, nutlike flavor produced from an annual tropical or subtropical herbaceous plant. Sesame is native to Asia, and has been cultivated in India, China, and Africa for thousands of years. Most likely the oldest crop grown for its edible oil, sesame dates back to 1600 B.C. Sesame seed, then known in Africa as *benne,* was first brought to America by slaves during the sixteenth and seventeenth centuries. Besides being edible, the seeds were thought to be tokens of good luck. The oil extracted from the seeds was often used for medicinal purposes.

The tiny seeds ripen inside a pod which bursts open upon maturation with a sharp pop. This sound, like the springing open of a door lock, may well be the source for Ali Baba's famous saying, "Open Sesame," which opened the door to riches in the tales of *The Thousand and One Nights.*

When the pods containing the sesame seed are well formed but green, they are harvested to minimize seed loss due to shattering. The crop is shucked like corn after being cut and tied in bundles.

Most sesame seed is hulled during processing. Whole sesame seed is available in most markets and sesame seed oil is found in specialty shops. It takes more than 12,000 seeds to make one ounce. Sesame seed oil, used as a cooking or salad oil as well as an ingredient in margarines and other shortenings, is produced by pressing the oil from the seeds.

Toasting sesame seed

Toasting brings out the flavor of sesame seeds and gives them a crunchy texture. If sprinkled atop breads or casseroles before baking, they will be toasted as the food cooks. If used as an ingredient, toast the seeds first.

To toast sesame seeds, spread seeds in a thin layer in a shallow, ungreased pan. Heat them in a preheated, moderate oven 10 to 15 minutes, stirring once or twice.

Sesame seed gives the distinctive flavor to the Turkish confection called halvah. You'll find both the flavor and texture of the seeds most enjoyable in cookies, on breads, with vegetables, chicken, and fish. Keep toasted sesame seed handy, too, to sprinkle onto salads, soups, and plain buttered vegetables just before serving.

Chicken-Sesame Balls

Combine two 5-ounce cans boned chicken, finely chopped; 1 tablespoon finely chopped onion; 2 tablespoons finely chopped, canned pimiento; 4 drops bottled hot pepper sauce; 1 tablespoon prepared mustard; and ¼ cup mayonnaise or salad dressing. Mix till thoroughly blended.

Form into balls, using about 1 teaspoon of mixture for each. Chill thoroughly, about 1 hour. Roll chilled balls in ¼ cup sesame seed, toasted. Makes 3 dozen appetizers.

Sesame Biscuits

Sift together 2 cups sifted all-purpose flour, 4 teaspoons baking powder, 2 teaspoons sugar, ½ teaspoon salt, and ½ teaspoon cream of tartar. Cut in ½ cup shortening till mixture is like coarse crumbs. Add ⅔ cup milk; stir only till dough follows fork around bowl.

Knead gently on lightly floured surface for 30 seconds. Roll ½ inch thick; cut in 2½-inch rounds. Place biscuits on *ungreased* baking sheet. Brush tops with a little milk. Sprinkle tops of biscuits with 1 tablespoon sesame seed. Bake biscuits at 450° for 10 to 12 minutes. Makes 16 biscuits.

Spiced Sesame Bars

Coat tiny bar cookies with sesame seed—

    ½ cup sifted all-purpose flour
    ¼ teaspoon salt
    ¼ teaspoon baking soda
    ¼ teaspoon ground allspice
    ¼ teaspoon ground mace
    ½ teaspoon ground cinnamon
    1 egg
    ¾ cup brown sugar
    3 tablespoons butter, melted
    ¼ cup sesame seed, toasted

Sift together flour, salt, soda, and spices; set aside. Beat egg; gradually add sugar and mix well. Stir in butter, then dry ingredients. Sprinkle *half* the sesame seed over bottom of greased 8x8x2-inch baking pan; pour in batter; top with remaining seed. Bake at 350° for 20 minutes. Let cool; cut in bars. Makes 32.

Sesame Cake

Sesame seed adds a delicate, nutlike flavor—

    2¼ cups sifted cake flour
    1½ cups sugar
    3 teaspoons baking powder
    ½ teaspoon salt
    ¼ teaspoon ground mace
    ½ cup sesame seed, toasted
    ½ cup shortening
    1¼ cups milk
    2 eggs
       Sea Foam Frosting (See *Sea Foam*)

Sift together dry ingredients; stir in sesame seed. Add shortening and ¾ *cup* milk. Beat 2 minutes on electric mixer. Add remaining milk and eggs; beat 1 minute. Pour into 2 greased and floured 8x1½-inch round pans. Bake at 350° for 25 minutes. Remove from pans. Frost the cooled cake with Seafoam Frosting.

SEVICHE *(sa vesh')* — A South American fish dish served as an appetizer. This dish is prepared by soaking delicate white fish meat, such as red snapper or lemon sole, in lime or lemon juice or sour orange juice with onions and hot peppers.

Brush biscuit tops with milk and sprinkle with sesame seed before baking. The baked biscuits will have a crunchy, toasted top.

SEVILLE ORANGE *(suh vil', sev' il)* — A variety of orange with bitter pulp and peel. Seville oranges are used in making marmalade with an aromatic bitter tang; they are also used in the manufacture of orange-flavored bitters which are used in making mixed drinks. (See also *Orange*.)

SHAD — A food fish related to the herring. These fish grow to a length of 30 inches and a weight of 14 pounds. They have a silvery coloring with a bluish-green tint on the back, and a dark spot and several lighter spots just behind the gills. The shad migrate upstream to spawn (like salmon), then journey to the sea. They are found in the Mediterranean Sea and the Atlantic and Pacific oceans.

Shad has been fished in America for centuries. The American Indians along the eastern coast were using shad for food long before the Europeans discovered America. The Indians' fishing and cooking techniques were picked up by the early settlers and many are still used today.

In colonial times, shad was so plentiful and inexpensive in America that it became known as food of the poor classes. However, the wealthier colonists were unable to resist its fine flavor, and shad soon appeared in menus at parties and dinners attended by early statesmen such as George Washington.

Americans made several attempts to spread the shad to new waters. In the 1870s, shad were successfully planted along the Pacific coast. However, they never flourished in the inland streams and lakes. Today shad is found on the market from January to June. The fish are sold whole, drawn, or in fillets. Upon request, the fish market will remove the bones so the fish will be easier to eat.

Shad can be baked, broiled, boiled, steamed, fried, planked, and stuffed. Whatever method you use, the skin should be left on during cooking to hold the delicate, pink flesh together.

The roe from shad is also considered gourmet fare when it is used in making many appetizers and entrees. It can be purchased fresh or canned.

Shad supplies protein, minerals and B vitamins in the diet. A four-ounce serving of baked shad contains 200 calories, and three and a half ounces of raw roe contains 130 calories. (See also *Fish*.)

SHAKER COOKERY — The cooking techniques and dishes developed by an offshoot Quaker group, called Shakers, in Massachusetts. It is characterized by genuine simplicity and excellent quality.

The Shakers, so named because of a ritual dance, were among English Quakers who fled to the American Colonies seeking freedom to exercise their religious beliefs. They advocated communal living and pacifism. Shakers settled in the northeast, founding a handful of small communities. Even though only a few of these settlements remain today, several museums and restored or preserved villages retain furniture, handwritten recipes, and numerous ingenious cooking or homemaking aids that the Shakers skillfully created.

Because of the philosophy of communal living, the Shaker women cooked for the entire community. To make this as efficient as possible, the Shakers devised a number of ideas for large-scale cooking: piping water to cooking areas; stone sinks; baking and canning kitchens; a type of re-

volving oven that allowed many pies to be baked together; and baskets and wooden firkins for holding foods.

As much as possible, the Shakers grew their own food, or gathered it from the surrounding woodland. Herbs were grown in abundance, and milk, cream, butter, and lard were favored cooking ingredients. Such sought-after items as lemons, which were valued for many cooking uses, and refined sugar had to be obtained from non-Shaker communities.

Also, because of the Shakers' austerity, they were most particular about not wasting food. They dropped the traditional, rather sloppy method of measuring ingredients by plops, globs, or describing amounts as "walnut- or egg-sized" and established exact weights and measures for their ingredients. They cherished every scrap of food, a philosophy that led to large-scale canning. Any edible portion of food that could be canned was used—for example, the Shakers made apple peel jelly and pickled fruit peel.

The Shaker diet, at one time completely meatless, consisted of many vegetables, fruits, cereals, eggs, cheese, and dairy products. Religious practices prompted a meat ban observed by many Shakers during the 1830s and 1840s.

Baking was an important part of Shaker cookery. Bread was basic, made from flour milled to retain the germ (whole wheat) and homemade yeast. Thus, the daily loaf was often a true wheaten bread. But they turned out other types, including salt-rising bread, potato bread, muffins or gems, tea breads—nearly two dozen kinds in all.

Cakes were made with precisely proportioned and measured ingredients. Maple syrup and sugar, honey, and molasses were used when ordinary sugar was scarce. A plentiful supply of sugar meant delectable pound cakes, sponge cakes and cookies would emerge from the ovens. Rosewater was prepared for use as a flavoring, and herb seeds were used in cookies. Butternuts and hickory nuts, gathered in the woods, supplied a crunchy taste that made layer and loaf cakes special treats.

Shakers baked pies of infinite variety, the crusts plain, buttery rich, or puffy, depending on the filling. There were fruit and berry pies and such favorites as pumpkin, maple custard, and cider syrup pies. Plus, when there was no ban on it, meat pies supplemented the roasts, steaks, chops, hams, and salt pork more commonly used as main dishes. The Shaker cooks also produced a variety of puddings, velvety custards, dumplings of many flavors, and apples gelled in boiled syrup.

The herbs of the garden, fresh in the summer and dried for winter use, were added to many Shaker foods. There was likely to be a touch of rosemary in spinach, savory in beans, a rose geranium leaf in a glass of apple jelly, a sprig of marjoram or thyme in a stew, or a few nasturtium leaves in a lettuce salad. Mixed herbs seasoned the meat dishes.

The Shakers' significant way of living and their pride in workmanship has led to a number of enduring recipes. Excellence in quality and simplicity, along with the overwhelming responsibility women felt toward their families' need for wholesome food, guided the recipe development.

Shaker Baked Beans

Develop rich bean flavor with long, slow cooking—

>   1 pound dry navy beans (2 cups)
> 1½ quarts cold water
>   1 teaspoon salt
>   1 small onion, peeled and sliced
>   4 tablespoons butter or margarine
>   ¼ cup catsup
>   ¼ cup molasses
>   1 teaspoon dry mustard
>   ½ teaspoon salt

Rinse beans; add to cold water. Bring to boiling; simmer 2 minutes. Remove from heat. Cover and let stand for 1 hour. Add 1 teaspoon salt; cover and simmer till beans are tender, about 1 hour. Drain, reserving bean liquid.

Place onion into a 2-quart bean pot or casserole. Add beans. Combine 2¼ cups of the bean liquid with butter or margarine, catsup, molasses, dry mustard, and the ½ teaspoon salt. Pour mixture over beans; cover and bake at 325° for 4 to 4½ hours. Add more liquid to beans, if necessary, during baking. Remove cover last half hour of baking to brown well.

Special Cabbage Salad

>   4 cups shredded cabbage
>   ½ cup light cream
>   2 tablespoons sugar
>   1 teaspoon salt
>   Dash pepper
>   2 tablespoons vinegar
>   2 hard-cooked eggs

Heap shredded cabbage in bowl. Combine cream, sugar, salt, pepper, and vinegar. Pour over cabbage; toss lightly. Slice eggs; sieve yolks. Arrange egg white rings around rim of bowl; put sieved yolk in center. Serves 6.

Shaker Daily Loaf

>   1 package active dry yeast
> 6½ to 7 cups sifted all-purpose
>   flour
> 2½ cups milk
>   2 tablespoons butter or margarine
>   2 tablespoons sugar
>   2 teaspoons salt

In mixer bowl combine yeast and 2¾ *cups* of the flour. Heat milk, butter, sugar, and salt just till warm, stirring occasionally to melt butter. Add to dry mixture in bowl. Beat at low speed with electric mixer for ½ minute, scraping sides constantly. Beat 3 minutes at high speed. By hand, stir in enough of remaining flour to make moderately stiff dough.

Let rise in warm place till double, about 1½ hours. Turn out and knead on lightly floured surface till smooth and elastic. Cover and let rest 10 minutes. Shape in 2 loaves. Place in greased 8½x4½x2½-inch loaf dishes. Cover and let rise till double in warm place, about 1¼ hours. Bake at 350° for 35 to 40 minutes.

SHALLOT (*shuh lot'*)—A mild-flavored vegetable related to onions. The bulbs grow in segments, like garlic cloves. At the market shallots resemble small, dried onions with reddish-brown skins having purple-white cloves underneath.

Although several areas on the eastern Mediterranean coast are credited with growing the first shallots, it is known that ancient Greeks obtained this vegetable from the village of Ascalon, Palestine. In fact, shallots, called *echalotes* in French, get their name from this ancient seaport, which is located in the Middle East.

Shallots were first brought into Europe by the French, probably during the first or second century. During the next several centuries the shallot became known and used throughout Europe. In the early sixteenth century, this vegetable was introduced into America, reportedly by followers of the Spanish explorer De Soto.

Fresh shallots should be selected and stored like dry onion varieties. Paper-thin, clean, bright-colored skins and thin-necked, dry, firm bulbs indicate good quality. Shallots are also sold chopped in freeze-dried and frozen forms.

The shallot's segmented structure makes it easy to use a portion of the bulb. Or, you can simply measure out the needed amount of the frozen or freeze-dried forms. Frozen or freeze-dried, shallots substitute equally for chopped, fresh shallots.

Shallots add mellow flavor to any dish in which onions are used. Slice fresh shallots and add them to tossed salads; or dice and cook them in butter, and place them atop broiled steaks. When browning fresh shallots, take care. Overbrowning causes a bitter flavor. (See also *Onion*.)

Barquette of Tiny Shrimp

1½ cups sifted all-purpose flour
½ teaspoon salt
½ cup shortening
4 to 5 tablespoons cold water
1 tablespoon salt
3 cups water
1 pound tiny shrimp in shell *or* 2 4½-ounce cans shrimp
2 tablespoons finely chopped celery
1 tablespoon chopped shallots
½ teaspoon dried dillweed
½ cup catsup
2 tablespoons lemon juice
2 tablespoons mayonnaise
2 teaspoons prepared mustard
1 teaspoon prepared horseradish
Chopped black olives
Sieved egg yolk

Sift together flour and salt. Cut in shortening with pastry blender till pieces are size of small peas. Sprinkle *1 tablespoon* of the water over part of mixture. Gently toss with fork; push to one side of bowl. Repeat till all is moistened. Gather up the mixture with fingers; form the dough lightly into a ball.

On lightly floured surface, roll dough to 14x15-inch rectangle. Top with same size aluminum foil; mark in 3x2-inch rectangles. Cut small rectangles with scissors, cutting through pastry and foil at the same time. Turn each rectangle pastry side up; prick well with fork. Moisten 2-inch ends of pastry; pinch together (along with foil) to form "boats," (foil will help keep the shape while baking). Place "boats" on baking sheet; spread sides to keep upright. Bake at 425° till lightly browned, about 10 minutes. Cool. Remove the foil.

Add the salt to water; bring the mixture to boiling. Add shrimp; cover and heat to boiling. Reduce heat; simmer gently till shrimp turn pink, about 5 minutes. Drain. Peel and devein shrimp; chop fine. Combine with remaining ingredients; mix well. Chill. Fill pastry with shrimp; garnish with olives and egg yolk. Serve as appetizer. Makes about 36 appetizers.

SHANDYGAFF *(shan' dē gaf')*—An English alcoholic drink consisting of ale or beer mixed with ginger beer or ginger ale. The two ingredients are simply mixed by stirring together gently. This cold drink was introduced to India as the beverage to accompany dishes made with curry.

SHANK—A cut of beef, veal, lamb, or pork, taken from the upper part of the front leg. Retail beef cuts include shank cross cuts, while the cuts in lamb and veal are termed fore shanks. In pork, the fore shank is often called hock. Because the shank is less tender than some other cuts, moist cooking methods such as braising and cooking in liquid are recommended.

International outdoor cooking

Feature Lamb Shanks, Armenian-Italian at →
your next outdoor barbecue. Lamb shanks are marinated in an herb-tomato mixture.

Lamb Shanks, Armenian–Italian

  1 cup tomato juice
  ½ cup lemon juice
  ½ cup dill pickle juice
  1 large onion, finely chopped
  1 green pepper, finely chopped
  1 teaspoon salt
  1 teaspoon coarse-cracked pepper
  1 teaspoon cumin
  1 teaspoon dried marjoram leaves,
    crushed
  6 meaty lamb shanks
    Salt

For marinade, combine first 9 ingredients; pour over lamb shanks in deep bowl and let stand 4 hours. Remove from marinade. Salt the meat. Broil over *slow* coals till tender, about 1 hour, brushing with marinade and turning occasionally. Heat the remaining marinade; serve as a relish. Makes 6 servings.

SHAPED COOKIE—A cookie molded by hand from a pliable dough. Roll the dough into a simple ball or form a long, pencil-thin roll and shape into tiny twists of artistry such as candy canes or Christmas wreaths. Select your favorite filling such as dates, candied fruits, or nut pieces around which to wrap a small bit of the cookie dough. Concentrate on keeping the cookies about the same size so they will bake evenly.

Before baking, flatten the cookie balls with the bottom of a glass which has been dipped in sugar or flour. Then use the tines of a fork to make crisscross patterns across the top of the cookie. Or, before baking, press your thumb in the center of the cookie. Fill this indentation with a chocolate piece or a dab of your favorite jelly or jam after baking. (See also *Cookie*.)

Macaroon Bonbons

  2 egg whites
  1 teaspoon vanilla
    Dash salt
  ½ cup sugar
  2 tablespoons all-purpose flour
  1 cup grated coconut
  3 drops red food coloring

Shape cookies into smooth 1-inch balls by rolling between hands. Make a design on cookie by pressing tops with tines of fork.

Beat egg whites with vanilla and salt till soft peaks form. Gradually add sugar, beating to stiff peaks. Fold in flour and coconut. Remove a *third* of dough to second bowl. With food coloring, tint remaining ⅔ of dough pink. Roll pink dough in ½-inch balls; place on greased cookie sheet. With thumb, make small indentation; top with ¼-inch balls of the white dough. Bake at 350° about 8 to 10 minutes. Let stand 1 minute; remove to rack. Makes 30.

Cream Cheese Dainties

  ½ cup butter or margarine
  1 3-ounce package cream cheese,
    softened
  ½ cup sugar
  ¼ teaspoon almond extract
  1 cup sifted all-purpose flour
  2 teaspoons baking powder
  ¼ teaspoon salt
  1½ cups crisp rice cereal, coarsely
    crushed
    Red and green candied cherries

Cream together butter or margarine, cream cheese, sugar, and almond extract till light. Sift together flour, baking powder, and salt; stir into butter mixture just till combined. Chill 1 to 2 hours. Shape into balls; roll in cereal and place on *ungreased* cookie sheet. Top each with a cherry. Bake at 350° for 12 to 15 minutes. Cool on racks. Makes 4 dozen.

Double Buttercups

Press candies in center of each cookie—

Combine 2 sticks piecrust mix, crumbled; one 3-ounce can chow mein noodles, crushed; and 1/3 cup brown sugar. Blend in 1/4 cup peanut butter, 1 beaten egg, 2 teaspoons water, and 1/2 teaspoon vanilla. Shape into 1-inch balls. Place on *ungreased* cookie sheet. Make a large depression in center of each. Bake at 375° for 8 minutes. Using one 11-ounce box bite-sized chocolate-covered peanut buttercup candies (40), press a candy in each center. Bake 2 to 3 minutes. Cool 5 minutes; remove. Makes 40.

Coconut Dainties

       1 cup butter or margarine
    1/4 cup sifted confectioners' sugar
       2 teaspoons vanilla
       1 tablespoon water
       2 cups sifted all-purpose flour
       1 cup chopped pecans
             . . .
         Light cream
       2 cups sifted confectioners'
            sugar
         Tinted Coconut

Thoroughly cream butter or margarine, 1/4 cup sifted confectioners' sugar, and vanilla. Stir in water. Add flour and mix well. Stir in nuts.

Shape in 1-inch balls. Bake 1 inch apart on an *ungreased* cookie sheet at 300° till firm to the touch, about 20 minutes. Cool thoroughly before removing from pan.

Add sufficient light cream to 2 cups sifted confectioners' sugar to make of spreading consistency. Dip cookies in icing and roll in Tinted Coconut. Makes 4 dozen.

Tinted Coconut: Shake flaked coconut in covered jar with few drops food coloring.

SHARPENING STONE—A smooth piece of soapstone or a manufactured, shaped carborundum piece used to sharpen knives.

SHASHLIK *(shäsh lik', shäsh' lik)*—The Russian and Turkish name for shish kabob. The marinated meat, usually lamb, is broiled along with vegetables on a skewer.

Lamb Shashlik

Brush melted butter over the skewers of lamb cubes and bright vegetable pieces during broiling—

In deep bowl combine 1/2 cup olive *or* salad oil; 1/4 cup lemon juice; 1 teaspoon salt; 1 teaspoon dried marjoram leaves, crushed; 1 teaspoon dried thyme leaves, crushed; 1/2 teaspoon pepper; 1 clove garlic, minced; 1/2 cup chopped onion; and 1/4 cup snipped parsley. Mix well.

Cut 2 pounds boneless lamb into 1 1/2-inch cubes. Add lamb to marinade; stir to coat. Cover; refrigerate overnight or let stand at room temperature 2 to 3 hours. Turn occasionally.

Fill skewers, alternating the meat cubes with green pepper and sweet red pepper quarters and thick onion slices. Broil 5 inches from heat till done, about 8 to 10 minutes, brushing frequently with melted butter or margarine. Turn often. Makes 6 servings.

SHEDDAR—The term used for lobsters and crabs whose shells are soft, due to the annual shedding of the old shell and growing of the new one. Blue crabs, commonly sold as soft-shell crabs, and lobster claws that can be broken open with the fingers instead of a nutcracker or similar device are called sheddars.

SHEEPBERRY—A wild berry from the hawthorn shrub. Also called black haw, it is used in jams and jellies. (See also *Berry*.)

SHEEPSHEAD—**1.** A saltwater fish related to the porgy. **2.** Another name for the freshwater drum found in the midwestern and southern United States.

Generally, the saltwater sheepshead lives along the Atlantic, Pacific, and Gulf coasts of the United States. A few of these fish are caught in rivers.

The sheepshead is noted for strong teeth which it uses to crush the shellfish it catches for food. It has a thick body banded with seven or eight dark stripes. The sheepshead can grow as large as 30 inches long and weigh up to 15 pounds. The market size averages 1 1/2 pounds.

The white, tender flesh of this fish has 113 calories in a 3 1/2-ounce serving before it is cooked. (See also *Fish*.)

SHELLFISH

Complete directions on selecting, cleaning, and cooking delicacies from the seas.

A shellfish is a saltwater or freshwater animal with a shell, but no fins, skull, or vertebrae like a fish. Some of the most familiar are the shrimp, lobster, crab, oyster, clam, scallop, and crayfish.

These creatures have been used as a source of food since the beginning of history. Early man undoubtedly found shellfish abundant along the shores and could capture them easily. Then, as he began to migrate, he followed water courses for supplies of food and drink. Even after he settled into an agricultural way of life, man continued to depend on shellfish as a supplement to his daily diet.

He eventually came to consider shellfish as a highly prized delicacy. In Julius Caesar's time, oysters and various forms of shellfish were the first course served at dinners for high state officials. Similarly, the Chinese included shellfish among the 200 or more dishes that were usually served at banquets.

The pilgrims who came to America found the coast teeming with shellfish. They used them as basic food just as the American Indians did. But when the settlers began to move westward, they were too far from the coast to get shellfish.

With the development of modern freezing methods and rapid transportation, Americans throughout the country have been able to obtain fresh shellfish. Since this relatively recent development, shellfish has become universally popular.

Crab and shrimp star in menu

← Plan a dinner around rich shellfish baked in coquilles. A vegetable, salad, white wine, and peaches complement Seafood Bake.

Nutritional value: Shellfish, like fish, are an excellent source of easily digestible protein, minerals, and vitamins. They are particularly rich in the minerals—calcium, phosphorous, iron, copper, magnesium, and iodine. The B vitamins, vitamin A, and vitamin D are also present.

All shellfish are lean and low in salt content, which makes them suitable for low-calorie or low-sodium diets.

In addition to being a very healthful food, they appeal to most palates.

Types of shellfish

The various types of shellfish have a number of common characteristics. Most are hatched from eggs in a form quite different from the adult. They pass through a series of developmental phases before they finally reach adulthood.

Shellfish eat both animal and vegetable matter. Since they do not have to exert much energy to hunt for food, their muscles do not become tough, and they have especially tender meat.

There are basically two types of shellfish—the mollusks and the crustaceans. The mollusks have a soft body partially or completely enclosed in a shell. Those with shells of only one part, such as the abalone, conch, and periwinkle, are univalve mollusks. The clam, cockle, mussel, oyster, and scallop are bivalve mollusks because of their two-part shell.

The crustaceans usually have elongated, segmented bodies with crustlike shells. Their eyes are mounted on movable stalks and their bodies are not always symmetrical. For instance, a pair of claws are sometimes different sizes. Those in this category include the lobster, crab, shrimp, crayfish, and prawn.

Each type of shellfish has individual characteristics and habits which distinguish it from the others in this group.

Abalone: These marine snails are found on the coasts of California, France and South Africa. The large footlike muscle tastes like clam, but needs tenderizing and must be pounded with a mallet. Fresh abalone is available only near the coast. Canned and frozen abalone can be found elsewhere in seafood stores. Because the Chinese-Americans have incorporated abalone into many of the dishes of their cuisine, abalone is also available in many oriental specialty food stores.

Conch: This shellfish with the beautiful spiral shell inhabits southern waters such as the Florida coast, the Caribbean Sea, and the Mediterranean Sea. The large muscle of the conch has a fine flavor, but it must be tenderized before cooking. Conchs are available canned. Many Italian specialty food stores carry them.

Periwinkle: Small marine snails, called periwinkles, are found in salt or fresh water in Europe and on the eastern coast of North America. The muscle has gained much popularity in the British Isles.

Clam: Hard, soft-shell, surf, butter, littleneck, and pismo clams are found along the various coasts of America. Because the clams burrow deeply into the sand and are difficult to harvest, certain species were expensive for many years. In the 1950s, the invention of a hydraulic dredge made harvesting easier. Now more abundant supplies are available to those who enjoy the traditional clambake, clam chowder, and clam entrées.

Cockle: Cockles are found in the salt waters that surround England, France, and America. The sweet meat is eaten raw or cooked like clams. Although cockles have never been a popular dish in America, these small delights are available in American markets canned or shelled.

Mussel: These small shellfish are found in both salt and fresh water, but only those from salt water are eaten. They have long been a favorite in Europe, especially in France. Mussels have not been widely used in the United States even though they are abundant. They are usually cooked with white wine, butter, and shallots.

Oyster: In America most oysters are found along the East and Gulf coasts from Massachusetts to Texas and along the West Coast from Washington to Mexico. The principal types of oysters include the Eastern, Pacific, and Olympia.

Oysters are cultivated underwater with the same attention that truck gardens are given. Oysters are eaten either raw or cooked, and are used in stews, and as appetizers, and entrées.

Scallop: These shellfish are found along the coast from New England to the Gulf and off Alaska. Most Americans eat only the "eye" or large muscle that opens the shell. Europeans, however, eat the entire scallop. The sweet, white, firm meat of scallops is eaten raw or cooked as appetizers, salads, and main dishes.

Crab: The most common types are the king, Dungeness, stone, tanner or snow, and blue crabs, which are found along all United States coasts. Long, coarse fibers make up the crab meat, which is generally tender and sweet. Crab is cooked and eaten hot or cold, either alone or in mixtures. It is used in appetizers, soups, chowders, gumbos, salads, and entrées.

Crayfish: These shellfish quite closely resemble a lobster in appearance and taste. In fact, saltwater varieties, which live along the southern Atlantic, Pacific, and Mediterranean shores, are called spiny or rock lobsters.

Lobster: Northern or Maine lobsters in America are found along the eastern coast from Virginia to Maine. Spiny lobsters are in Florida, southern California, South Africa, Australia, and the Mediterranean.

Lobsters are the largest shellfish and the sweet meat is picked from the shell after cooking, for eating plain or for combining with other ingredients.

Prawn: Prawns resemble large shrimps with which they are frequently confused. They are found in temperate and tropical waters, both fresh and salt. Prawns are used in the same way as are shrimp.

Shrimp: Proclaimed by many as the most popular shellfish, shrimp is enjoyed for its sweet, firm meat. These small, slender shellfish are caught in south Atlantic, Gulf, Maine, California, and Alaskan waters. They are cooked and served hot or cold, either alone, with a sauce, or in combination with other ingredients.

Selection of shellfish

Going to the fish market or supermarket to buy shellfish can be an adventure when you know what you want and how to select the best products. Decide how much will be needed and which form will best fit the recipe preparation—live in the shell, fresh, frozen, or canned.

How much to buy

Shellfish	Amount for 1 person*
Abalone	5 ounces
Clam (in shell)	15 to 20
(shucked)	½ to ¾ cup
Crab, whole blue	2 to 4
whole Dungeness	½ to 1
Crab meat	4 ounces
Crayfish	10
Lobster, whole	1 pound
Lobster meat	4 ounces
Lobster tails	1 tail
	8 ounces
Mussels	12
Oysters (in shell)	6
(shucked)	½ to ¾ cup
Prawns	6 large
Scallops	4 to 5 ounces
Shrimp	6 large
(shelled)	4 ounces

*The amounts listed are average servings as an entrée. If persons are hearty eaters, larger amounts may be needed. When served as an appetizer or with a rich sauce, less is needed.

Fresh: Each type of shellfish can be purchased in a wide variety of fresh forms. Some shellfish are sold alive and the consumer does all the preparation, while others have been shucked or cooked before they are sold at the market.

Those that are marketed alive must be active. Crabs and lobsters should show movement in the legs. Hard clams, oysters, and scallops should close their shells tightly when they are tapped gently. If the shellfish do not show these signs of life, then probably they are dead and should not be purchased or eaten.

Most of the shellfish are available shucked, which means that the scallops, oysters, clams, or mussels have been removed from their shell while alive and then packed in clear liquid. This saves the consumer much time and work.

Shrimp and prawns are usually sold with the heads removed. A greenish or pink color, firm texture, and mild odor are indications that shrimp are fresh.

Lobsters and crabs are also sold cooked. The market cooks the shellfish and sells them whole or the meat is picked from the shell and is packaged and chilled.

Frozen: Shellfish are frozen in practically every form: cooked, uncooked, in the shell, and out of the shell. Some are sold breaded and ready to fry or bake.

Canned: Whole shellfish, lumps of meat, minced meat, and smoked meat are canned for wide distribution. These may be "dry packed" in a vacuum without liquid, or "liquid packed" in a brine or juice.

The federal and state governments have adapted standards to assist the consumer in purchasing shellfish. These standards are reflected in the listing of correct contents and amounts on the label.

The U.S. inspection shield on shellfish indicates that the product was processed under the supervision of a trained government inspector. Shellfish that meet specifications can also be given the Grade A rating just as fish are graded.

Many coastal states have inspection programs to make sure that shellfish are not taken from polluted waters or processed under unsanitary conditions.

Storage of shellfish

Shellfish are quite perishable. They must be carefully handled and refrigerated to preserve quality. Cook live ones immediately and use cooked meat quickly.

For longer storage, freeze fresh and live shellfish. Oysters, clams, and scallops should be shucked before freezing; use within three months. Lobster and crab should be cooked before freezing; use within a month. Freeze uncooked shrimp, in shells or shelled; and keep as long as three months. Thaw shellfish in the refrigerator or cook while frozen.

Commercially frozen shellfish will keep about four months in a home freezer. Canned products will keep a year.

Preparation of shellfish

The most important principle in cooking shellfish is to cook them only until done, for overcooking toughens the meat. Mollusks, such as oysters and clams, are done when the meat curls around the edges or when the shells open, and crustacea, such as lobster and shrimp, are done when they turn a bright pink or red color.

Shellfish are eaten raw, steamed, boiled, broiled, baked, or fried. Each method of cookery should be explored to discover the flavor of shellfish in various forms.

Raw: Oysters, clams, and scallops are the shellfish most commonly eaten raw. Because the muscles are tender and the flavor delicate, they are regarded as gourmet fare. The only preparation necessary is to open the shells (insert knife between halves, pry open, and cut muscle free).

Serve these raw shellfish very cold. Placing one half of the shell and the muscles on a bed of cracked ice keeps them cold and is an attractive way of serving them. Lemon juice, lime juice, freshly ground pepper, or horseradish can be served to accent the flavor as desired.

Boiling or steaming: These methods of cooking shellfish require a short time and minimum preparation. Some shellfish need scrubbing or cleaning, but some clean themselves if placed in salted water.

Shellfish should be alive when put into boiling water or steamed, but you need not worry—the shellfish are killed instantly. With a little practice, one learns to do this quickly and easily.

Plunge the lobsters and crabs into boiling salted water or court bouillon for about 20 minutes. With clams, oysters, and scallops, boil or place them on a rack in a deep pot or kettle with a small amount of boiling water (water does not touch them). In about 5 minutes, the shells open, showing they are cooked. Any shells that do not open with the majority must be discarded. This indicates the shellfish was not alive when cooking began.

Once cooked, serve these shellfish in the shell and let each person pick out the meat for himself. You can remove the meat before serving if you prefer.

Boiled or steamed shellfish meats are frequently combined with ingredients for an entrée, casserole, appetizer, salad, soup, chowder, or sauce. Cook the meat at home, or buy it already cooked in a can or in a package of fresh-cooked meat.

Spinach–Shrimp Salad

⅔ cup salad oil
⅓ cup orange juice
2 tablespoons sugar
1 tablespoon vinegar
½ teaspoon grated orange peel
¼ teaspoon salt
¼ teaspoon dry mustard
    Dash bottled hot pepper sauce
    • • •
1 large avocado
1 tablespoon orange juice
1 pound fresh spinach, torn in
    pieces (12 cups)
2 cups cooked, shelled shrimp
3 oranges, sectioned

In screw-top jar combine salad oil, the ⅓ cup orange juice, sugar, vinegar, orange peel, salt, dry mustard, and hot pepper sauce. Shake well and chill. Makes 1⅓ cups dressing.

Just before serving, peel avocado and slice into rings; sprinkle with orange juice. Combine avocado, spinach, shrimp, and oranges in salad bowl. Toss with dressing. Serves 6 to 8.

Seafood Salad

3 tablespoons lemon juice
2 cups cooked shrimp, crab, *or*
   lobster meat
1 cup chopped celery
   Mayonnaise or salad dressing
3 hard-cooked eggs, sliced
   Lettuce
   Lemon wedges

Sprinkle the 3 tablespoons lemon juice over shellfish. Add celery. Moisten with mayonnaise; season with salt and pepper. Fold in hard-cooked eggs. Arrange salad in lettuce-lined bowl with lemon wedges. Makes 4 to 6 servings.

Crab-Filled Abalone Shell

1 cup cooked crab meat
1 tablespoon diced celery
1 tablespoon mayonnaise
1 teaspoon prepared horseradish
½ teaspoon lemon juice
   Salt
   Pepper
   Abalone shell
   Lettuce

Combine crab meat, celery, mayonnaise, horseradish, and lemon juice. Add salt and pepper to taste. Line an abalone shell with lettuce; fill with the crab salad. Makes 1 serving.

Tossing Spinach-Shrimp Salad with a slightly sweet, orange French dressing brings out the best in all the fresh flavors. Serve this meal-in-one salad for lunch or a light supper.

Split jumbo shrimp about halfway through and stuff with a well-seasoned clam mixture for the unusual Clam-Stuffed Shrimp.

Seafood Soufflé Pie

    1 stick piecrust mix
    2 3-ounce packages lime-flavored
       gelatin
  ½ teaspoon salt
    2 cups boiling water
    1 cup cold water
    1 cup mayonnaise or salad
       dressing
    2 tablespoons lemon juice
              • • •
 1½ cups diced, cooked shrimp
    2 cups diced, peeled avocado
  ½ cup diced celery
    2 tablespoons finely chopped
       onion

Using piecrust mix, prepare and bake one 9-inch pastry shell following package directions. Dissolve gelatin and salt in 2 cups boiling water. Stir in 1 cup cold water, mayonnaise, and lemon juice; beat till smooth. Chill till partially set. Whip till fluffy. Fold in shrimp, avocado, celery, and onion. Chill till mixture mounds when spooned. Pour the shrimp mixture into the baked pastry shell. Chill till firm, about 4 to 5 hours. Garnish with additional whole, cooked shrimp, if desired. Makes 6 servings.

Crab Meat Suzette

Adapted from the famous dessert, Crepes Suzette—

  ⅓ cup sifted all-purpose flour
    1 tablespoon sugar
       Dash salt
    1 egg
    1 egg yolk
  ¾ cup milk
    1 tablespoon butter or margarine,
       melted
              • • •
    1 tablespoon butter or margarine
    1 tablespoon all-purpose flour
       Dash salt
       Dash white pepper
  ½ cup milk
    1 cup crab meat *or* 1 6-ounce
       package frozen crab meat,
       thawed
    1 tablespoon lemon juice
    2 teaspoons dry sherry
       Dash bottled hot pepper sauce
       Dash Worcestershire sauce
  ½ cup hollandaise sauce
       (See *Hollandaise Sauce*)

Measure the first 7 ingredients into a blender container or a mixing bowl; blend or beat till the batter is smooth.

In a saucepan melt the 1 tablespoon butter over low heat. Blend in the tablespoon flour, dash salt, and white pepper. Add the ½ cup milk all at once; cook quickly, stirring constantly, till mixture is thickened and bubbly. Add crab meat, lemon juice, sherry, hot pepper sauce, and Worcestershire sauce; heat through and keep warm while cooking crepes.

Lightly grease a heavy 6-inch skillet and heat till a drop of water dances on the surface. Lift skillet off heat and pour in 2 tablespoons of the batter. Tilt from side to side till batter covers bottom of skillet evenly. Return skillet to heat and cook till underside is lightly browned, about 1½ minutes. Remove crepe by inverting skillet over paper toweling. Cook remaining crepes the same way, on one side only. Spread 1 tablespoon of the hot crab meat filling across the unbrowned side of each crepe.

Place in a 400° oven and heat till edges of crepes begin to toast. Remove from oven and spoon hollandaise sauce over. Serve as appetizers or entrée. Makes about 11 crepes.

Broiling: All types of shellfish are appropriate for broiling. The direct heat of this method cooks the meat quickly, thus, leaving it moist and tender.

Broiling shellfish expands beyond the kitchen and the range. Other equipment cooks the shellfish in the same manner and moves out-of-doors with the festivities. Cooking on a grill, hibachi, rotisserie, portable appliance, and with kabobs uses the same type heat and techniques.

Shucked mollusks, lobster tails, crab legs, shelled shrimp, and whole shellfish are popular to broil. Whole shellfish must be killed just before broiling. Plunge the shellfish into boiling water for a few minutes or sever the spinal cord. After either method, split open the shellfish and remove the inedible organs. During broiling, brush the meat with melted butter and season with salt and pepper.

Over-the-Coals Lobster Tails

⅓ cup salad oil
¼ cup sauterne
½ cup soy sauce (optional)
1 small clove garlic, crushed
¼ teaspoon ground ginger
¼ teaspoon paprika
Dash pepper
. . .
6 frozen lobster tails (about 6 ounces each), thawed
3 lemons, halved crosswise

Combine salad oil, sauterne, soy sauce, garlic, ginger, paprika, and pepper. Let stand 1 hour. Cut underside membrane of lobster tails around edges and remove meat from shell. Thread lobster tail lengthwise on skewers alternately with lemon halves. Brush lobster meat with sauce.

Broil, meat side up, over *hot* coals 10 minutes, brushing occasionally with sauce. Turn and broil till lobster is cooked through, about 20 minutes longer, brushing meat occasionally with sauce. Remove from skewers; serve with hot lemon halves. Makes 6 servings.

To cook on rotisserie: Thread lobster tails and lemons on spit. To keep tails from turning, insert skewers parallel to spit, through 2 or 3 tails. Let revolve over *hot* coals 35 to 40 minutes; brush occasionally with sauce.

Scallops à la Jimmy

1 pound fresh or frozen scallops
¼ cup butter or margarine, melted
⅓ cup fine soft bread crumbs
⅛ teaspoon garlic salt
⅛ teaspoon dry mustard
⅛ teaspoon paprika
2 tablespoons dry sherry
Lemon wedges

Thaw frozen scallops. Slice large scallops in half horizontally. Pour *2 tablespoons* of the butter in a shallow baking pan; arrange scallops in single layer. Combine bread crumbs, garlic salt, dry mustard, paprika, and remaining butter; sprinkle over scallops. Broil 4 inches from heat till lightly browned, 6 to 8 minutes. Drizzle wine over scallops; serve hot with lemon wedges. Serves 6 to 8.

Barbecued Shrimp with Lemon

During the cold months, broil shrimp in the oven and cut the cooking time by a few minutes—

12 ounces fresh or frozen shelled shrimp
3 large cloves garlic, sliced
¼ cup butter or margarine
½ lemon, sliced *paper-thin*
Chopped parsley

Thaw frozen shrimp. Cook garlic in butter 2 or 3 minutes. Line a shallow pan with foil (or use a shallow, foilware pan); arrange shrimp in a layer over bottom. Dash with salt and pepper. Place lemon slices over shrimp. Drizzle with garlic butter; sprinkle with parsley. Cook over *hot* coals till done, about 6 to 8 minutes; turn the shrimp frequently.

Baking: Two forms of shellfish are used in baking—the raw shellfish and cooked meat. The raw form bakes in much the same way as it broils. Butter, lemon juice, sauce, and seasonings are added for flavor.

Shellfish that are eaten raw can be included in a baked dish without previous cooking. Cooked meat is frequently combined with other ingredients and baked for an appetizer entrée, or casserole.

Crab-Swiss Bites

Crisp water chestnuts garnish these delicious, cheesy appetizers—

1 7½-ounce can crab meat, drained, flaked, and cartilage removed
1 tablespoon sliced green onion
4 ounces process Swiss cheese, shredded (1 cup)
½ cup mayonnaise or salad dressing
1 teaspoon lemon juice
¼ teaspoon curry powder

. . .

1 package flaky-style refrigerated rolls (12 rolls)
1 5-ounce can water chestnuts, drained and sliced

Combine crab meat, green onion, Swiss cheese, mayonnaise or salad dressing, lemon juice, and curry powder. Mix well. Separate rolls; separate each into three layers. Place on *ungreased* baking sheet; spoon crab meat mixture onto rolls. Top each with a few water chestnut slices. Bake at 400° till golden brown, about 10 to 12 minutes. Makes 36 appetizers.

Seafood Bake

Pictured on page 2052—

1 10½-ounce can condensed cream of celery soup
¼ cup milk
1 beaten egg
2 tablespoons grated Parmesan cheese

. . .

1 7½-ounce can crab meat, drained, flaked, and cartilage removed
1 4½-ounce can shrimp, drained
1 3-ounce can sliced mushrooms, drained

. . .

3 tablespoons fine dry bread crumbs
2 tablespoons grated Parmesan cheese
1 tablespoon butter or margarine melted
Parsley
Lemon twists

Combine cream of celery soup, milk, egg, and the two tablespoons Parmesan cheese in a saucepan. Stir over low heat till cheese is melted and mixture is hot. Stir in crab, shrimp, and mushrooms. Spoon into 4 large baking shells.

Toss dry bread crumbs with 2 tablespoons Parmesan cheese and melted butter. Sprinkle crumbs over the mixture in shells.

Bake the mixture at 375° for about 20 minutes. Garnish each serving with parsley and a lemon twist. Makes 4 servings.

Cassola de Peix

French version of seafood casserole—

2 tablespoons butter or margarine
2 tablespoons all-purpose flour
¼ teaspoon salt
1 cup milk
12 medium shrimp, cooked and split, or 1 4½-ounce can shrimp
1½ cups crab meat *or* 1 7½-ounce can crab meat, drained, flaked, and cartilage removed
1 cup steamed lobster *or* 1 5½-ounce can lobster
1 3-ounce can sliced mushrooms, drained
2 tablespoons dry sherry
1 tablespoon lemon juice
Dash bottled hot pepper sauce
¼ teaspoon Worcestershire sauce

. . .

2 ounces sharp process American cheese, shredded (½ cup)
1 cup soft bread crumbs
2 tablespoons butter or margarine, melted

Melt the 2 tablespoons butter over low heat. Blend in flour and salt. Add milk all at once. Cook quickly, stirring constantly, till sauce thickens and bubbles; remove from heat. Add shrimp, crab meat, lobster, mushrooms, sherry, lemon juice, hot pepper sauce, and Worcestershire sauce; mix well. Place mixture in a 1-quart casserole dish. Sprinkle cheese over top. Combine bread crumbs and 2 tablespoons melted butter; sprinkle over cheese. Bake at 375° till heated through, about 40 minutes. If desired. garnish top with mushroom caps and additional seafood. Serves 4 to 6.

Clam-Stuffed Shrimp

   1 pound large shrimp in shells
   ¾ cup rich, round cracker crumbs
   3 tablespoons butter, melted
   1 7½-ounce can minced clams,
      drained
   2 tablespoons snipped parsley
   ⅛ teaspoon garlic powder
   ⅓ cup dry white wine

Shell and devein shrimp. Slit each along vein side about halfway through. Combine crumbs and butter. Stir in clams, parsley, garlic powder, ⅛ teaspoon salt, and dash pepper. Stuff each shrimp with clam mixture. Arrange in an 11¾x7½x1¾-inch baking dish. Bake at 350° for about 18 to 20 minutes; baste occasionally with wine. Makes 4 servings.

Shrimp Saki

   1 pound fresh or frozen jumbo
      shrimp, shelled
   Dash salt
   Dash pepper
   Dash paprika

      •   •   •

   2 tablespoons lemon juice
   ⅓ cup butter or margarine
      melted

Split shrimp from back and wash thoroughly under running water; place on a baking sheet. Season with salt and pepper; sprinkle with paprika. Bake at 425° for 8 minutes. Remove from oven and place under broiler for 5 minutes. Combine lemon juice and melted butter or margarine; serve with shrimp. Serves 4 to 6.

Choose Crab Meat Suzette, a variation of crepes suzette, or Cassola de Peix for an experience in elegant dining. Cassola de Peix is garnished with shellfish and mushroom crowns.

Crab-Shrimp Bake

Bake in one casserole or in individual bakers—

> 1 cup shelled, cooked shrimp
> 1 cup diced celery
> ¼ cup chopped green pepper
> 2 tablespoons finely chopped
>   onion
> 1 7½-ounce can crab meat, drained,
>   flaked, and cartilage removed
> 1 teaspoon Worcestershire sauce
> ¾ cup mayonnaise or salad dressing
> 1 cup soft bread crumbs
> 1 tablespoon butter or margarine,
>   melted

Cut large shrimp in half lengthwise. Combine shrimp, celery, green pepper, onion, crab meat, ½ teaspoon salt, dash pepper, Worcestershire sauce, and mayonnaise or salad dressing. Turn into 1-quart casserole or individual bakers. Combine crumbs and butter. Sprinkle atop casserole. Bake at 350° till hot, 30 to 35 minutes for casserole, and 20 to 25 minutes for individual bakers. Makes 4 servings.

Frying: Shellfish fry in a matter of minutes. Most shellfish deep-fat fry in 2 to 5 minutes and panfry in 5 to 10 minutes to a delicious crispness.

Prepare for frying by shucking or removing any bits of shell and inedible parts. Then, dip the whole shellfish or chunks of meat in an egg batter and roll in a coating mixture of crumbs and flour, cornmeal, or a commercially prepared, packaged mixture. You also can combine the meat with other ingredients for fritters, croquettes, and other fried dishes.

Serve fried shellfish with a sauce, such as tartar or cocktail sauce, or with lemon juice. (See also *Fish.*)

French Fried Shrimp

> 2 pounds fresh or frozen shrimp
>   in shells
> 1 cup sifted all-purpose flour
> ½ teaspoon sugar
> 1 slightly beaten egg
> 2 tablespoons salad oil

Thaw frozen shrimp. Combine flour, sugar, egg, salad oil, ½ teaspoon salt, and 1 cup ice water. Beat smooth. Shell shrimp, leaving last section and tail intact. Butterfly shrimp by cutting almost through at center back without severing tail end; remove vein. Dry.

Dip shrimp into batter; fry in deep, hot fat (375°) till golden. Drain. Serve with a cocktail or seafood sauce. Makes 5 servings.

Clams Parmesan

Cheese adds a unique flavor—

> 48 large, shucked clams
> 2 beaten eggs
> 2 tablespoons milk
>   • • •
> ½ cup fine saltine cracker crumbs
> ½ cup grated Parmesan cheese
> ½ teaspoon salt
>   Dash pepper
>   Shortening
>   Lemon wedges

Dry clams with paper toweling. Combine beaten eggs and milk. Mix cracker crumbs, Parmesan cheese, salt, and pepper together. Dip clams in egg mixture, then roll in cracker mixture. Panfry on both sides in small amount of hot shortening, about 4 to 5 minutes. Serve with lemon wedges. Makes 4 to 6 servings.

SHEPHERD'S PIE—A hash of chopped meat, vegetables, tomato sauce or gravy, and mashed potatoes. The potatoes can form a cover over the hash or a wall around the edge. Forcing the mashed potatoes through a pastry tube adds an artistic touch.

Shepherd's pie makes very good use of leftover meats and vegetables. Use convenience products for a speedy dish, or substitute for any of the leftovers that may happen to be missing.

Modern version of traditional dish

Serve supper in a hurry by making Shortcut→ Shepherd's Pie from frozen vegetables, canned beef, and instant mashed potatoes.

Shepherd's Pie

½ cup finely chopped celery
2 tablespoons chopped onion
2 tablespoons butter or margarine
2 tablespoons all-purpose flour
1 cup milk
¾ cup beef *or* lamb broth
2 cups cooked lamb, cut in cubes
1 tablespoon snipped parsley
½ teaspoon salt
⅛ teaspoon pepper
⅛ teaspoon dried dillweed (optional)
¼ teaspoon Kitchen Bouquet
2 cups seasoned mashed potatoes
¼ cup shredded sharp process
American cheese

In a skillet cook celery and onion in butter till tender but not brown. Blend in flour. Add milk and broth all at once. Cook and stir till mixture thickens and bubbles. Stir in lamb, parsley, salt, pepper, dillweed, and Kitchen Bouquet. Pour meat mixture into a 1½-quart casserole and top evenly with the mashed potatoes. Sprinkle with cheese. Bake at 400° till brown, about 20 to 25 minutes. Serves 6.

Short-cut Shepherd's Pie

1 10-ounce package frozen mixed
    vegetables
1 tablespoon instant minced onion
2 tablespoons butter or margarine
2 tablespoons all-purpose flour
1 14½-ounce can evaporated milk
1 12-ounce can roast beef, cut
    into cubes
  Packaged instant mashed potatoes
    (enough for 4 servings)
2 slices process American cheese

Cook vegetables and onion following package directions; do not drain. Stir in butter. Combine flour and 1 *cup* milk; stir into vegetables. Cook and stir till mixture thickens. Add beef and juices to vegetables; heat to boiling. Turn into 4 casseroles. Prepare potatoes following package directions, *except substitute ⅔ cup evaporated milk for milk called for.* Pile atop meat. Top each with a triangle of cheese. Broil 4 inches from heat for about 3 to 4 minutes. Makes 4 servings.

SHERBET (*shûr' bit*)—**1.** A frozen dessert made with milk and sugar, usually flavored with fruit. Familiar types of sherbets include the fruit-flavored sherbets that are commercially prepared and the kinds that are prepared in the home freezer, some of which may be flavored with wines or liqueurs. **2.** A sweetened fruit drink.

Although sherbet, ice cream, and ices are all frozen desserts, they differ somewhat in ingredients. Ice cream is a richer product made with cream, while ices are made with water. Home-frozen sherbets on the other hand, are prepared with milk.

Commercially, sherbet is made with an ice cream mix and acidulated fruit syrup. Stabilizers and emulsifiers are added for uniform body and texture.

Each of the basic ingredients has its own particular function in the preparation of homemade sherbet.

The fruit gives the sherbet mixture its flavor, which generally is tart. Fruit incorporated into sherbets is generally in the form of a purée or a juice.

Milk contributes to the creamy texture of a sherbet. Both the solids and fat in milk help interfere with crystal formation, giving a finer-textured product with many small crystals. Even though sherbets are made with milk, they are considered to be low in fat and milk solids content compared to most frozen dairy products.

Sugar is also an important ingredient in sherbets. Surprisingly, you will find more sugar in sherbet than in ice cream. This is one of the reasons why sherbets are not that much lower in calories. Sugar not only adds sweetness, but it decreases the freezing point of the sherbet mixture. Therefore, it is important that the freezer section of your refrigerator maintain a low temperature in order to keep the sherbet as firmly frozen as possible.

Homemade sherbets are also improved with a stabilizer. Gelatin and marshmallows are two stabilizing ingredients frequently used in recipes. Stabilizers are added to slow down the formation of large crystals, important for a creamy sherbet.

There are two factors in the preparation that are important for a creamy product: the agitation the mixture receives and the temperature used for freezing.

SHERRY—A blended, amber appetizer or dessert wine with a characteristic nutty flavor. Although sherry is traditionally made from the juice of palomino grapes, today many other grape varieties also are used. And because brandy is added to the grape juice during production, its alcoholic content is often as high as 20 percent.

People have been sipping sherry for centuries. It was first made about 31 B.C. in the region around Jerez de la Frontera in southeastern Spain. But there was no wide recognition of sherry until centuries later when some of the wine was taken to England under the name Vino de Jerez. The English translated this first to jerries, then sherries, and finally, just sherry.

The elegant flavor of sherry has been praised by many notables, including Shakespeare, who said of the amber colored wine: "If I had a thousand sons, the first human principle I would teach them should be to foreswear thin potations and to devote themselves to sherry."

How sherry is produced: Today, sherry production is centered largely in the United States, Spain, South Africa, and Australia. Two methods of production are commonly used. The first, the traditional method, is still used in Spain and in some of the other countries, too. The second, a modern approach to production, is more often used in the wineries in the United States.

The traditional method follows some unique stages of fermentation, aging, and blending. The fully ripe grapes are first picked and laid in the sun to dry slightly, then crushed. At one time, the grapes were placed in wooden troughs and crushed by men wearing specially designed cleated shoes. The dancing movements they used to crush the grapes illustrated the jubilant atmosphere that pervaded the harvest. But due to high labor costs and sanitary considerations, most, if not all, grapes are crushed mechanically today.

Following crushing, the grape juice is transferred to bulk casks called butts where fermentation begins. The lightly covered butts of fermenting juice are often placed out of doors and are subjected to direct sunlight. This technique helps the development of the sherry flavor.

Since no two butts ferment in the same way, an essential element of good wine production is the accurate evaluation of the developing wine by tasters. After the wine has fermented for several months, it is analyzed and divided into two major categories. Judgments are based on flavor, bouquet, and the amount of *flor,* or flower. (*Flor* is the unique yeast that develops on the surface of the sherry.) The wines that are clean, light-bodied, and that have good bouquet and *flor* are destined for the drier sherries, called finos and have brandy added to about 15 percent alcohol. Heavier, fuller-bodied wines with less bouquet and *flor* are labeled oloroso and contain from 16 to 18 percent alcohol. The smaller alcohol content of the finos enables the *flor* to continue developing its unique flavor, while the higher alcoholic content of the oloroso kills the *flor*. Both finos and olorosos rest for a year or two more, during which time they are periodically classified into more specific groups.

At last the wines are admitted to the beginning phases of the solera, a system of blending which enables vintners to maintain a uniform style and quality of sherry from year to year. The solera consists of pyramids of butts, usually about three butts high. Age of the wines progresses from the top of the stack on down.

Again astute tasters are needed to determine how and when the wines in the solera are to be blended. Up to a third of the wine in the bottom cask is drawn off for either bottling or more blending. The amount that has been lost in the bottom butt is then replaced by wine in the middle butt. Likewise, that in the middle is replaced by wine from the top butt and newly fermented wine or wine from a more recent solera is added to the top butt. Thus solera-blended sherry may be a blend of only one or many soleras.

Although a few select sherries are prepared by this method in the United States. most American sherries are blended before fermentation. The grape juice, a blend of varieties, is fermented into a dry white wine; then brandy is added. At this point in the processing, the wine may be made into sherry by the flor method or baked in large tanks at 120 to 140 degrees for about two or three months. This baking replaces sun aging, yet, at the same time, helps to give the same characteristic sherry flavor. The wine is then aged in barrels.

Types of sherry: Sherries are divided into distinct categories according to their relative dryness or sweetness. Spanish-produced sherries often are labeled with the Spanish designations as well as the better-known American names.

Spanish sherries are generally classified as being finos (dry) or olorosos (sweet). Well-known finos, starting with the driest, include manzanilla, fino, and amontillado. From slightly sweet to very sweet olorosos are amoroso, oloroso, cream, and brown sherries. Finos tend to be pale in color with rich flavor and bouquet; olorosos are usually dark and heavier flavored.

Sherry terminology used in the United States has been simplified. A pale, dry sherry is very dry, while a cocktail sherry usually is less dry. Medium, straight, or golden sherry, is not really dry or sweet. Cream sherry, on the other hand, is the sweet dessert wine. Some wines that are marketed as select sherries contain the traditional palomino grapes, which are prepared in the age-old way.

How to use: Sherry is one of the most popular aperitif and cooking wines. Drier sherries are usually designated for appetizer uses, while sweeter sherries are more appropriate for dessert courses.

When sherry is served as a beverage, there are several guidelines that are recommended for the homemaker to follow. It is common, for example, to serve sherry chilled as an appetizer beverage, and at room temperature (60 to 70 degrees) as a dessert. Plan on at least three ounces of sherry for each serving. As an appetizer, chilled sherry in a wine glass or sherry "on the rocks" is superb by itself or served with hors d'oeuvres, nuts, or cheeses. At the dessert course of a meal, serve cream sherry with fresh fruit, cookies, nuts, cheese, or thin slices of fruitcake.

Sherry is also one of the most versatile wines for cooking. Sherry accents dips and soups for the first course. For entrées, it is particularly suitable in poultry, fish, shell-fish, or ham dishes. And for desserts, the flavor of sherry excels in compotes, cakes, and pies. (See also *Wines and Spirits*.)

Marinated Broiled Chicken

    ½ cup dry sherry
    ½ cup salad oil
    ½ cup soy sauce
    1 teaspoon ground ginger
    ⅛ teaspoon garlic powder
            . . .
    1 2½- to 3-pound ready-to-cook
        broiler-fryer chicken, cut up
    1 tablespoon sesame seed

Combine first 5 ingredients. Pour over chicken in flat dish and marinate in refrigerator for 4 hours or overnight. Broil, skin side down, in broiler pan (without rack) 5 to 7 inches from heat till lightly browned, about 20 minutes. Turn; broil 15 to 20 minutes longer. When almost done, brush the chicken with the marinade. Sprinkle with sesame seed; return the chicken to broiler and brown. Makes 4 servings.

Tenderloin Deluxe

    1 2-pound beef tenderloin
    2 tablespoons butter, softened
            . . .
    ¼ cup chopped green onion
    2 tablespoons butter
    2 tablespoons soy sauce
    1 teaspoon Dijon-style mustard
        Dash freshly ground pepper
    ¾ cup dry sherry

Remove the surface fat and the connective tissue from meat; spread with 2 tablespoons butter. Place on rack in shallow roasting pan. Insert meat thermometer. Roast at 425° for 20 minutes. Meanwhile, in small saucepan cook green onion in 2 tablespoons butter till tender but not brown. Add soy sauce, mustard, and pepper. Stir in wine; heat the mixture just to boiling. Remove the roast from the oven; pour wine sauce over tenderloin. Return roast to the oven; continue roasting at 425° for 25 to 30 minutes for rare (140°). Baste frequently with sauce. Pass remaining wine sauce with meat. Makes 6 to 8 servings.

Vary shirred eggs with a sprinkling of shredded process cheese. Add cheese the last 5 to 10 minutes of baking just till melted.

Turkey-Ham Casserole

  ½ cup chopped onion
  2 tablespoons butter or margarine
  3 tablespoons all-purpose flour
  ½ teaspoon salt
  ¼ teaspoon pepper
  1 3-ounce can broiled, sliced
      mushrooms, undrained
  1 cup light cream
  2 tablespoons dry sherry
          • • •
  2 cups diced, cooked turkey
      or chicken
  1 5-ounce can water chestnuts,
      drained and sliced
  1 cup diced, fully cooked ham
  2 ounces Swiss cheese, grated
      (½ cup)
1½ cups soft bread crumbs
  3 tablespoons butter or margarine,
      melted

Cook onion in 2 tablespoons butter or margarine until tender but not brown. Blend in flour, salt, and pepper. Stir in mushrooms with liquid, cream, and sherry. Cook, stirring constantly, till thickened and bubbly. Add turkey, water chestnuts, and ham. Turn into an 8¼x1¾-inch round ovenware cake dish. Cover with Swiss cheese. Mix bread crumbs with 3 tablespoons melted butter and sprinkle over cheese. Bake at 400° until sauce starts to bubble and top is brown, about 35 minutes. Serves 6.

Sherried-Date Sauce

  2 cups pitted dates
  ¾ cup light corn syrup
  ½ cup sherry
  1 tablespoon chopped, preserved
      ginger
  1 teaspoon shredded orange peel

Cut dates lengthwise in quarters. Combine with remaining ingredients; cover and refrigerate at least 24 hours. Serve the sauce over ice cream. Makes about 2½ cups sauce.

Fruit Refresher

  ½ cup brown sugar
  ¼ cup honey
  ¼ cup dry sherry
  2 tablespoons lemon juice
  1 teaspoon grated lemon peel
          • • •
  2 medium unpeeled apples, sliced
  2 medium nectarines, peeled
      and sliced (1½ cups)
  2 medium pears, peeled and
      quartered (1½ cups)
  2 medium bananas, peeled and
      sliced
  1 cup dark sweet cherries, halved
      and pitted

In saucepan combine brown sugar, honey, sherry, lemon juice, and lemon peel. Cook over low heat 5 minutes, stirring occasionally. Remove the mixture from heat and cool.

Combine fresh fruits. Pour dressing over; toss lightly. Cover; chill thoroughly, stirring occasionally. Drain, reserving dressing. Serve fruit on lettuce-lined plates. Pass dressing with salad. Makes 6 to 8 servings.

SHIRR—To bake in a shallow dish till set, usually with reference to eggs. The ramekins, shallow baking dishes, or custard cups that are used should be buttered. Either one or two eggs are added to each dish with a dash of cream and seasonings.

Since eggs are best cooked at a low temperature, place the dishes in a pan of hot water and bake in 325° oven till firm. If soft yolks are preferred, remove the eggs

Marinate chunks of lamb in an herbed mixture. Then, brush Lamb Shish Kabobs with the marinade during broiling.

from the oven when the white is cooked and the yolks quiver when the dish is shaken gently. The eggs will continue to cook as they travel from oven to table.

Variations include a sprinkling of shredded cheese or crumbs over the top of the eggs, or the addition of precooked sausage, ham, or crumbled bacon before the egg is cooked. (See also *Egg*.)

SHISH KABOB, KEBAB *(shish' kuh bob')*— The Near Eastern name for meat, traditionally lamb or mutton, that is broiled on a skewer. The word shish means skewer, while kabob refers to the small pieces of meat that are roasted. This dish has several names—The Russian refer to it as *shashlik;* the French, *en brochette.*

Shish kabob, or more often just kabob, is now used for any combination of meat and vegetables or just vegetables that are cooked on a skewer. Beef and seafood are incorporated in some versions. Many recipes suggest marinating the meat in a sauce for flavor. (See also *Kabob*.)

Lamb Shish Kabobs

        ½ cup salad *or* peanut oil
        ¼ cup lemon juice
        1 teaspoon salt
        1 teaspoon dried oregano leaves,
            crushed
        ½ teaspoon pepper
        1 clove garlic, minced
                •   •   •
        3 pounds boneless lamb, cut in
            2-inch cubes
        5 medium onions
        4 medium green peppers
        3 medium tomatoes, quartered

Combine the first 6 ingredients. Add lamb cubes, stirring to coat. Marinate in refrigerator for 2 days, turning meat several times.

Peel and quarter onions; make each quarter into a cup by removing a few center pieces. Cut the four sides off the green peppers. From each side, carve an oval. On four 12-inch skewers alternately thread pieces of onion, lamb, green pepper, and tomato. Brush kabobs with marinade. Broil 4 inches from heat for 15 minutes. Turn and brush with marinade. Broil 10 minutes longer. Makes 4 servings.

Kau Kau Kabobs

            Instant seasoned meat tenderizer
        1½ pounds beef round steak, cut in
            1½-inch cubes
        4 medium green peppers
        6 7-ounce frozen lobster tails,
            thawed and quartered
            Preserved kumquats (optional)
                •   •   •
        ¼ cup sauterne
        ¼ cup lemon juice
        ¼ cup salad oil

Use meat tenderizer on meat cubes according to label directions. Cut sides from green peppers and trim to form ovals. Alternate beef, lobster, and green pepper ovals on 4 long or 8 medium skewers. Finish off each skewer with a preserved kumquat, if desired.

Combine sauterne, lemon juice, and salad oil. Broil kabobs over *hot* coals till desired doneness, about 20 minutes, turning often and basting with wine mixture. Makes 4 servings.

Garlic Lamb Kabobs

1½ pounds boneless lamb, cut
in 1-inch cubes
1 cup garlic salad dressing
or 1 envelope *dry* garlic
salad dressing mix*
2 medium green peppers, cut
in squares
1 16-ounce can small onions

Place meat in shallow dish. Pour dressing over meat. Let stand 2 hours at room temperature or overnight in refrigerator, turning occasionally. Drain meat, reserving liquid. Thread meat and vegetables on skewers in the following order: lamb, green pepper, lamb, onion. Broil 4 inches from heat for about 15 minutes, turning once. Baste meat and vegetables occasionally with dressing. Makes 6 servings.

*Prepare mix following package directions.

Shish Kabobs Italiano

½ cup Italian salad dressing
¼ cup lemon juice
1 teaspoon dried oregano leaves,
crushed
2 pounds boneless lamb, cut in
2-inch cubes

Combine salad dressing, lemon juice, oregano, ¼ teaspoon salt, and ⅛ teaspoon pepper. Place lamb in shallow dish; pour marinade over. Cover; marinate 2 hours at room temperature or in refrigerator overnight, turning meat several times. Thread meat on skewers. Grill over hot coals for 20 to 25 minutes, turning skewers occasionally and brushing with marinade. Makes 5 or 6 servings.

Marinated Beef Cubes

½ cup salad oil
¼ cup vinegar
¼ cup chopped onion
1 teaspoon salt
1 teaspoon coarsely ground pepper
2 teaspoons Worcestershire
sauce *or* steak sauce
2 pounds beef round steak, cut in
1½-inch cubes

Combine oil, vinegar, onion, salt, pepper, and Worcestershire sauce. Place beef in shallow dish; pour marinade over. Cover; marinate 2 hours at room temperature or in refrigerator overnight, turning meat several times. Thread on skewers. Broil kabobs over *hot* coals till desired doneness, about 20 minutes. Turn often and baste with marinade. Serves 6.

SHOE PEG CORN—A sweet, white corn with thin, narrow kernels. This type of corn is available either in canned and frozen forms at most supermarkets.

SHOESTRING POTATO—A thin, match-stick size piece of potato that has been deep-fat fried, then salted. Shoestring potatoes are available in packages and various sized cans packed with a vacuum seal, making them easy to keep on the shelf.

Eat shoestring potatoes by the handfuls or dress them up with a cheese coating. Or, use the potatoes in a casserole to add flavor and texture. (See also *Potato*.)

Parmesan Shoestrings

Empty one 4-ounce can shoestring potatoes into a shallow baking pan. Sprinkle potatoes with ½ cup grated Parmesan cheese. Heat at 350° till potatoes are toasty, about 15 minutes, stirring occasionally. Makes 3 cups.

Tuna Jackstraw Bake

1 4-ounce can shoestring potatoes
1 10½-ounce can condensed cream
of mushroom soup
1 6½- or 7-ounce can tuna, drained
1 6-ounce can evaporated milk
• • •
1 3-ounce can sliced mushrooms,
drained
¼ cup chopped, canned pimiento

Reserve 1 cup of the potatoes. Combine remaining potatoes with soup, tuna, and evaporated milk. Stir in mushrooms and pimiento. Turn into a 1½-quart casserole. Top with reserved potatoes. Bake at 375° till hot, about 25 minutes. Makes 4 to 6 servings.

Trim Scotch Shortbread with gumdrops. Attach decorations with corn syrup.

SHOOFLY PIE—A dessert-type open-face pie that is made with molasses, sugar, and a crumb mixture all baked in a pastry shell. The origin of this pie is credited to the Pennsylvania Dutch homemakers. Some say that it got its name because the flies, attracted to this sweet, molasses dessert, had to be shooed away. (See also *Pennsylvania Dutch Cookery*.)

Shoofly Pie

> 1½ cups sifted all-purpose flour
> ½ cup sugar
> ¼ teaspoon baking soda
> ¼ cup butter or margarine
>   • • •
> ½ cup light molasses
> ¼ teaspoon baking soda
> ½ cup hot water
>   • • •
> 1 *unbaked* 8-inch pastry shell
>   (See *Pastry*)

Sift together flour, sugar, and ¼ teaspoon soda. Cut in butter till crumbly. Combine molasses, ¼ teaspoon soda, and hot water. Pour ⅓ of liquid in *unbaked* pastry shell; sprinkle with ⅓ of flour mixture. Repeat layers, ending with flour mixture. Bake at 375° about 40 minutes. Cool the pie before serving.

SHORT—A term used to describe a product having a high proportion of shortening. When referring to a pastry or cookie, a short product is rich, tender, and flaky and will break apart or crumble readily. A dough that is short, such as shortcake, has a high proportion of shortening.

SHORTBREAD—A thick, rich cookie made with a high proportion of shortening. Because of the high amount of shortening, usually butter, shortbread is a crumbly type of cookie. The other two ingredients of this Scottish favorite are sugar and flour. Because there are so few ingredients, and because it's easily shaped for baking, shortbread is a very simple cookie to prepare. (See also *Cookie*.)

Scotch Shortbread

> 1 cup butter or margarine
> ½ cup sugar
> 2½ cups sifted all-purpose flour

Cream butter and sugar till light and fluffy. Stir in flour. Chill several hours. Divide in half. On *ungreased* cookie sheet pat each half into 7-inch circle. With fork, prick each mound deeply to make 16 pie-shaped wedges. (Or on floured surface, roll dough ¼ to ½ inch thick. Cut in 2x½-inch strips or with 1¾-inch cutter.

Bake on *ungreased* cookie sheet at 300° for 30 minutes. Cool slightly; remove from pan. Makes 32 wedges or 42 cookies.

SHORTCAKE—**1.** A dessert or main dish of fruit or a creamed meat mixture served over baking powder biscuits. **2.** The biscuit used for the dessert or main dish. **3.** A cake that is prepared with a large amount of shortening.

Shortcake is a dessert that is as American as apple pie, especially the strawberry version served with whipped cream. Variations are just as popular as the traditional baking powder biscuit-based dessert. Some people prefer sponge cake cups or pound cake for the dessert base. Occasionally, the baking powder biscuits are made with slightly more sugar, egg, or additional shortening to make a sweeter and richer

Springtime favorite

Finish off an all-American Strawberry Short- → cake, featuring a jumbo baking powder biscuit, with mounds of fluffy whipped cream.

product. The biscuit dough can be baked in one large cake that is split apart for filling, instead of the individual portions familiar to many. Whether the biscuit is buttered or not is also a matter of individual preference.

The toppings, too, can vary just as much as the bases for a shortcake. While strawberries are probably the most popular fruit for the dessert favorite, fresh peaches or other types of in-season fruits and berries are enjoyed. No matter what fruit is chosen, it should be ripe, slightly crushed and sugared, and spooned onto the warm biscuits so that the juices will soak in. Some people prefer a shortcake without the embellishments of cream or ice cream, while others maintain that the shortcake isn't complete if it isn't topped with mounds of whipped cream.

Main dish shortcakes are probably not as familiar as the dessert variety. The base, either a baking powder biscuit, square of corn bread, or split cornmeal muffin, can be topped by creamed meat, seafood, or poultry. (See also *Dessert*.)

Use a serrated knife to split the king-sized biscuit for Strawberry Shortcake. Then, spread the warm bottom layer with butter.

Strawberry Shortcake

    2 cups sifted all-purpose flour
    2 tablespoons sugar
    3 teaspoons baking powder
  ½ teaspoon salt
  ½ cup butter or margarine
    1 beaten egg
  ⅔ cup light cream
     Butter
    1 cup whipping cream
    3 to 4 sugared, sliced
       strawberries

Sift together flour, sugar, baking powder, and salt. Cut in ½ cup butter till mixture resembles coarse crumbs. Combine egg and cream; add all at once, stirring just enough to moisten.

Spread dough in a greased 8x1½-inch round baking pan, building up edges slightly. Bake at 450° for 15 to 18 minutes. Remove from pan; cool on rack for about 5 minutes.

Split in two layers. Lift top off carefully. Butter bottom layer. Whip the cream. Spoon berries and whipped cream between layers and over top. Serve the shortcake warm.

Peach Shortcakes

    2 cups sifted all-purpose flour
    1 tablespoon sugar
    3 teaspoons baking powder
  ½ teaspoon salt
    6 tablespoons butter or margarine
    1 beaten egg
  ⅔ cup milk
    1 quart fresh, sliced peaches
       Lemon juice
       Granulated sugar
    1 cup whipping cream
    2 tablespoons brown sugar
       Butter

Sift together flour, 1 tablespoon sugar, baking powder, and salt. Cut in 6 tablespoons butter till mixture resembles coarse crumbs. Combine egg and milk; add all at once, stirring just enough to moisten. Turn dough out on floured surface; knead gently about 30 seconds. Pat or roll to ½-inch thickness. With floured 2½-inch cutter, cut out 6 biscuits. Bake on *ungreased* baking sheet at 450° about 10 minutes.

Meanwhile, dip sliced peaches in lemon juice to prevent them from darkening. Add granulated sugar to desired sweetness. Whip cream with brown sugar. Fold *half* the peaches into *half* the whipped cream. Split shortcakes in half, and butter bottom layers. Spread peaches and cream mixture on bottom layers of biscuits. Cover top half of biscuit with remaining peaches and cream. Makes 6 servings.

SHORTENING – 1. The preparation process of making a food short. **2.** A solid or liquid fat or oil including lard, butter, margarine, hydrogenated shortening, and vegetable oils. The main purpose of shortening is to contribute shortness to the product. For example, shortening provides tenderness to cakes, cookies, and breads; aids in leavening; and adds strength to batters. Some shortenings, such as butter or margarine, contribute flavor to the final product.

When a recipe specifies shortening, it usually means one of the solid hydrogenated vegetable shortenings. (See *Fat, Oil, Short* for additional information.)

SHORT RIB – A less tender cut of beef from the ends of the ribs immediately below the rib section. It contains a cross section of the rib bone and has alternating layers of lean and fat. Since it is a less tender cut of beef, it should be cooked in liquid or braised. Short ribs are perfect for soups and stews. (See also *Beef*.)

Barbecued Short Ribs

Trim excess fat from 4 pounds beef short ribs. Season. Place ribs in Dutch oven; add water to cover. Simmer, covered, till tender, about 2 hours. Drain. Place ribs on broiler pan rack.

Combine ⅓ cup catsup, 2 tablespoons molasses, 1 tablespoon lemon juice, 2 teaspoons dry mustard, ¼ teaspoon chili powder, and dash garlic powder; brush over ribs. Broil 4 to 5 inches from heat 15 minutes, turning often and brushing with the sauce. Serves 4.

Braised Short Ribs have a flavor bonus—Onion Gravy with a hint of sauerbraten flavor. These short ribs are not only hearty enough for man-sized appetites, but easy on the budget.

Short Rib-Vegetable Stew

```
     2 pounds beef short ribs
   ¼ cup all-purpose flour
     2 teaspoons salt
   ¼ teaspoon pepper
     2 tablespoons shortening
     2 16-ounce cans tomatoes
     2 cloves garlic, minced
     1 tablespoon Worcestershire sauce
     4 to 5 carrots, peeled
         and sliced
     2 medium onions, sliced
     1 medium potato, peeled
         and diced
  1½ teaspoons salt
       Dash pepper
       Parsley Dumplings
```

Cut short ribs in serving-sized pieces. Combine flour, 2 teaspoons salt, and ¼ teaspoon pepper; coat ribs with flour mixture. In Dutch oven brown meat in hot shortening. Combine tomatoes, garlic, and Worcestershire sauce; pour over ribs. Cover and simmer 1½ hours.

Add carrots, onions, and potato to meat. Simmer till meat and vegetables are tender, about 45 minutes. Skim off fat. Season with salt and pepper. Thicken slightly, if desired.

For *Parsley Dumplings:* Sift together 1 cup sifted all-purpose flour, 2 teaspoons baking powder, and ½ teaspoon salt. Blend in ¼ cup snipped parsley. Combine ½ cup milk and 2 tablespoons salad oil; add to dry ingredients, stirring just till moistened. Drop mixture from tablespoon atop bubbling stew. Cover tightly; bring to boiling. Reduce heat (don't lift cover) and simmer 15 minutes. Makes 4 or 5 servings.

Braised Short Ribs

Trim excess fat from 3 pounds beef short ribs. Roll ribs in all-purpose flour. Brown ribs in 2 tablespoons hot shortening; spoon off fat. Season with 1 teaspoon salt and dash pepper. Add 1 medium onion, sliced, and ½ cup water. Cover; simmer till tender, 2 to 2½ hours. (Add more water, if needed.) Remove meat; keep hot.

Prepare *Onion Gravy:* Skim fat from meat juices, reserving 2 tablespoons fat. Measure juices, and add enough water to make 2 cups. Brown ¼ cup sugar in reserved fat. Add 2 medium onions, thinly sliced; cook till tender.

Shred a cabbage for coleslaw by first cutting the head of cabbage in half. Then, use a sharp knife to cut the cabbage in fine shreds.

Push the onions to one side. Add 2 tablespoons all-purpose flour; brown the flour slightly. Stir in meat juices, 1 tablespoon vinegar, and ¼ teaspoon Kitchen Bouquet. Return to heat; cook and stir till gravy thickens and bubbles. Boil 2 to 3 minutes. Season to taste with salt and pepper. Serve gravy with short ribs. Makes 6 servings.

SHOYU (*shō′ yōō*)—The Japanese word for soy sauce. (See also *Soy Sauce.*)

SHRED—To cut foods with a knife or grater or to tear foods into thin strips or slivers. For example, cabbage, lettuce, and carrots are often shredded for salads. Cheese is another food that is shredded and used as an ingredient in recipes.

SHREDDED WHEAT—A whole wheat cereal made of long, thin shreds of cooked wheat that are shaped into large, oblong, or round biscuits or into bite-sized squares. One shredded wheat biscuit adds 85 calories to the diet in addition to some protein, phosphorus, and B vitamins. When used as an ingredient, shredded wheat adds both flavor and crisp texture. (See also *Cereal.*)

SHRIMP—A small, long-tailed shellfish related to the crab and lobster. The shrimp resembles a lobster in miniature. It has 10 legs, tiny claws, an arched back, and a segmented shell. The shell is grayish green, pink, red, or brownish red. The meat is white and has a tender texture and a sweet taste that are popular with Americans.

Shrimp has been included in many countries' cuisines. The Greeks, Romans, and Chinese began using it centuries ago. Today, shrimp is still a prominent food in typical Italian and oriental dishes.

In the United States, shrimp were first available to the people who lived near the Gulf and Pacific coasts. Only within the last century have Americans throughout the nation had access to supplies of shrimp. Developments in canning, freezing, and shipping have made this possible.

How shrimp live: Shrimp live along muddy inshore and offshore waters. In the United States, they inhabit the waters along the Gulf coast from North Carolina to Texas and along the Pacific coast from San Francisco Bay to Alaska. Shrimp also are found in the waters off the coasts of South America, Japan, Europe, and Asia.

The shrimp of each area possess distinguishing characteristics. Those from the Gulf of Mexico are large, and are white, brown, red, or pink. Pacific shrimp are much smaller and are usually pink. South American shrimp look brownish red.

All shrimp, regardless of the area in which they are found, lead similar lives. The life cycle begins during the spawning season, which takes place in offshore waters from March to September. The tiny shrimp eggs settle to the bottom of the ocean rather than being carried by the mother as are some shellfish eggs. Within a few weeks time, the eggs hatch and the larvae return to the water's surface. The young shrimp, like other shellfish, undergo

Grill shrimp on a hibachi

Baste Sweet-Sour Sauced Shrimp with pimiento-dotted sauce. Use small shrimp for appetizers and large ones for an entrée.

a series of changes, and eventually they develop into a form that looks similar to that of the adult shrimp.

The developing shrimp move toward the coastline and go to the bottom of inland waters and rivers. These shrimp are caught in harvest from August to December.

As winter approaches, the smaller shrimp stay near the coast, but the larger ones travel offshore toward warmer waters. These large shrimp are the ones taken in offshore waters from March to June.

Shrimp are caught by the crews of shrimp boats or trawlers, who drag nets along the bottom of the water. The majority of the catch goes to processing plants where the head and thorax are removed (these parts have very little meat). Then, machinery separates the shrimp by size, removes the shells, and cleans the shrimp. Machinery also applies breading to some of the shrimp. Then, they are canned or frozen for nationwide distribution.

Nutritional value: Shrimp, like other fish and shellfish, are a good source of protein. The B vitamins and minerals (calcium, phosphorus, copper, and iodine) are also present. The calories in a serving of shrimp depend on the method of cooking used and the sauce or breading added. A 3½-ounce serving, uncooked, has 90 calories, while french-frying increases the calorie count to 225. If frozen shrimp are purchased breaded, a 3½-ounce serving, uncooked, will average about 140 calories.

Buying shrimp: Shrimp on the market range from fresh, whole ones to frozen, breaded tails. Whole shrimp are rarely found except along the coast. Most of the fresh ones are sold headless, peeled or unpeeled, and with sand vein still present or deveined. The name "green shrimp," which is applied to some shrimp, does not refer to color; rather, it means that they have not been cooked. When buying fresh shrimp, look for those with a mild odor and firm, glossy shells that fit the body.

Canned shrimp—cooked, peeled, and deveined—come in both dry pack and wet pack. Smoked or dried shrimp, shrimp paste, shrimp in cocktail sauce, and frozen entrées are also available.

Frozen shrimp come in various combinations of processing—cooked or raw, peeled or unpeeled, deveined or with vein, and breaded or plain. They may be frozen together or individually. The separate ones are convenient especially for those who cook only a portion of the package at a time. The number of shrimp needed can be removed without having to thaw the whole package; the remainder can then be returned to the freezer for future use.

Frozen entrées, such as shrimp creole and chow mein, and frozen soups are among the many products that can be found in the super market.

When purchasing shrimp, allow approximately 6 of them per person or ¼ pound of shrimp without shells per person.

How Much Shrimp You Need	
Shrimp in 1 pound	
Size	Number of raw shrimp in shell from 1 pound
Jumbo size	15 to 18
Average size	26 to 30
Tiny	60 or more
Buy in shell or shelled	
Amount needed	Amount to buy
For each 1 cup cleaned, cooked shrimp	12 ounces raw shrimp in shell *or* 7 or 8 ounces frozen shelled shrimp *or* 1 4½- or 5-ounce can shrimp
Shrimp in casserole or sauce	
Servings	Amount needed
For 4 servings of casserole or creamy sauce (approximate)	1 pound shrimp in shell *or* 1⅓ cups cleaned, cooked shrimp *or* 1 or 2 4½- or 5-ounce cans (1 or 2 cups) shrimp

Storing shrimp: Fresh shrimp should be wrapped and stored in the coldest section of the refrigerator for a day or two. For longer storage, freeze uncooked, headless shrimp either with or without shells.

Be sure commercially frozen and home-frozen shrimp are wrapped in moisture-vaporproof material and sealed securely.

Use frozen shrimp within three months. If possible, cook them while still frozen. If you can't do this, thaw shrimp in the refrigerator and use them immediately. Never refreeze shrimp.

Cleaning shrimp: Shrimp are cleaned either before or after boiling. Those cleaned before boiling have a more delicate flavor, while those cleaned after boiling have a more attractive appearance. The choice depends on personal taste.

When cleaning fresh shrimp, remove the head and thorax if the shrimp are whole. Peel off the shell and devein the shrimp. Butterfly large shrimp for frying by cutting to but not through the back.

Devein shrimp by making a slit along the arch of the back with a knife. Rinse under cold water and remove the black vein.

The secret of cooking shrimp

Cook shrimp only a short time. They're done when firm and a reddish pink color. Avoid overcooking because this shrinks them, and avoid rinsing with cold water as this toughens them. Cool and then refrigerate.

Cooking shrimp: Shrimp are delicious cooked in a number of ways. The most popular methods are frying and boiling. However, other methods should be explored, for there are many delicious ways of preparing shrimp. Shrimp can be baked, broiled, barbecued, or made into casseroles, salads, appetizers, stuffings, pizzas, and breakfast entrées. (See also *Shellfish*.)

Fresh Cooked Shrimp

In large saucepan combine 6 cups water, 2 tablespoons salt, 2 tablespoons vinegar, 2 bay leaves, 1 teaspoon mixed pickling spices, and 2 branches celery; bring to boiling.

Add 2 pounds fresh or frozen shrimp in shells or shelled. Heat the mixture to boiling, then lower heat and simmer gently till the shrimp turn pink, about 1 to 3 minutes. Drain. If cooked in shell, peel shrimp and remove black vein that runs down the back.

Note: When cooking shrimp for highly seasoned dishes, omit the vinegar and the spices.

Jiffy Shrimp Skillet

In skillet place one 10-ounce can frozen condensed cream of shrimp soup, thawed; add ¾ cup water and stir to blend. Cover; bring just to boiling. Stir in ⅔ cup uncooked packaged precooked rice; 7 or 8 ounces frozen, shelled shrimp, ⅓ cup chopped celery, ⅓ cup chopped green pepper, ¼ teaspoon salt, and ½ to 1 teaspoon curry powder. Cover; return to boiling. Reduce heat; simmer till rice and shrimp are done, 10 minutes, stirring occasionally.

Just before serving the shrimp mixture, add ⅓ cup sliced, pitted ripe olives. Sprinkle with 2 tablespoons toasted, slivered almonds. Makes 3 or 4 servings.

Arrange individual servings of French Shrimp in Shells around
a dish of green vegetables, and present the meal at the table.
This simple menu makes an unbeatably delicious combination.

French Shrimp in Shells

    1 pound small, shelled shrimp
   ¼ cup butter or margarine
    3 tablespoons all-purpose flour
1½ cups milk
   ½ teaspoon salt
     Dash pepper
     Dash paprika
   ¼ cup dry sherry
     Grated Parmesan cheese

Cook shrimp; drain. Melt butter in saucepan;
stir in flour. Add milk; cook and stir till thickened. Stir in salt, pepper, paprika, sherry, and
shrimp. Pour into 5 baking shells; sprinkle each
with 1 tablespoon Parmesan cheese. Place under broiler 3 to 4 inches from heat; broil till
cheese browns. Makes 5 servings.

Shrimp de Jonghe

    2 pounds shelled shrimp
   ½ cup butter or margarine
    2 cloves garlic, minced
   ⅓ cup snipped parsley
   ½ teaspoon paprika
     Dash cayenne pepper
   ½ cup dry white wine
     • • •
    2 cups soft bread crumbs

Cook shrimp; arrange in an 11¾x7½x1¾-inch
baking dish. Melt butter; add garlic, parsley,
paprika, cayenne, and wine; mix. Stir in bread
crumbs. Spread crumb mixture over shrimp.
   Bake at 350° till crumbs brown, about 25
minutes. Sprinkle with more snipped parsley,
if desired. Makes 6 to 8 servings.

Shrimp à l'Imperatrice

    1 cup mayonnaise
    1 teaspoon dry mustard
    3 tablespoons chopped, canned
        pimiento
    ¼ cup finely diced green pepper
    ½ teaspoon salt
    1½ pounds shrimp in shells, cooked
        and shelled, *or* 2 4½-ounce cans
        shrimp
    3 avocados, peeled and halved
    2 teaspoons fine dry bread crumbs
        Paprika
        Lemon wedges

Thoroughly combine mayonnaise and mustard. Add chopped pimiento, green pepper, and salt; mix well. Fold in shrimp. Fill each avocado half, cut side up, with shrimp mixture (you may have to slice off bottom of avocados to get them to stand upright). Sprinkle tops with bread crumbs and paprika. Serve hot or cold. To serve hot, bake at 350° till heated through, about 10 to 15 minutes. To serve cold, chill shrimp mixture before filling avocado halves. Pass lemon wedges. Makes 6 servings.

Sweet-Sour Sauced Shrimp

Grill these outdoors for a rare treat—

    1 cup sugar
    ½ cup white vinegar
    1 tablespoon chopped green pepper
    1 tablespoon chopped, canned
        pimiento
    ½ teaspoon salt
    2 teaspoons cornstarch
    1 tablespoon cold water
    1 teaspoon paprika
        Shelled, raw shrimp

In saucepan mix sugar, vinegar, ½ cup water, green pepper, pimiento, and salt. Simmer 5 minutes. Combine cornstarch and cold water; add to hot mixture. Cook and stir till sauce is thickened and bubbly. Cool. Add paprika.

Cook the shelled, raw shrimp on fine wire grill over *hot* coals till done, about 6 to 8 minutes, turning once and brushing often with sweet-sour sauce. *Don't overcook!* Pass extra sauce with the shrimp. Makes 1½ cups sauce.

Shrimp à la King

Make ahead and freeze till ready to serve—

    1 7-ounce package frozen, shelled
        shrimp
    1 3-ounce can sliced mushrooms,
        drained
    ¼ cup chopped green pepper
    ¼ cup butter or margarine
        •   •   •
    2 tablespoons all-purpose flour
    ½ teaspoon salt
        Several dashes white pepper
    2 cups milk
    1 tablespoon lemon juice
    6 to 8 toast cups

Cook shrimp according to package directions; drain. In medium saucepan cook mushrooms and green pepper in butter or margarine till tender. Blend in flour, salt, and white pepper. Add milk all at once. Cook and stir till thickened and bubbly. Stir in shrimp and lemon juice. Heat through; serve in toast cups.

Or pour mixture into 1-quart casserole; cool. Cover and freeze. When ready to serve, bake frozen casserole, covered, at 375° till heated through, about 50 to 60 minutes. Stir occasionally while heating. Makes 6 to 8 servings.

Shrimp and Rice Deluxe

    ½ cup milk
    1 cup water
    1 10½-ounce can condensed
        cream of celery soup
    1 7-ounce package frozen rice
        and peas with mushrooms
    1 4½- or 5-ounce can shrimp,
        drained, *or* 1½ cups cooked
        shrimp
    2 tablespoons snipped parsley
    ½ teaspoon curry powder
        Toasted slivered almonds

In a 2-quart saucepan gradually blend the milk and water into cream of celery soup. Add frozen rice and peas with mushrooms, shrimp, the 2 tablespoons snipped parsley, and curry powder. Cover and simmer gently for 30 minutes. Stir mixture occasionally. Garnish with toasted, slivered almonds. Makes 4 to 6 servings.

Shrimp Sandwiches

Cut into tiny triangles for tea sandwiches or into halves for a luncheon entrée—

    1 3-ounce package cream cheese,
        softened
    2 tablespoons mayonnaise or
        salad dressing
            . . .
    1 tablespoon catsup
    1 teaspoon prepared mustard
        Dash garlic powder
            . . .
    1 cup chopped, cooked shrimp
    ¼ cup finely chopped celery
    1 teaspoon finely chopped onion
    8 to 10 slices lightly buttered
        white bread

Blend cream cheese with mayonnaise or salad dressing; mix in catsup, prepared mustard, and garlic powder. Stir in shrimp, celery, and onion. Spread mixture between bread slices. For tea sandwiches, use 10 slices; for luncheon size, size, use 8 slices. Trim crusts from bread, if desired. Cut each tea sandwich diagonally in 4 triangles; cut luncheon size in half. Makes 4 luncheon or 20 tea sandwiches.

Spear a Gourmet Shrimp on wooden picks for dipping into a special sauce. A chafing dish keeps the appetizers warm.

Shrimp-Curry Luncheon

    1 avocado, peeled and sliced
    1 tablespoon lime juice
    1½ teaspoons butter or margarine
    ½ teaspoon curry powder
    1 small tomato, peeled and chopped
    2 tablespoons chopped onion
    ¾ cup cooked shrimp
    ½ cup dairy sour cream
    2 English muffins, split

Brush avocado slices with lime juice; heat at 300° for 5 to 10 minutes.

Melt butter in small saucepan; add curry, ½ teaspoon salt, tomato, and onion. Cook till onion is tender, 5 minutes. Add shrimp; heat through. Stir in sour cream; heat, *but do not boil.* Toast muffins. Top muffins with warm avocado; spoon shrimp curry over. Serves 2.

Shrimp-Cheese Fondue

    1 10-ounce can frozen condensed
        cream of shrimp soup, thawed
    ½ cup milk
    2 teaspoons instant minced onion
    ¼ teaspoon dry mustard
    1 pound process Swiss cheese,
        shredded (4 cups)
    2 tablespoons dry sherry
        French bread or hard rolls

In a saucepan heat soup and milk till blended. Stir in onion, mustard, and Swiss cheese. Heat and stir till cheese melts. Stir in wine, Serve immediately in fondue pot or chafing dish. Cut bread in bite-sized pieces with crust on each. Spear cube on long-handled fork and swirl in cheese mixture. Serves 6 to 8.

Gourmet Shrimp

Combine 1 cup catsup, ¼ cup sauterne, and 2 tablespoons snipped parsley; chill thoroughly.

Melt ¼ cup butter or margarine in skillet or blazer pan of chafing dish. Add 1 clove garlic, minced, and 1 teaspoon dried dillweed. Cook several minutes. Add 2 cups shelled, raw shrimp and cook till shrimp turn pink, about 5 to 10 minutes. Turn occasionally. Salt to taste. Serve with chilled sauce. Serves 4.

Shrimp Sauce

Try this sauce with egg dishes—

Melt 2 tablespoons butter; blend in 2 tablespoons all-purpose flour. Stir in one 10-ounce can frozen condensed cream of shrimp soup, thawed, and 1 soup can milk. Cook and stir till bubbly. Add ½ cup shredded sharp process American cheese; stir to melt. Makes 3 cups.

SHRIMP SPICE—A blend of seasonings, also called shrimp boil or crab boil. Commercial blends of shrimp spice contain a combination of red pepper, bay leaf, mustard seed, allspice, clove, black pepper, savory, and dillseed, all in whole form. Placing shrimp spice in the boiling water with shrimp, crab, or other seafood gives the food extra flavor. Bundling the spices together in a cheesecloth bag makes them easy to remove at the end of cooking time.

SHRUB—A beverage made of fruit juice, sugar, and sometimes alcohol. The juice, usually orange or lemon, gives the drink a tart flavor, and the sugar adds sweetness. Rum or brandy can be added for an alcoholic drink. These mixtures are drunk cool from tumblers either straight or diluted.

Shrubs have been a popular drink since colonial times. The pioneers were fond of the refreshing flavor, and they were able to store the drink year-round.

SHUCK—**1.** The outer covering on corn, nuts, oysters, and clams. **2.** To remove this covering. To shuck corn, peel the husks off the ears. Shuck nuts by cracking and removing the shell. Shuck oysters and clams by cutting around the shell, forcing it open, and cutting out the muscle.

SIDECAR—An alcoholic cocktail made of brandy, lemon juice, and orange liqueur. (See also *Wines and Spirits.*)

SIEVE *(siv)*—**1.** A circular utensil with a wire mesh or fine holes. **2.** To force food through a sieve or a sifter.

Sieves come in various sizes. Most of them have a handle attached. The bottom and sides are of wire mesh.

Sieve foods by pushing them through the wire mesh. Begin with utensil about half full and press with back of a large spoon.

Sieving serves various purposes in the home. Drain liquids from a food by balancing the sieve over a container and pouring the food into the sieve. Purée foods by forcing them through the sieve. Recipes for cheesecake, for example, often call for cottage cheese to be puréed. This may be done with a sieve.

A sieve can even double as a sifter. Shake flour or dry ingredients through the mesh part of the sieve. Use a spoon to press the food through, if necessary.

SIFT—To force foods through a sieve or sifter. Many functions in the kitchen involve sifting. Dry ingredients are blended together, foods are fluffed, and foreign particles are removed. Lumps are broken up, and foods are sprinkled, such as confectioners' sugar over a cake.

Follow correct procedures when sifting flour—sift the flour onto waxed paper or a plate; spoon lightly into a measuring cup designed for dry ingredients, being careful not to pack or shake the cup; and level off with a knife or spatula. This will give a measurement that is consistent with that used in testing the recipe. Thus, the best **results** will be achieved.

SIFTER—A small kitchen utensil that is similar to a sieve or a strainer, used for aerating flour or confectioners' sugar. Sifters, in the form of variously sized metal cups, have a screen bottom through which the flour or sugar is forced. Revolving disks or wires rub across the fine mesh screen bottom propelled by a lever which is most often connected to the handle of the sifter.

Many baked products are dependent upon the use of a sifter for producing a light and airy product. For example, a sifter is very important in the making of a light and tender angel food or sponge cake. The dry ingredients are usually sifted together three times so as much air as possible is incorporated into the mixture.

Besides aerating dry ingredients, a sifter breaks up or holds back possible lumps, as in the case of confectioners' sugar, which is often used in making a smooth, creamy frosting. Also, a sifter is used to blend together dry ingredients, such as flour, leavening agents, salt, and spices before they are combined with the liquid ingredients. (See also *Equipment*.)

SIMMER—To cook food in liquid at a temperature of 185 to 210 degrees, where bubbles form at a slow rate and burst before reaching the surface. Simmering is a slow method of cooking and is preferred over faster cooking temperatures for a number of reasons: High protein foods, such as fish, meat, and eggs toughen at higher temperatures, which makes simmering a more suitable cookery method. Soups and sauces develop a rich flavor and smooth consistency if allowed to simmer on the range for several hours. And tougher cuts of meat become surprisingly tender and dried fruits turn out plump and juicy when allowed to simmer. Foods also retain their shapes better during gentle simmering.

SIMNEL CAKE *(sim' nuhl)*—A rich, fruitcake with a filling and topping of almond paste. A British Lenten cake, it is also called Mothering Sunday Cake because, years ago, indentured servant girls were allowed to bake the simnel cake to take to their mothers on the fourth Sunday in Lent —their only visiting day. The cake is now popular at holiday times as a fruitcake.

Simnel Cake

½ cup butter
⅓ cup sugar
3 eggs

•   •   •

½ cup raisins
½ cup currants
¼ cup mixed candied fruits
    and peels
2 teaspoons grated lemon peel
1 cup sifted all-purpose flour
½ teaspoon baking powder
½ teaspoon salt
½ teaspoon ground nutmeg
¼ teaspoon ground cinnamon
1 tablespoon water
1 tablespoon light molasses

•   •   •

8 ounces almond paste
1 beaten egg
    Confectioners' Icing

In small mixer bowl cream together butter and sugar. Add eggs, one at a time, beating well after each addition. Combine raisins, currants, mixed fruits and peels, and lemon peel; set aside. Sift together flour, baking powder, salt, nutmeg, and cinnamon; sprinkle over fruits, tossing to coat. Stir into creamed mixture. Add water and molasses; mix well.

Pour *half* of the batter into greased and floured 8x1½-inch layer cake pan. Divide almond paste into thirds. Roll ⅓ of the paste between waxed paper to a 7-inch round; remove waxed paper. Place almond paste round on cake batter in pan. Cover with remaining batter. Bake at 325° till done, 40 to 45 minutes. Cool.

Roll another ⅓ of the almond paste to a 7-inch round; place atop cake. Shape remaining almond paste into 11 balls; arrange around top edge of cake. Brush with beaten egg; bake at 400° till golden, 7 to 8 minutes. When cool, drizzle with *Confectioners' Icing*: Combine 1 cup sifted confectioners' sugar, ½ teaspoon vanilla, and 1 to 2 tablespoons milk.

SIMPLE SYRUP—Equal parts or two parts granulated sugar to one part water cooked for five minutes to make a thin syrup. It is used in some canning, as sweetener for punches and drinks, and as a glaze for some breads and coffee breads.

Thread chunks of fruit and meat onto skewer for broiling. Make sure the food pieces are centered so they will cook evenly.

SIPPET *(sip' it)* — Small triangles of freshly made toast that are used to complete or garnish a food, such as seafood Newburg or creamed chicken dishes.

SIRLOIN — A cut of meat—steak or roast—from the hip area of the hindquarters of beef, pork, lamb, or veal. Often a hip bone is present—round, flat, or wedge in shape. However, some steaks and most roasts are boneless. The sirloin is usually an excellent cut of meat.

Sirloin steaks are broiled, and high quality roasts are roasted. Less-tender roasts are cooked with moist heat. (See *Beef, Meat, Steak* for additional information.)

Braised Sirloin Roast

Sprinkle one 3- to 4-pound beef sirloin tip roast lightly with 2 tablespoons all-purpose flour and rub in. In Dutch oven, brown roast slowly on all sides in 2 tablespoons shortening. Season with 2 teaspoons salt and ¼ teaspoon pepper. Add 1 medium onion, sliced; 2 bay leaves; 1 clove garlic, minced; and ½ cup hot water to roast. Cover and cook at 350° till meat is almost tender, about 2 hours.

Add 8 small onions, peeled; 8 medium carrots, peeled; and 8 small potatoes, peeled. Sprinkle vegetables with 1½ teaspoons salt. Cook, covered, till meat and vegetables are tender, 1½ hours. Make gravy. Serves 6 to 8.

Sirloin Tip Roast

    1 3- to 4-pound sirloin tip roast
    2 tablespoons all-purpose flour
    2 tablespoons shortening
    2 teaspoons salt
    ½ cup pineapple juice
    1 tablespoon instant minced onion
    1 tablespoon lemon juice
    1 teaspoon Italian salad
        dressing mix
    1 teaspoon Worcestershire sauce
    ⅛ teaspoon pepper
      Gravy

Sprinkle meat lightly with flour; brown slowly on all sides in hot shortening in roasting pan. Season with salt. Combine pineapple juice and next 5 ingredients; pour over meat. Cover; roast at 325° till meat is tender, about 2 to 2¾ hours. Remove to serving platter. Allow 3 or 4 servings per pound of meat.

To prepare *Gravy*, pour pan juices into large measuring cup. Skim off excess fat; return 1½ cups juices to pan. Combine ½ cup cold water and ¼ cup all-purpose flour in shaker; shake well. Stir into juices; cook, stirring constantly, till gravy is thickened and bubbly. If desired, add a little Kitchen Bouquet for a richer, brown color. Makes 2 cups gravy.

SKATE — A saltwater fish that has large side winglike fins. These Pacific coast fish have a broad, flat body and measure two to eight feet in length.

The fins are delicious when poached or fried. To eat these fins, scrape off the flesh with the knife and fork instead of cutting it into bites. (See also *Fish.*)

SKEWER — 1. Short, sharp metal or wooden pins used to hold stuffed meat roasts, chops, or fish together as they cook. 2. Long metal or bamboo pins used for threading food to form kabobs for broiling.

When used to hold together the stuffing in poultry, the small metal skewers are laced together with heavy cord. When used in fish or chops, the metal skewers act as pins to hold in the stuffing. Wooden skewers are used by butchers to hold together boned meats or roasts with pockets cut in them for stuffing.

Skewers used for kabobs, called *brochettes* in French, vary in length. Foods, such as meat chunks and vegetable or fruit pieces, are threaded onto the long metal pins for broiling. Because it is an attractive and unusual way to serve food, marinated fruits or vegetables are sometimes strung on short skewers for serving.

Marinated Skewered Fruit

    1 20½-ounce can pineapple chunks
    ¼ cup honey
    1 tablespoon brandy
    1 teaspoon snipped fresh mint *or*
       dried mint flakes
    1 apple, cut in wedges
    1 pear, cut in wedges
    1 nectarine, cut in wedges

Drain pineapple chunks, reserving the syrup. To the syrup add honey, brandy, and snipped fresh mint *or* dried mint flakes. Place apple, pear, and nectarine wedges in shallow dish; add the honey mixture. Marinate in refrigerator 2 to 3 hours, turning fruit wedges occasionally. Thread on skewers, or serve in sherbet dishes with marinade. Makes 4 servings.

Use skewers for serving marinated fruit chunks. Select fresh or canned fruits of assorted colors for an interesting effect.

SKILLET—A frying pan, sometimes called a spider, an old-fashioned name that dates back to the days when iron skillets were made with three legs.

Made of metal, ceramic, or enamel, skillets have a long handle and usually are quite shallow. Electric skillets, controlled by an adjustable thermostat, maintain a constant cooking temperature.

Skillets are most popularly used for pan-frying, panbroiling, and sautéeing. They are sometimes appropriate for preparing stews, one-dish meals, vegetables, and desserts. (See *Appliance, Pots and Pans* for additional information.)

SKIM—1. To remove floating particles from a liquid with the aid of a flat, perforated utensil. 2. To remove the cream that rises to the surface of whole milk that has not been homogenized.

The floating particles, in the form of a layer, are often referred to as the foam, froth, or scum. Examples of skimming include removing the foam that forms on the top of jam or jelly during the cooking process, and removing the floating fat from the surface of soups or stews before they are spooned into serving dishes.

SKIM MILK—Whole milk from which almost all the fat has been removed. States have different standards as to the minimum percentage of nonfat milk solids or total milk solids that skim milk must have.

In the shopper's mind, there often is some confusion about those milks which contain less fat than whole milk. Carefully reading the labeling of each of them individually, one can see the differences in each type of milk.

Skim milk has the least amount of milk fat—ordinarily 0.5 percent or less milk fat content. *Low fat milk* has slightly more fat than skim milk—0.5 to 1.9 percent, while *two percent milk* has just a bit more fat—two percent, as the name indicates. Most of these milks are usually enriched with nonfat milk solids.

The nutritive value of skim milk is less than that of whole milk as is the calorie count. Because of the reduction in fats, skim milk contains lesser amounts of vitamin A, although this vitamin is frequently added along with vitamin D in commercial production. Other nutrients in skim milk are the same as in whole milk.

Among skim milk products are instant nonfat dry milk and evaporated skim milk. Skim milk is used to make some cheeses, cottage cheese, and cultured buttermilk. It is also a popular beverage and recipe ingredient for those people who find it necessary to count calories. One cup of enriched skim milk contains about 105 calories, while one cup whole milk provides 160 calories. (See also *Milk*.)

Raspberry Bavarian Cake

A make-ahead dessert that is low in calories—

    1 ⅞-ounce package low-calorie
        raspberry-flavored gelatin
        (2 envelopes)
    1 cup evaporated skim milk
    1 cup fresh raspberries, sweetened
        or 1 10-ounce package frozen
        raspberries, thawed and drained
    1 10-inch angel cake

Dissolve gelatin in 2 cups *boiling* water. Chill till partially set. Meanwhile, place evaporated skim milk in shallow pan; freeze just till ice crystals form around edges. In chilled mixer bowl, beat milk with electric beater till stiff; fold milk into partially set gelatin. Gently fold in fresh or thawed raspberries.

Cut angel cake into 3 layers. Spread about 1¼ cups of the raspberry mixture between each cake layer; spread sides and top of cake with remaining mixture. Chill till serving time.

Banana Milk Shake

Fresh banana flavor in a low-calorie snack—

    1 medium-large banana
    1 cup skim milk
        Noncaloric sweetener equal to
        1 tablespoon sugar

Peel banana; wrap in foil and freeze. Cut frozen banana into chunks. Place milk and sweetener in blender container. Gradually add banana; blend till smooth. Makes 2 servings.

SKIRRET *(skir′ it)* — An Asiatic pot herb that is culivated in Europe for its sweet, edible, tuberous roots that resemble a cluster of small parsnips.

SLAW — The shortened name for the shredded cabbage salad tossed with mayonnaise or vinegar-type dressing. It is most often called coleslaw. (See also *Coleslaw*.)

SLICE — 1. A flat piece, thin or thick as desired, cut from or across a larger piece of food, such as a roast of meat, whole carrot, loaf of bread, or cake. **2.** To cut into flat pieces, usually with a knife.

SLING — An alcoholic drink popular in tropical countries. Although gin is most frequently used in a sling, it often is prepared with whiskey or brandy. The drink is a combination of liquor, confectioners' sugar, fruit peel or juice, and ice. A Singapore Sling contains gin and cherry-flavored brandy. (See also *Cocktail*.)

Singapore Sling

In highball glass combine cracked ice, ½ ounce cherry-flavored brandy, ½ ounce lemon juice, 1 teaspoon confectioners' sugar, and 1½ to 2 jiggers gin. Fill glass with cold water or carbonated water; stir. Garnish with maraschino cherry and orange slice, if desired. Serve with straws. Makes 1 serving.

Vegetables, such as yellow squash, are often sliced before cooking. A sharp knife and cutting board ensure smooth, even slices.

SLIT—A small, narrow incision made into a food to allow steam to escape. When preparing a two-crust pie, several slits are made in the top layer of the pastry to allow steam to escape during cooking. Slits are sometimes cut into a roast, such as leg of lamb, beef, or ham, as seasonings, such as garlic, herbs, or spices, are inserted to add flavor during roasting.

SLIVER—1. A long, thin piece of such foods as almonds, cheese, fruits, vegetables, or meats. 2. To cut food in long, thin pieces.

Use a sharp knife or coarse grater blade to cut the slivers. Slivered almonds are among the most popular toppings for such desserts as ice cream and for many main dishes. Slivered fruits and vegetables, as well as meat and cheese, add interest to crisp, tossed salads.

Tuna-Noodle Casserole

Slivered almonds add a crunchy topping to creamy tuna and noodle casserole—

```
    6 ounces medium noodles (3 cups)
    1 6½- or 7-ounce can tuna,
        drained
    ½ cup mayonnaise or salad
        dressing
    1 cup sliced celery
    ⅓ cup chopped onion
    ¼ cup chopped green pepper
    ¼ cup chopped, canned pimiento,
        drained
    ½ teaspoon salt
    1 10½-ounce can condensed cream
        of celery soup
    ½ cup milk
    4 ounces sharp process American
        cheese, shredded (1 cup)
    ½ cup slivered almonds, toasted
```

Cook noodles according to package directions; drain. Combine noodles, tuna, mayonnaise, celery, onion, green pepper, pimiento, and salt.

In saucepan blend soup with milk; heat and stir till smooth. Stir in cheese; heat and stir till cheese melts. Stir into noodle mixture.

Turn mixture into 2-quart casserole. Sprinkle casserole with almonds. Bake, uncovered, at 425° for 20 minutes. Makes 6 servings.

SLIVOVITZ *(sliv' uh vits, -wits, shliv'-)*—A golden brown plum brandy made in Balkan countries, particularly Yugoslavia. The brandy is doubly distilled, aged for a year, after which more plums are added. Slivovitz is the national beverage of two of the Yugoslavian republics, Bosnia and Serbia. (See also *Brandy*.)

SLOE *(slō)*—A small, wild, plumlike fruit of the blackthorn, a European bush of the rose family. The bush grows in the southern and midwestern sections of the United States and is known by other names, including haw bush and bullace tree.

Although the astringent fruit is edible, sloe is rarely gathered for eating as a fresh fruit. The tart, bluish black fruit is used primarily for flavoring sloe gin, although it is also for use in making jams, jellies, and some kinds of conserves.

SLOE GIN—A liqueur made by steeping sloe berries in gin. The liqueur takes on the flavor and color of the berries. (See *Gin, Liqueur* for additional information.)

SMEARCASE (SMIERCASE) CHEESE—The Pennsylvania Dutch name for creamed cottage cheese. It means "spread cheese."

SMELT—A small, slender fish with silvery, olive green coloring. Smelts are usually seven or eight inches long and weigh about 1½ to 2 ounces. The rich-flavored smelts can be fat or lean, and either freshwater or saltwater fish.

Smelts have been abundant along both the Atlantic and Pacific coasts for centuries. They were caught by Indians and used for food and trading purposes. The Pacific coast Indians dried one oily type and burned it for light. And in 1906, smelts were planted in the Great Lakes to feed the salmon that were introduced into those waters. The salmon did not survive, but the smelt flourished.

Like their relative, the salmon, smelt travel up rivers and streams to spawn. This annual event occurs when the ice begins to break. At this time, when the smelts are running, people throng to the river banks to scoop up fish with all types of makeshift equipment.

For those who are not near streams to catch their own, smelt is available fresh, frozen, and canned at the market. Most of these are whole or dressed. Precooked and breaded smelt are also available in the frozen-food section.

Smelt is usually cooked whole by frying, broiling, baking, boiling, or steaming. Before cooking, four or five fish have about 100 calories if fresh, and 200 calories if canned. (See also *Fish*.)

Smelts

    1 pound fresh or frozen smelts
    ¼ cup milk
    ½ cup cornmeal
    ½ teaspoon salt
    ¼ cup butter or margarine
        . . .
    2 tablespoons snipped parsley
    Tartar sauce
    Lemon juice

Clean fresh smelts. (If using frozen smelts, thaw them.) Rinse smelts thoroughly and wipe dry. Dip smelts in milk, then in mixture of cornmeal and salt. In large skillet cook the smelts in butter or margarine till done, about 5 minutes on each side. Sprinkle snipped parsley over smelts and serve with tartar sauce or lemon juice. Makes 2 or 3 servings.

Smelts in Barbecue Sauce

    1 pound fresh or frozen smelts
    1 8-ounce can tomato sauce
    ½ cup chopped onion
    2 tablespoons brown sugar
    2 tablespoons vinegar
    1 tablespoon Worcestershire sauce
    1 tablespoon water
    2 teaspoons prepared mustard
    ¼ teaspoon salt

Thaw frozen smelts; clean, rinse, and wipe dry. Combine all ingredients *except* smelts. Marinate smelts in tomato mixture, covered, in refrigerator for several hours. In large skillet bring smelts and tomato mixture to boiling. Reduce heat and simmer, uncovered, till fish are done, 8 to 10 minutes. Makes 3 or 4 servings.

SMITANE—Indicates that sour cream is one of the ingredients in a dish when used in a recipe title. It is a French variation of *smetana,* the Russian word for sour cream.

SMITHFIELD HAM—A special type of ham from the meat of hogs cured, smoked, and aged in Smithfield, Virginia, at the mouth of the James River.

Historically, Smithfield hams have always enjoyed an international reputation. England's Queen Victoria had these hams shipped to her, and both Sarah Bernhardt and Germany's Kaiser William rated the Smithfield ham far above any delicacy of their own cuisine. Reportedly, gourmand Diamond Jim Brady ate entire Smithfield hams in just one meal.

It was an Englishman, Mallory Todd, who set into motion the Smithfield ham industry. He set up a curing plant and smokehouse near the present-day site.

Dry salt curing and dehydration are the basic principles involved in the production of the famous Smithfield hams. The hams are first covered with salt and a curing agent. As the salt penetrates the ham, some of the natural juice is drawn out. Before smoking, hams are coated with

Recognize famous Smithfield hams by their coarse black pepper coating. The rich, lean meat should be served in paper-thin slices.

ground pepper for protection from insects. The dehydration process during the aging period continues for at least six months and may go as long as one and one-half years. The tenderness of the aged ham is believed to be caused, in part, by the protein breakdown during aging.

Directions for ham preparation are in the cloth bag used to cover the meat. The ham is usually soaked for 24 to 48 hours, washed and scraped, simmered in water, skinned, and glazed if desired. It is best sliced and panfried or baked whole then served thinly sliced. (See also *Ham*.)

SMOKE COOKER—Equipment specially designed so that the food hangs in a chamber away from the direct heat of the fire and is cooked by hot smoke. Originally a Chinese apparatus, the cooker has a chimney at one end of the firebox in which the food is hung from hooks. Openings at the top of the chimney and at the firebox opening control the draft. The cooking chamber fills with hot smoke as the wood chips burn in the firebox. Smoke cooking imparts a special flavor to the meat, depending upon the type of wood. (See also *Barbecue*.)

SMOKE COOKERY—A method of outdoor cookery in which the food is cooked by hot smoke in a smoke cooker instead of directly over hot coals. (See also *Barbecue*.)

SMOKED FISH—Fish that has been exposed to smoke from hardwoods, in the presence of low heat, until the flavor of smoke has penetrated throughout the fish. Undoubtedly man learned thousands of years ago that by stringing the fish on a stick over the fire he obtained a good, smoky taste and was able to store the fish for a long time. The commercial smoking of fish is a controlled process.

It essentially involves hanging the fish above the smoke of a dampened wood fire for a specified length of time. The fish is generally cured in a brine solution before it is smoked. During the smoking process, the fish absorbs the aroma of the smoke, which depends upon the particular type of wood that is used. Hickory is the most popular wood, but other hardwoods such as maple are also used.

Fish are smoked both whole or in pieces. Whole fish are drawn before they are smoked, while some large fish are cut into steaks or chunks. The whole process— splitting, cleaning, salting, drying, and smoking such fish as herring or salmon— is commonly known as kippering.

You will find some smoked fish by the pieces or sliced to order in fish markets and delicatessens. They are also available in cans or packages.

Look for these popular kinds of smoked fish: anchovy, bloaters or herring, butterfish, carp, chub, black cod, eel, finnan haddie, haddock, halibut, kippers, mackerel, salmon (lox), sardine, shad, sturgeon, trout, and whitefish.

While smoked fish need not be cooked before eating, you may cook them if you wish. Panfried or poached bloaters, for example, make a good breakfast dish. Finnan haddie or smoked haddock is delicious broiled and served with a sauce, or baked in milk. Smoked salmon or halibut makes a hearty casserole with rice and seasonings. Smoked whitefish or chub is a good lunch dish with potato salad and tomatoes.

Smoked eel, thin slices of smoked sturgeon or salmon, and smoked anchovies are tasty appetizer foods. Serve with crackers or rye bread slices. (See also *Fish*.)

Smoked Salmon and Macaroni

1 3⅔-ounce can sliced, smoked salmon
1 15-ounce can macaroni and cheese
1 3-ounce can chopped mushrooms, drained
¼ cup chopped green pepper
1 teaspoon instant minced onion
3 hard-cooked eggs, chopped
2 tablespoons butter or margarine
1½ cups soft bread crumbs

Rinse, drain, and cut salmon into small pieces. Combine all ingredients *except butter and crumbs*. Turn into a 1-quart casserole. Melt butter; toss with crumbs. Sprinkle over casserole. Bake, uncovered, at 350° for 30 to 35 minutes. Garnish with green pepper rings or hard-cooked egg slices, if desired. Serves 3 or 4.

Smoked Eel Canapés

   6 thin slices party pumpernickel
      Butter or margarine
12 thin slices skinned, smoked eel or
      other dry, smoked fish (about
      one 4-ounce fish)
  ¼ cup dairy sour cream
   1 teaspoon finely chopped onion
      Capers, drained

Spread bread slices with butter or margarine;
cut each slice of bread in half. Lay one slice fish
atop each half. Combine sour cream and onion.
Spoon a dollop over smoked fish; garnish with
capers. Makes 12 appetizers.

SMOKED MEAT—Meat that is cured by ex-
posing it to smoke in the presence of low
heat. Like smoked fish, the meat is hung
above the smoke for a specified length of
time until the flavor of smoke has penetrated throughout the meat. In commercial
smoking of meat, special care is taken to
ensure that the meat is not too dry after
smoking, that the smoke is circulated properly for even penetration, and that the degree of smoke is just right for the specific
meat product. Hickory is the traditional
smoking wood, but other hardwoods, including maple, apple, and cherry, also are
popular for preparing smoked meat.

    More cuts of pork than any other type

Use a handy dry soup mix and prepared frozen patty shells to
make Smoked Beef Luncheon. Bits of smoked, sliced beef are
in the sauce. Spiced Peaches makes a delicious accompaniment.

of meat are smoked. People have learned to enjoy the flavor of pork and smoke together. It's the smoking after the meat curing that makes ham and bacon taste so different from the flavor of fresh or cured (pickled) pork.

Many sausages made of all pork or a mixture of meats, are smoked to add flavor and keeping quality. Some of these sausages require cooking before eating while others are safe for immediate eating.

A small amount of beef is cured and smoked. Smoked sliced beef differs from dried beef, though they look alike. Smoked sliced beef is made from coarsely ground beef formed into round or square logs that are cured, cooked, and smoked. Breakfast beef (erroneously called beef bacon) is another smoked beef product, packaged in slices that resemble bacon in size, but they are much more lean.

Birds, too, are smoked for good eating. But the small supply of smoked turkey, duckling, goose, and pheasant that comes to the market is very much in the luxury food category. Both smoked turkey and smoked pheasant are made into a pâté and canned, to use as an appetizer spread.

You can add smoke flavor to meats when you cook them over heat on a grill or rotisserie. Or you can brush liquid smoke on oven-cooked meats or sprinkle them with smoke-flavored seasoning.

As with fresh meats, a meat thermometer is best to test doneness of smoked meat.

Smoking does not change the nutritional value of meats. They are as good sources of protein, the B vitamins, and minerals after smoking as before.

Smoked Beef Luncheon

      6 frozen patty shells
      1 envelope leek soup mix
    1¾ cups water
      1 6-ounce can evaporated milk
        (⅔ cup)
      3 drops bottled hot pepper sauce
      1 3-ounce package smoked, sliced
        beef, coarsely snipped
      2 tablespoons chopped, canned
        pimiento
        Spiced Peaches

Bake patty shells according to package directions. Prepare soup according to package directions, using the water and evaporated milk as the liquid. Stir in hot pepper sauce, beef, and pimiento; cook and stir till thick and bubbly. Spoon into patty shells. Serves 6.

Spiced Peaches: Heat canned peach halves for 5 minutes in syrup with stick cinnamon, a few whole cloves, and a dash of vinegar.

SMOKE POINT—The temperature at which heated fat starts to break down, giving off smoky vapor, and taking on an acrid flavor. The smoking point determines whether a fat is a suitable one to use for frying. Olive oil and butter have low smoking points and can only be used for panfrying or sautéeing with careful temperature control to make sure they do not overheat. Vegetable oils and shortening are the choices for deep-fat frying, for they can withstand high frying temperatures without breaking down. (See also *Fat.*)

SMORGASBORD (*smôr′ guhs bōrd′, -bôrd′*)—A Swedish style luncheon or dinner buffet at which a variety of foods is offered. Smorgasbords are now very popular in the United States and other countries. (See also *Scandinavian Cookery.*)

SMORREBROD (*smoe′ ruh broeth*) — The name for the tiny, open-face sandwiches of Denmark. (See also *Scandinavian Cookery.*)

SMOTHER—To cook food in a tightly covered container or massed together in their own juices or in a small amount of liquid.

SMYRNA FIG (*smûr′ nuh*)—A yellowish or greenish fig native to the Near East.

Smyrna fig cuttings, ancestors of California-grown Calimyrna figs, were brought to the United States in 1880. Although the trees thrived, the fruit from the trees did not develop properly until 1899 when the unique cross-pollination process of this fig type was discovered and could be put to use commercially. (See also *Fig.*)

SNACK—A small amount of food eaten at any time other than at mealtime. Sandwiches, fruits, and sweets are snacks.

SNAIL—A small mollusk with a one-part, spiral shell. Market-sized snails usually measure about 1 to 1½ inches in diameter. They feed on green plants and move by means of a muscular foot. They frequently are referred to as escargots on menus.

Snails live either in water or on land. The water type, usually smaller than the land ones, are found in Europe and the east coast of America, and are called periwinkles. Land snails live in France, Switzerland, Japan, Italy, and the middle United States. Some are caught wild and some are raised on farms. These are the ones most used as food; however, land and water snail are used interchangeably.

You can purchase fresh, canned, and frozen snails. Cook fresh ones immediately. First, soak them in warm water till they emerge from the shell. (Those that do not emerge should be discarded.) Then boil them in salted water of court bouillon. Afterwards rinse the snails and shells. Canned snails and shells can be bought together or separately. Both canned and frozen ones are ready to use.

Cook snails by frying, making into a sauce, or putting into the shells with a seasoned butter and baking. There are special plates designed to use when baking in shells. These have indentions so the shells will not slide or move on the tray.

When you are eating snails from the shell, use pincers or snail tongs and a small fork, such as a snail or oyster fork. Place the tongs, in the left hand, to hold the shell steady while you remove the snail with the fork. Then, eat the snail. Delicious. Do not waste the snail butter. Pour it onto the plate and dip French bread into the tasty mixture.

SNAP BEAN—A green or yellow-podded kidney bean eaten with the pod. The green varieties are called green beans; the yellow varieties, wax beans. When bent in half, fresh beans snap crisply. (See also *Bean.*)

SNAPPER—A group of large fish that live in warmer ocean areas. The red snapper is one of the best known. The gray snapper, muttonfish, schoolmaster, and yellowtail are also included as members of the snapper family. (See also *Red Snapper.*)

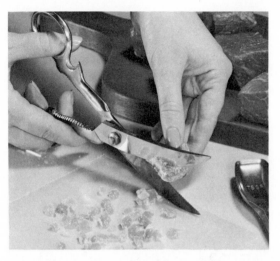

Use kitchen shears to snip foods, such as candied ginger, dates, parsley, or chives. Snip the food in small, uniform pieces.

SNICKERDOODLE—A spiced, shaped cookie. Often rolled in a cinnamon-sugar mixture, they may contain fruit. (See also *Cookie.*)

Snickerdoodles

      ½ cup shortening
      ½ cup butter or margarine
    1½ cups sugar
      2 eggs
    2¾ cups sifted all-purpose flour
      2 teaspoons cream of tartar
      1 teaspoon baking soda
      ¼ teaspoon salt
      3 tablespoons sugar
      3 teaspoons ground cinnamon

Cream together first 3 ingredients. Add eggs; beat till fluffy. Sift together flour, cream of tartar, baking soda, and salt; stir into creamed mixture. Shape into balls the size of small walnuts. Mix 3 tablespoons sugar and cinnamon; roll balls in sugar mixture. Place on *ungreased* baking sheet 2 inches apart. Bake at 400° for 10 to 12 minutes. Makes 7 dozen.

SNIP—To cut a food, such as parsley or chives, into little bits by clipping with quick, short strokes of scissors or shears.

SNIPE—A small game bird related to the woodcock. Although more slender than the woodcock, the snipe has a similar long, slender bill used for probing in the mud for food. The bird is most often cooked whole in a casserole or stuffed for roasting.

SNOW—A lovely refrigerator dessert made with stiffly beaten egg whites, gelatin, sugar, and fruit pulp or juice. Snow Pudding is an example. (See also *Dessert*.)

Pineapple Fluff

A delicate dessert to complete the menu—

1 20-ounce can crushed pineapple (juice pack)
1 envelope unflavored gelatin (1 tablespoon)
¼ cup sugar
¼ teaspoon salt
· · ·
2 unbeaten egg whites
3 to 4 drops yellow food coloring

Drain pineapple, reserving juice; add water to reserved pineapple juice to make 1½ cups. In medium saucepan combine gelatin, sugar, and salt; add the reserved pineapple juice mixture. Stir over low heat till gelatin and sugar dissolve. Remove from heat; chill in the refrigerator till mixture is partially set.

Turn into large mixer bowl; add egg whites and yellow food coloring. Beat at high speed with electric mixer till light and fluffy, about 5 minutes. Fold in pineapple and chill again till partially set. Turn into 5½-cup mold; chill. Unmold to serve. Makes 8 servings.

SNOWBALL—A round-shaped dessert such as cookie, cake, or ice cream which has been rolled in confectioners' sugar or frosted with white frosting and rolled in coconut to give a snowball appearance. You can also cover snowballs with whipped cream and serve them with your favorite fruit or chocolate sauce.

SNOW CRAB—The name for a species of crab previously known as tanner or queen crab, which weighs less than the king crab.

SNOW PEA—A flat podded pea with under-developed seed that is eaten with the pod. It is common to oriental cooking and is also widely known by the name of Chinese pea pod. (See also *Chinese Pea Pod*.)

SODA (*beverage*)—1. A soft drink that consists of carbonated water, flavoring, and syrup, often referred to as soda pop. 2. A soft drink made with ice cream. Often referred to as an ice cream soda, it is sometimes topped with whipped cream, cherries, and nuts. (See *Beverage, Ice Cream Soda* for additional information.)

SODA (*leavening agent*)—The common name for sodium bicarbonate or baking soda. The crystalline salt is used in making baking powder. (See also *Baking Soda*.)

SODA WATER—A carbonated beverage that has been charged under pressure with carbon dioxide gas. Ironically, soda water, a nonalcoholic beverage, came about through experimental tests done on gas for the production of beer.

Initially sold in Philadelphia drug and perfume stores as a medicine, soda water now is used for a variety of purposes—as a beverage, as a beverage mixer, and as an ingredient in soft drinks.

Its popularity as a mixer stems from its ability to reduce the heat in water. This is brought about by the escaping gas. Furthermore, its bubbly, sparkling characteristic upon opening makes it a pleasant mixer for punches and some alcoholic drinks. It is one of the basic ingredients, along with fruit juice and syrup, in most commercial soft drinks.

SODIUM BICARBONATE—The chemical name that is used for baking soda or bicarbonate of soda. (See also *Baking Soda*.)

SOFT DRINK—Nonalcoholic carbonated beverages including soda pop, soda water, ginger ale, root beer, and some fruit drinks. It is called "soda" in some areas, "pop" in others, and "tonic" in still other areas. A number of fruit-flavored powders are on the market for making a type of soft drink at home. Soft drinks can be used either for making several glasses of beverage at one time or to provide the fruit flavor for a punch. (See also *Beverage*.)

SOFT-SHELL CLAM—A type of clam that is found along the Atlantic coast from Chesapeake Bay to the Arctic Ocean. This clam differs from the hard and surf clams in that its shell is oval and thin. The clam's long neck, or siphon, prevents the shell from closing completely.

These clams can be eaten raw, but are usually steamed. In fact, they are often called "steamers." (See also *Clam*.)

SOFT-SHELL CRAB—A crab that has shed its hard shell during molting. The new shell, not yet hardened, is delightful when eaten with the crab meat. Soft-shell crabs that are sold in markets are usually blue crabs. (See also *Crab*.)

SOFT WHEAT—Any of several varieties of wheat low in gluten, including red winter and white wheat. Also known as pastry wheats, their flour is used in cakes, cookies, piecrusts, doughnuts, biscuits, and crackers. Soft white wheat is also used in breakfast cereals. (See also *Wheat*.)

SOLE—A saltwater or brackish water flatfish. A relative to the flounder, this fish has a flattened body, brown to gray coloring, black markings, and a small mouth. Both eyes are on the right side and the teeth are on the left or blind side. The flesh is white, firm, and delicately flavored.

The sole from the European coasts are of excellent quality, but the American ones are small and bony. Imported sole available in American markets is labeled Channel, Dover, or English sole. The fillet of sole, lemon sole, and gray sole in markets and on menus usually comes from flounder rather than from a true sole.

Packages of sole fillets and whole fish are sold both fresh and frozen. Some are available breaded and stuffed. Cook this fish like other lean fish by boiling, steaming, or frying. Or bake or broil it. If you do the latter, add butter.

One serving of uncooked sole (3x3x⅜-inch) contains 68 calories. This fish supplies protein, minerals, and B vitamins to the diet. (See also *Flounder*.)

Sole with Grapes

Spoon creamy wine-based sauce with seedless green grapes over fish before serving—

> 1 pound fresh or frozen sole fillets or other fish fillets
> 1 cup dry sauterne
> Salt
> ½ cup light cream
> 2 teaspoons cornstarch
> ¼ teaspoon salt
> ½ cup seedless green grapes, halved

Thaw frozen fish. Cut into 3 or 4 portions. Place fillets in greased 10-inch skillet. Add wine. Bring to boiling; reduce heat and simmer, covered, till fish flakes easily when tested with a fork, about 4 to 8 minutes. Remove fish to platter; sprinkle with salt. Keep the fish warm in a slow oven. Strain the wine.

Return ⅓ cup wine to skillet. Blend together light cream, cornstarch, and salt. Stir into wine in skillet; cook and stir till thickened and bubbly. Add grapes; heat through. Spoon sauce over fillets. Serves 3 or 4.

Sole-Shrimp Kettle

> 1 pound fresh or frozen sole fillets or other fish fillets
> 1 large onion, thinly sliced
> ¼ cup butter or margarine
> 3 chicken bouillon cubes, crushed
> 4 cups hot water
> 2 tablespoons lemon juice
> 1 teaspoon salt
> ⅛ teaspoon white pepper
> 1 pound fresh or frozen shelled shrimp
> 2 medium tomatoes, peeled and chopped
> 1 tablespoon snipped chives

Thaw frozen fillets. Cut fillets into 1-inch chunks. In large saucepan cook onion in butter till tender. Add fish, bouillon cubes, water, lemon juice, salt, pepper, shrimp, and tomatoes. Bring to boiling. Reduce heat and simmer till fish flakes easily when tested with a fork and shrimp turns pink, 2 to 3 minutes. Sprinkle top with snipped chives. Serves 8.

SOLID-STATE—A type of small, lightweight electronic control used in a variety of household appliances. The controls need no heating power or warm-up time, use little electricity, and are very rugged. For example, solid-state components are used for speed controls in blenders and mixers, giving an unlimited range of speeds.

SORGHUM—1. A canelike grass similar to corn used for food, forage, and syrup. 2. A thick sweet syrup that is prepared from the juices of sweet sorghum.

Originating in Africa and Asia, sorghum was one of the first wild plants to be adapted for domestic use by man. The Egyptians grew sorghum before 2200 B.C., and the Chinese and Indians cultivated it several thousands of years ago.

This annual grows from three to fifteen feet tall and yields smaller, rounder grains than other cereals. The sorghum grasses are divided into four main types; broomcorn, grain, grass, and sugar. Broomcorn sorghum has a cluster of long branches, referred to as the brush, that is used for carpet and whisk brooms. Grain sorghums are used for livestock feed and in alcoholic beverages, oil, and starch. Grass sorghum is used for hay and pasture usage. The sweet juice that sugar sorghum or sorgo yields from its stalks is used in making a pungent syrup.

This thick, sweet syrup is quite often used as a substitute for molasses in recipes. The sorghum syrup is most common in the southeastern portion of the United States. (See also *Grain*.)

SORREL (*sôr′ uhl, sor′-*)—A perennial herb of the buckwheat family with long, oblong leaves. Some varieties of sorrel are cultivated, while others grow wild in Asia, Europe, and North America.

The varieties differ from one another in the intensity of the sharp acid flavor of the leaves. The least mild variety, referred to as dock, has foot-long leaves which are added to green salads or used as a potherb. French sorrel, with its shield-shaped leaves, and sour dock or garden sorrel, the most acid of these varieties, are used in breads, vegetable dishes, and as meat accompaniments. You will also find that chopped sorrel in an egg and sour cream broth forms the base for the Jewish specialty chilled soup, *schav*.

Sorrel, marketed in bunches, is available in limited amounts during the summer and early fall in some eastern markets. Choose fresh, green clean leaves. Clean and store sorrel like lettuce.

Sorrel leaves contain high amounts of vitamin A with some calcium, phosphorous, and vitamin C. (See also *Herb*.)

SOUFFLÉ (*soo flā′, soo′ flā*)—1. A baked egg dish, based on a thick sauce with puréed or chopped ingredients added, and made high and puffy with beaten egg whites. 2. An unbaked egg dish, with a whipped gelatin base which is chilled and served as a light, airy dessert.

The true baked soufflés are a pleasure to the palate and delight to the eye when handled correctly. These include nonsweet soufflés for appetizer or accompaniments, main-dish soufflés with relatively hearty ingredients, and sweet soufflés for dessert.

Appetizer or accompaniment soufflés have similar ingredients to main-dish soufflés, with fewer such ingredients as meat or cheese. Appetizer soufflés can be served in small, individual soufflé or custard dishes as can main-dish soufflés.

Combinations of hearty and satisfying ingredients make main-dish soufflés a treat. Combine two or more food items and let your cooking creativity take over. Think of such combinations as liver and onions, mushrooms and chicken or turkey, spinach and ham, and cheese and bacon. Main-dish soufflés are an elegant way to use leftovers such as ham or chicken.

The sweet or dessert soufflés are made much in the same way as nonsweet soufflés, except sugar is added to the sauce. Select a flavoring ingredient, such as chocolate or vanilla, and combine with a puréed fruit, nuts, or liqueur. Replace the liquid ingredients with a fresh fruit juice or a combination of juice and liqueur.

Basic preparation: A combination of procedures leads to a perfect soufflé. Some of these factors include: a smooth sauce base, perfectly beaten egg whites, correct beating equipment, proper preparation of mold, proper folding in of whites, and the correct baking temperature.

Begin by separating the egg yolks from the egg whites. Do this as you remove the eggs from the refrigerator when they are easiest to separate. Then, while you prepare the sauce base, let the egg whites stand in a clean, dry bowl. Take care that there is no trace of fat or egg yolk in the bowl. A speck of egg yolk has enough fat in it to keep the white from beating properly. In a clean bowl, the whites beat to a great volume, especially when the egg whites are at room temperature.

The sauce is made basically as you make any white sauce. Make sure it is very smooth before adding the puréed or chopped meats, cheese, or vegetables. Beat the egg yolks until thick and lemon-colored. Then, slowly add hot sauce to yolks, a little at a time, stirring constantly.

You can refrigerate the sauce mixture till ready to use, if desired. Just reheat sauce before folding in beaten egg whites.

The important thing to remember is that the success of the soufflé is largely dependent upon the stiffly beaten egg whites which expand during heating, thus making the soufflé rise. Your goal is to incorporate as much air as possible into the beaten egg whites. This is most satisfactorily achieved with a wire whip. Lift the eggs as you whip, using a down, up, and over action. An electric mixer or a rotary egg beater can also be used, as long as you remember this action. When using the electric mixer, use a rubber spatula to lift the egg whites. Most recipes call for stiffly beaten egg whites, which means beating the egg whites till the peaks stand up straight but are still moist and glossy.

While it's convenient to have a special soufflé dish, you can substitute with a casserole dish with straight sides. The soufflé dish, because it's made for this specialty, is best with its round shape and straight sides. Made of metal, porcelain, or glass, it ranges in size anywhere from one to eight cups. In any case, use the right size baking dish.

The soufflé climbs as it bakes, so collar the dish to keep it in bounds if you want the soufflé to rise above the dish. To do this, simply fasten a piece of buttered

waxed paper around outside rim of the dish. A string or paper clip will hold it in place. Most soufflés climb best in an ungreased dish, but some do well in a buttered dish, often sprinkled with crumbs or sugar. However, follow recipe directions.

Folding the stiffly beaten egg whites into the base ingredients is the last preparation step. Before beginning, make sure you preheat the oven. This is very important for the best results are achieved in a well-regulated oven. Use a folding up and over motion, using a rubber spatula, when combining the egg whites with the base ingredients. Avoid mixing too thoroughly and perform the operation as quickly as

Trace a circle in soufflé mixture one inch from edge of dish and about one inch deep for a top hat that will puff in the oven.

Fasten a piece of buttered waxed paper around the outside rim of dish for an extra high soufflé. Secure with a string or clip.

possible. For a soufflé with a top hat that puffs in the oven, trace a circle through the mixture one inch from the edge and one inch deep.

Put the soufflé in the oven. You can forget about it till the end of the baking time. The length of the baking time often becomes a difference of opinion. The French prefer baking the soufflé in less time so it will have a soft runny center which may serve as a sauce for the firmer baked part. Americans prefer the soufflé baked completely throughout. Generally, you can test the doneness of a soufflé by inserting a knife off-center. The knife should come out clean. However, do not open oven door to peek, for drafts can damage the structure of the baked dish. Test doneness only at end of baking time.

Serve soufflés immediately

For the least amount of damage and to lessen the normal sinking of the soufflé, use two forks to break soufflé into servings. Then lightly spoon soufflé on individual plates. Pass an appropriate sauce or fruit garnish.

Easy Cheese Soufflé

In saucepan combine one 11-ounce can condensed Cheddar cheese soup and 4 ounces process American cheese, shredded (1 cup). Cook and stir over low heat till cheese melts. Remove from heat. Beat 4 egg yolks till thick and lemon-colored. Slowly add cheese mixture to beaten egg yolks, stirring constantly. Fold cheese mixture into 4 stiffly beaten egg whites. Pour into *ungreased* 2-quart soufflé dish or casserole. Bake at 300° till knife inserted off-center comes out clean, about 1 hour. Serve immediately. Makes 4 to 6 servings.

Elegant entertaining

←Set an elegant mood with light and rich Turkey Soufflé served with Dilled Mushroom Sauce. Another time make it with chicken.

Potato Puff Soufflé

  2 teaspoons minced onion
  ¼ cup butter or margarine
  ¼ cup all-purpose flour
  1 teaspoon salt
    Dash pepper
  1 cup dairy sour cream
  2 cups hot mashed potatoes
  4 well-beaten egg yolks
  4 stiffly beaten egg whites

Cook onion in butter till tender. Blend in flour, salt, and pepper. Heat till bubbly. Remove from heat. Stir in sour cream and potatoes; beat smooth. Add small amount of hot mixture to egg yolks, stirring constantly. Return to hot mixture; mix well. Fold in whites. Pour into *ungreased* 1½-quart soufflé dish. Bake at 350° till knife inserted off-center comes out clean, 30 to 35 minutes. Serves 6.

Spinach Soufflé

  1 10-ounce package frozen, chopped spinach
  2 tablespoons butter or margarine
  2 tablespoons all-purpose flour
  ½ teaspoon salt
  ½ cup milk
  ¼ cup grated Parmesan cheese
  5 egg yolks
  5 stiffly beaten egg whites
    Cheddar Cheese Sauce

Cook spinach following package directions. Drain *very thoroughly*. Add butter to spinach; cook and stir over high heat till butter is melted. Blend in flour and salt; add milk all at once. Cook and stir over medium heat till mixture thickens and bubbles. Remove from heat; stir in grated Parmesan cheese.

Beat egg yolks till thick and lemon-colored. Stir spinach into egg yolks. Pour spinach mixture over egg whites; fold together carefully. Pour into an *ungreased* 1-quart soufflé dish. Bake at 350° till knife inserted off-center comes out clean, about 30 to 35 minutes. Makes 4 to 6 servings. Serve with Cheddar Cheese Sauce.

Cheddar Cheese Sauce: Combine one 10½-ounce can condensed cream of mushroom soup and ⅓ cup milk; heat. Add 4 ounces sharp natural Cheddar cheese, shredded (1 cup); stir.

Macaroni Puff Soufflé

  ½ cup elbow macaroni, cooked and
      drained
  1 3-ounce can mushrooms, drained
  1 cup milk
  3 egg yolks
  ½ small onion, cut in pieces
  3 tablespoons all-purpose flour
  ½ teaspoon salt
  ¼ small green pepper, cut in
      pieces
  4 ounces sharp process American
      cheese, cut in cubes (1 cup)
  3 egg whites
  ¼ teaspoon cream of tartar

Place macaroni and water to cover in blender; blend till coarsely chopped. Drain. Pour macaroni into saucepan; add mushrooms. Place milk, egg yolks, onion, flour, and salt in blender container; blend smooth. Add green pepper and cheese; blend till coarsely chopped. Pour over macaroni. Cook and stir till thick and bubbly. Beat egg whites with cream of tartar till stiff peaks form. Fold into macaroni mixture. Bake in an *ungreased* 1½-quart soufflé dish at 325° till knife inserted off-center comes out clean, 50 to 55 minutes. Makes 6 servings.

Crab Soufflé Bake

  3 tablespoons butter or margarine
  3 tablespoons all-purpose flour
  1 teaspoon salt
  1 cup milk
  3 eggs, separated
  1 7½-ounce can crab meat, drained,
      flaked, and cartilage removed
  1 3-ounce can chopped mushrooms,
      drained

In a saucepan melt butter; blend in flour, salt, and dash pepper. Add milk. Cook and stir till thick and bubbly. Remove from heat. Beat egg yolks till thick and lemon-colored. Slowly add the sauce mixture to the egg yolks, stirring constantly. Stir in crab and mushrooms. Beat egg whites till stiff peaks form. Fold into crab mixture. Turn into an *ungreased* 1-quart soufflé dish. Bake at 325° till a knife inserted off-center comes out clean, about 60 minutes. Serve immediately. Makes 4 or 5 servings.

Pour gelatin-type soufflé into collared soufflé dish for chilling. Gently remove the waxed paper collar before serving.

Turkey Soufflé

Select turkey or chicken to make this elegant soufflé, and serve it with dilled mushroom sauce—

In medium saucepan melt 3 tablespoons butter or margarine; blend in 3 tablespoons all-purpose flour, 1 teaspoon salt, dash pepper, and ¼ teaspoon paprika. Add 1 cup milk to mixture all at once. Cook quickly, stirring constantly, till mixture is thickened and bubbly. Remove from heat. Stir in 1 teaspoon grated onion, 1 cup finely chopped, cooked turkey or chicken, and 1 tablespoon snipped parsley.

Beat 3 egg yolks till thick and lemon-colored. *Slowly* add turkey mixture to egg yolks, stirring constantly. Cool slightly. Add gradually to 3 stiffly beaten egg whites, folding together thoroughly. Turn into *ungreased* 1 quart soufflé dish. Bake at 325° till knife inserted off-center comes out clean, 50 minutes. Serve with Dilled Mushroom Sauce. Makes 4 servings.

Dilled Mushroom Sauce: In saucepan cook 2 tablespoons chopped onion in 2 tablespoons butter or margarine till tender but not brown. Stir in 2 tablespoons all-purpose flour; ¼ teaspoon dried dillweed, crushed; ¼ teaspoon salt; dash pepper; and one 3-ounce can chopped mushrooms, drained. Add 1¼ cups milk to mixture all at once. Cook, stirring constantly, till mixture is thick and bubbly. Makes 1½ cups.

Tuna Soufflé

¼ cup butter or margarine
¼ cup all-purpose flour
¼ teaspoon salt
1 cup milk
4 ounces sharp process American cheese, shredded (1 cup)
1 6½- or 7-ounce can tuna, drained and flaked
2 tablespoons chopped, canned pimiento
4 eggs, separated

In saucepan melt butter; blend in flour and salt. Add milk; cook and stir till mixture is thickened and bubbly. Remove from heat. Add cheese, tuna, and pimiento; stir till cheese melts. Beat egg yolks till thick and lemon-colored. Slowly add cheese mixture, stirring constantly; cool slightly. Wash beaters. Beat egg whites to stiff peaks. Gradually pour yolk mixture over whites, folding together.

Pour into *ungreased* 1½-quart soufflé dish. For top hat that puffs, trace a circle through mixture 1 inch from edge and 1 inch deep. Bake at 300° till knife inserted off-center comes out clean, 65 to 70 minutes. Break apart into servings with two forks. Makes 4 servings.

Chocolate Cloud Soufflé

⅓ cup light cream
1 3-ounce package cream cheese
½ cup semisweet chocolate pieces
3 egg yolks
Dash salt
3 egg whites
¼ cup sifted confectioners' sugar

In saucepan blend cream and cream cheese over very low heat. Add chocolate pieces; cook and stir till melted. Cool. Beat egg yolks with salt till thick and lemon-colored. Gradually blend into chocolate mixture. Beat egg whites till soft peaks form. Gradually add confectioners' sugar, beating till stiff peaks form. Fold a small amount of beaten egg white into chocolate mixture; carefully fold chocolate mixture, half at a time, into egg whites.

Pour into *ungreased* 1-quart soufflé dish. Bake at 300° till knife inserted off-center comes out clean, 50 minutes. Makes 5 or 6 servings.

The chilled soufflés, made with a whipped gelatin base, are almost foolproof and look much like a true soufflé. Pile the gelatin mixture in a collared soufflé dish and chill. (See also *Egg*.)

Orange Dessert Soufflé

In saucepan combine ¼ cup sugar, 1 envelope unflavored gelatin (1 tablespoon), and ⅛ teaspoon salt; add 1½ cups cold water. Stir over low heat till dissolved. Stir small amount of hot mixture into 3 slightly beaten egg yolks; return egg mixture to saucepan. Cook and stir over low heat till mixture coats metal spoon, 2 to 3 minutes. Remove from heat; stir in ⅓ cup orange-flavored breakfast drink powder. Chill till partially set; stir occasionally.

Prepare one 2- or 2⅛-ounce package dessert topping mixture according to package directions; fold the topping mix into the gelatin mixture. Beat 3 egg whites to soft peaks. Gradually add ¼ cup sugar, beating the mixture till stiff peaks form. Fold into the gelatin mixture. Turn into a 5-cup soufflé dish with a foil collar. Chill till firm, 5 to 6 hours or overnight. Remove collar. If desired, garnish with chocolate curls. Makes 8 servings.

Relatively inexpensive, yet impressive, is Orange Dessert Soufflé prepared with flavored drink powder and dessert topping mix.

SOUP

Exciting ideas for nourishing soups, from clear broths to hearty chowders.

When the familiar call from the kitchen is "soup's on," this could mean that any one of hundreds of soups is set on the table waiting to be eaten. Technically, a soup is usually defined as any liquid food in which a solid is cooked. Solids can be meat and/or bones, poultry, seafood, pasta, vegetables, or fruit. Because of such variety, soups can be hearty or thin, clear or thick, hot or cold. There is seemingly no end to the types and kinds of soups from which to choose.

Even the word "soup" has many derivations. Some say that it was named after the bread, referred to as sops, that was dipped into a liquid before being eaten. Others say it came from the sound that was made when soup was drunk from a cup.

Early souplike mixtures were often referred to as pottages. They were thick and generally were made of vegetables. One of the earliest written references is made in the *Holy Bible*. Esau, in the book of Genesis, sold his birthright for a pottage of lentils, a red lentil soup.

As time went on meat was added to the vegetable mixtures. Then, as the art of cooking developed still further—or perhaps out of necessity—clear, broth-type soups were introduced. Thinner soups were often prepared that way because of a lack of solid ingredients during times of food scarcities. In earlier days in the United States, a pot of soup stock was often found simmering on the back of the stove.

Nutritional value: Soup is as nutritious as the ingredients that are used in the preparation. Hearty soup can play an important part in the daily diet for the entire family. Not only is it a source of liquid, which is a dietary necessity, but many soups furnish concentrated nutrients in a form easy to eat and digest. An example is soup prepared with milk, where you get the nutrients of the milk as well as the nutritional value of whatever other ingredients are used in the mixture.

In addition to being nutritious, soups have a wide range of caloric counts. Some are especially good for dieters. Soup is so filling that it should be planned in the calorie-counter's menu. A serving of chicken broth contains 11 calories, while beef broth has 23 calories. Other soups such as cream soups, chowders, bean and pea soups are among those that rank higher in calories. Regardless of the calories, soups can be used to vary the menu for dieters and nondieters alike. Everyone gains nutritionally from a bowl of soup.

National favorites

Soupmaking plays an integral part in the cuisines of almost every country. Practically any food you can think of is used in soup somewhere in the world. In some cases the ingredients and flavors that are used will tell you quickly in which country a soup originated. In others, the combination of ingredients is somewhat startling. There are thin soups and there are those nearly as thick as stew, brimming with vegetables and meat.

American favorites include the seafood chowders of the coast, the gumbos of New Orleans, and the highly popular tomato soup. Although vichyssoise is an adapted

Hearty soups to serve with crackers

← Ladle out steaming bowlfuls of Ham and Pea Soup, Supper Corn Chowder, or Meatball Chowder for a chilly-day supper.

French peasant soup, it was invented by a chef of a New York hotel. This potato soup, flavored with leeks, is generally served cold. It has become an elegant soup, standard at gourmet dinners as the appetizer course. Another typically American soup is Philadelphia pepper pot, a well-seasoned mixture of tripe and vegetables, which was first put together in a steaming pot during the American revolution.

Favorites of European countries include the broths, onion soup, and bouillabaisse, a hearty seafood chowder of France. Pot au feu, which translated, means pot on the fire, is another French favorite—a rich meat-and-vegetable soup—derived from the peasants but universally popular.

Other foreign favorites include the oxtail and beer soups of Germany, minestrone of Italy, Spanish gazpacho, and the mulligatawny of India. Soups typical of other countries are the Scandinavian buttermilk soups and yellow split pea soup with pork, Russian cabbage soup and borsch, and the bird's nest soup and custard soup of China. A favorite Greek soup is a soup called avgolemono.

Some of these soups have been adapted to the modern kitchen and make use of timesaving appliances and convenience products which can be purchased.

Blender Vichyssoise

    1 10¼-ounce can frozen condensed cream of potato soup
    1 10½-ounce can condensed cream of chicken soup
    1 soup can milk
        • • •
    1 cup light cream
    Snipped chives

In a saucepan heat frozen potato soup until thawed. Pour soup into a blender container. (Or use a mixing bowl.) Add cream of chicken soup and milk. Blend or beat till smooth.

Add light cream; blend a few additional seconds. Cover and chill thoroughly, 3 or 4 hours or overnight. (If desired, blend again just before serving.) Serve soup in chilled bowls or cups. Garnish each serving of soup with snipped chives. Makes 4 servings.

Blender Gazpacho

    3 cups tomato juice
    2 tablespoons olive *or* salad oil
    2 tablespoons wine vinegar
    1 clove garlic
    2 medium tomatoes, peeled and quartered
    1 small cucumber, cut in pieces
    1 small green pepper, cut in pieces
    3 medium stalks celery, sliced
    ¼ medium onion, cut in pieces
    4 sprigs parsley
    2 slices bread, torn in pieces
    1 teaspoon salt
    ¼ teaspoon freshly ground pepper
    1 cup croutons
    Cucumber slices

Put *1 cup* of the tomato juice, olive *or* salad oil, wine vinegar, and garlic in blender container. Blend till garlic is finely chopped.

Add *half each* of the tomato, cucumber, green pepper, celery, onion, parsley, bread, salt, and pepper to blender container. Blend till vegetables are pureed. Transfer to 2-quart container. Repeat with remaining tomato juice, vegetables, bread, and seasonings. Cover and chill. Serve in chilled mugs or bowls topped with croutons and cucumber slices. Serves 6.

Speedy Borsch

    1 16-ounce can beets
    2 10½-ounce cans condensed consommé
    2 tablespoons lemon juice

Drain beets, reserving liquid. Finely chop enough beets to make ⅔ cup. Combine beets, beet liquid, consomme, and lemon juice; chill. Stir just before serving; serve in chilled cups or bowls. If desired, top with dairy sour cream and snipped parsley. Makes 6 servings.

Festive soup from Spain

Blender Gazpacho is a chilled mixture chock-→ full of vegetables and thickened with bread. Make it easily with an electric blender.

Types of soups

Because of the number of ingredients that go into the making of soups, there are a large variety of soups. The gamut is anywhere from clear appetizer soups to the heartier soups served as a main course, alone, or with bread or crackers.

The clear soups include stock, broth, bouillon, and consommé, while the heartier soups include cream soups, bisques, chowders, puréed soups, and gumbos.

Fruit soups are a category that fit neither into the clear nor hearty groups. These specialized soups are often served as the first or last course of the meal.

No matter what type of soup you make, it takes time to make good soup from scratch. You can hurry up your soupmaking by using canned or packaged soup products available on the supermarket shelves. These convenience products often make a suitable base for another soup of your own concoction, or are delicious products in themselves.

Clear soups: While the three words, stock, broth, and bouillon are frequently used interchangeably, consommé is often set apart from the others.

A *stock* is basic to most types of clear soups. No doubt it gets its name from the kettle or stock pot that was kept on the old-time stoves ready for use. In the pot, and when used as an ingredient, the liquid was referred to as stock, but once ladled out and served, it was called a *broth*.

Essentially, stock is the liquid in which meat, fish, or vegetables are slowly cooked together, and it is usually the base for a soup, sauce, or gravy with other ingredients added. Use inexpensive cuts of meat and poultry, sometimes bones, and combine them with a liquid—generally cold water. Then bring the mixture slowly to a boil. Because the less tender cuts of meat are used, simmer the stock for a long period of time to extract the flavorful juices into the liquid.

The major types of stock include brown stock, made from meat, bones, and vegetables which have first been browned; white stock, made from unbrowned ingredients or from lighter colored meats such as veal or chicken; fish stock, prepared from trimmings of the fish; and meatless vegetable stock.

For shortcut cooking, canned broths are available. These ready-made convenience products include canned chicken and beef broth and lamb-flavored Scotch broth.

Bouillon, the French word for stock or broth, has come to mean a clarified, strained, and seasoned broth. Remove the fat, clarify the broth, and then skim and strain it. The result: A plain, clear soup.

If you want a well-flavored liquid—the familiar court bouillon—in which to poach fish and vegetables or for a soup base, cook cut up onion and carrots, spices, herbs, other seasonings, and wine, if desired, in the liquid. Then strain.

For a quick bouillon, dissolve chicken, beef, or vegetable cubes or granules in hot water or prepare bouillon with beef- or chicken-flavored base.

Consommé is different from the other clear soups in that the liquid is boiled down until reduced by half, thus intensifying the flavor. It, too, starts with stock or broth prepared from meat or poultry. When reduced still further, oftentimes consommé will gel by itself when chilled, especially when cooked with bones. Most canned consommés have gelatin added.

Consommé is one type of clear soup that is enjoyed either hot or cold. Pasta, rice, or finely cut vegetables are frequently added when it is served hot. When served cold, consommé is jellied and makes an ideal appetizer course for a heavy entrée.

Herbed Tomato Broth

    1 10½-ounce can condensed beef
      broth
    1 cup tomato juice
    ¼ teaspoon dried marjoram
      leaves, crushed
    ¼ teaspoon dried thyme leaves,
      crushed
    1 tablespoon snipped parsley

Combine beef broth, tomato juice, ¾ cup water, marjoram, and thyme. Heat to boiling. Reduce heat and simmer 2 minutes. Ladle into bowls. Garnish with parsley Makes 6 servings.

Serve Hot Sherried Consommé as an appetizer in a crystal glass. Pour hot soup over a silver spoon to prevent cracking of glass.

Hot Sherried Consommé

2 10½-ounce cans condensed consommé
6 tablespoons dry sherry

In a saucepan combine consommé, 1⅓ cups water, and dry sherry. Heat through. Serve warm as an appetizer. Makes 6 to 8 servings.

Hearty soups: As with the clear soups, there often is a fine distinction between the types of soups that are most generally served as the main course, or in small portions as the appetizer course of the meal. Hearty soups include cream soups, puréed soups, bisques, chowders, gumbos, and other meat, poultry, seafood, and vegetable soups of many kinds.

Cream soups come in thick and thin varieties. Thicken some with flour and actually begin with a basic thin white sauce recipe. Thicken others with egg yolk and cream, rice, or vegetables. Use milk or cream as the liquid, or substitute vegetable juice, puréed vegetables, or broth for part of the milk. An important step is to season adequately a cream soup, or it will taste bland. Do make sure that the sauce for a cream soup is velvety smooth, because it is worth the effort to avoid disconcerting lumps when you serve the soup to family or guests.

Common types of cream soups include tomato, mushroom, chicken, celery, corn, potato, asparagus, and cheese.

A *bisque* is actually a cream soup with a shellfish or vegetable purée added, and often there are bits of solid food as well. The word bisque is most frequently used in connection with shellfish; however, there are some familiar vegetable bisques, too, such as tomato bisque.

Puréed soups are similar to bisques or cream soups. The pulp of puréed vegetables acts as the thickening agent. Use fresh, canned, or dried vegetables for this type of soup. Speed the task of puréeing the vegetables into a smooth mixture with the aid of a food mill or blender. Familiar puréed soups include those prepared with peas, lentils, or beans.

Chowders are another type of hearty soup. Originally, chowders were primarily seafood mixtures, but now vegetable chowders, such as corn chowder and meat chowders, are also popular. A chowder contains solid ingredients. Familiar American-style fish chowders include the Manhattan and New England clam chowders.

Gumbo, the Creole-inspired New Orleans specialty, incorporates seafood, meat, or poultry, and vegetables in its unique combination. What makes this soup different from other types of soup is primarily the fact that it is thickened with okra or gumbo filé powder.

There are a number of other soups that are hearty enough to satisfy the hungriest of appetites. However, many of these soups don't fit into a special category. Many of the meat, poultry, fish, and vegetable soups are in this group. For example, old-fashioned vegetable soup could fit into the chowder category, but it seems to be in a class by itself.

Fruit soups are another group that stands alone. Prepare these soups by cooking fresh or dried fruit in water or wine. Sweeten and slightly thicken the mixture, then serve warm or cold for an appetizer or dessert.

Blender Bean Soup

    1 pound dry navy beans
    3 medium carrots, sliced
    1 meaty ham bone
    2 teaspoons salt
    ¼ teaspoon pepper
    1 bay leaf
    1 medium onion, cut in pieces

Place about a *third* of the dry navy beans in blender container; blend till chopped. Remove. Repeat process till all beans are chopped. Place carrots in blender container; cover with water. Blend till coarsely chopped; drain.

Combine chopped beans, carrots, 2 quarts water, ham bone, salt, pepper, and bay leaf in large kettle or Dutch oven. Cover; simmer 3 hours, adding onion the last half hour. Remove ham bone and bay leaf. Add about a *third* of the bean mixture at a time to blender container. Blend at low speed till nearly smooth. Cut ham off bone; add ham to soup. Serves 8.

Cheeseburger Chowder

    1 pound ground beef
    ½ cup finely chopped celery
    ¼ cup chopped onion
    2 tablespoons chopped green pepper
    3 tablespoons all-purpose flour
    ½ teaspoon salt
    4 cups milk
    1 tablespoon beef-flavored
        gravy base
    4 ounces sharp natural Cheddar
        cheese, shredded (1 cup)

Brown beef in saucepan. Add vegetables; cook till tender. Blend in flour and ½ teaspoon salt. Add milk and gravy base. Stir over low heat till bubbly. Add cheese; cook and stir just till cheese melts. Serves 4 to 6.

Supper Corn Chowder

    1 medium onion, thinly sliced
        and separated into rings
    3 tablespoons butter or margarine
    2 cups cooked or canned whole
        kernel corn
    1 cup diced, cooked potatoes
    1 10½-ounce can condensed
        cream of chicken soup
    2½ cups milk
    1 teaspoon salt
        Dash pepper

In large saucepan cook onion in butter or margarine till lightly browned. Add corn, potatoes, soup, milk, salt, and pepper. Heat to boiling. Reduce heat and simmer a minute or two. Dash each serving with paprika and top with butter, if desired. Makes 6 servings.

Vegetable-Beef Soup

    3 pounds beef shank
    1 18-ounce can tomato juice
    ⅓ cup chopped onion
    4 teaspoons salt
    2 teaspoons Worcestershire sauce
    ¼ teaspoon chili powder
    2 bay leaves
    1 16-ounce can tomatoes
    1 cup diced celery
    1 8¾-ounce can whole kernel corn
    1 cup sliced carrots
    1 cup diced, peeled potatoes
    1 10-ounce package frozen
        lima beans

Combine meat, tomato juice, onion, salt, Worcestershire sauce, chili powder, bay leaves, and 6 cups water in soup kettle. Cover and simmer 2 hours. Cut meat from bones in large cubes; strain broth and skim off excess fat. Add meat and vegetables to broth; cover and simmer 1 hour. Makes 8 servings.

A nourishing entrée

Chunks of ground beef, milk, and sharp →
Cheddar cheese all contribute to the heartiness of creamy, Cheeseburger Chowder.

Potato-Pea Potage

  1 10½-ounce can frozen condensed
    green pea with ham soup
  1 10¼-ounce can frozen condensed
    cream of potato soup
1½ soup cans water
  4 ounces sharp process American
    cheese, shredded (1 cup)

In saucepan combine soups, water, and cheese.
Heat, stirring occasionally. Serves 4.

Uses in menu

Soups fit into the appetizer, main dish,
or dessert course of the menu. Be sure to
include them often when planning meals.
Because of the varieties available, you're
sure to find many that will be favorites.
Perfect accompaniments are crackers.

Once you've decided on the soup, choose
a garnish that will enhance both flavor
and appearance. Some garnishes also add
texture to an otherwise smooth soup.

Prepare Chicken-Vegetable Chowder (see *Bean* for recipe) at
home, then take the hot soup along on a picnic in an insulated
plastic ice bucket or wide-mouth vacuum container.

Soup garnishes

Choose one of the following garnishes to add texture and enhance the appearance of soups.

For clear soups: Thin lemon slices; snipped parsley or chives; tiny meatballs or dumplings; avocado slices; sliced hard-cooked egg.

For cream soups: Dairy sour cream; salted whipped cream; sliced, chopped, or slivered nuts; snipped parsley or chives; croutons; shredded cheese; popcorn; puffed cereal.

For chowders and meat soups: Thin lemon slices; frankfurter slices; snipped parsley; crumbled, crisp-cooked bacon; corn chips; oyster crackers; croutons; popcorn.

For chilled soups: Dairy sour cream; thin unpeeled cucumber slices; thin lemon wedges.

As an appetizer: Start out the meal with a soup. Plan it in conjunction with the remainder of the meal so that it blends well, flavorwise. There should be no duplication of flavors in the various courses.

An appetizer soup should stimulate the appetite, not dull it. So, serve a light soup with a hearty entrée and a heartier type soup with a light main dish. Also remember that small bowls or cups of well-seasoned appetizer soups will be appreciated to start out a meal. Appealing appetizers include broths, bouillons, and consommés, as well as thin cream soups.

Confetti Consommé

Only 22 calories per serving—

   2 10½-ounce cans condensed
      chicken broth
½ cup shredded carrot
¼ cup chopped green pepper
¼ cup finely chopped green onion

In medium saucepan combine chicken broth, 1⅔ cups water, and vegetables. Heat to boiling. Serve hot. Makes 10 servings.

Savory Tomato Soup

¼ cup chopped celery
  2 tablespoons chopped green onion
  1 tablespoon butter or margarine
  2 teaspoons all-purpose flour
  1 8-ounce can stewed tomatoes
¼ cup dry white wine *or* water
  1 chicken bouillon cube
  2 slices crisp-cooked bacon

Cook celery and onion in butter till tender but not brown. Blend in flour. Add 1 cup water and remaining ingredients, except bacon; cook and stir till slightly thick. Reduce heat; cook for 15 minutes, stirring occasionally. Garnish with crumbled bacon. Serves 2.

Chilled Avo-Mato Soup

  2 avocados, pitted and peeled
½ cup dairy sour cream

   • • •

  3 medium tomatoes, peeled and
      finely chopped (2 cups)
  1 10½-ounce can condensed
      beef broth
¼ cup finely snipped green onion
  1 tablespoon lemon juice
    Dash bottled hot pepper sauce

Blend avocados and sour cream with electric blender. (Or sieve avocados; mix well with sour cream.) Stir in remaining ingredients and 1 teaspoon salt. Chill thoroughly. Trim with sour cream, if desired. Serves 4 to 6.

❦**MENU**❧

DINNER FOR TWO
Savory Tomato Soup
Broiled Chicken Halves
Asparagus Spears
Cranberry Sauce   *Hard Rolls*
Caramel Sundaes
Iced Tea

```
┌─────────────────────────────────┐
│        ❧MENU❧                   │
│                                 │
│     MAN-PLEASING SUPPER         │
│  Golden Cheese Soup   Parsley Dumplings │
│  Tossed Green Salad   French Dressing   │
│        Baked Apples             │
│           Coffee                │
└─────────────────────────────────┘
```

As a main dish: Choose one of the heartier, nourishing soups when featuring it as the main part of the meal. A hearty soup is a good supper dish, needing only a salad, a breadstuff, and dessert to complete the meal. Any not-too-heavy soup goes perfectly with a complementary-flavored salad or sandwich for a quickie luncheon.

Remember to serve hot soups steaming and cold soups well chilled.

Golden Cheese Soup

⅓ cup chopped carrots
⅓ cup chopped celery
2 tablespoons chopped onion
3 tablespoons butter or margarine
¼ cup all-purpose flour
2 cups milk
1 13¾-ounce can chicken broth
5 ounces sharp process American
   cheese, shredded (1¼ cups)
Dumplings

Cook carrots, celery, and onion till tender in 1 cup boiling, salted water. Do not drain. Melt butter in Dutch oven; blend in flour. Add milk; cook, and stir till thick. Add broth, cheese, and vegetables with liquid. Stir over low heat till cheese melts. Drop dumplings into bubbling soup. Cover tightly; cook over low heat for 20 minutes.

Dumplings: Sift together 1 cup sifted all-purpose flour, 2 teaspoons baking powder, and ¼ teaspoon salt. Add 2 tablespoons snipped parsley. Combine ½ cup milk and 2 tablespoons melted shortening. Add to dry ingredients all at once; stir just till moistened. Drop by teaspoons into soup. Serves 6.

Meat and Vegetable Soup

1 envelope dry onion soup mix

• • •

1 16-ounce can meatballs
   with gravy
1 16-ounce can cream-style corn
1 10¾-ounce can condensed
   tomato soup

Prepare the onion soup mix according to package directions. Add meatballs with gravy, corn, and tomato soup; stir till blended. Heat through. Makes 6 to 8 servings.

Cheesy-Asparagus Soup

2 tablespoons butter or margarine
2 tablespoons all-purpose flour
1 teaspoon salt
   Dash ground nutmeg
   Dash pepper
3 cups milk

• • •

1 10-ounce package frozen, cut
   asparagus, cooked and drained
6 ounces natural Cheddar
   cheese, shredded (1½ cups)
   Paprika
   Grated Parmesan cheese

Melt butter and blend in flour, salt, nutmeg, and pepper. Add milk all at once. Cook, stirring constantly, till mixture thickens and bubbles. Cook 2 minutes longer. Add asparagus (cut any large pieces) and cheese; stir till cheese melts. Garnish with a sprinkling of paprika and Parmesan cheese. Makes 6 servings.

```
┌─────────────────────────────────┐
│        ❧MENU❧                   │
│                                 │
│     QUICK-FIXING  LUNCH         │
│    Meat and Vegetable Soup      │
│  Melba Toast    or    Crackers  │
│  Pear and Cottage Cheese Salad  │
│       Assorted Cookies          │
│            Milk                 │
└─────────────────────────────────┘
```

Pacific Chowder

    4 slices bacon
    ¼ cup chopped onion
    2 tablespoons chopped green pepper
    1 10¼-ounce can frozen con-
        densed cream of potato
        soup *or* 1 10½-ounce can
        condensed cream of potato soup
    2 cups milk
    1 6½- or 7-ounce can tuna, drained

Cook bacon; drain and crumble, reserving drippings. Cook onion and green pepper in 2 tablespoons drippings just till tender. Add soup,
milk, and dash salt; heat to boiling. Break tuna
in chunks; stir into soup with *half* the bacon.
Heat. Dash with paprika, if desired, and trim
with remaining bacon. Makes 4 servings.

Shrimp Chowder

Goes together in a jiffy—

    ½ cup finely chopped onion
    1 tablespoon butter or margarine
    1 10½-ounce can condensed
        cream of celery soup
    1 10¾-ounce can condensed
        clam chowder
  1½ soup cans water
    1 4½-ounce can shrimp, drained
    1 tablespoon snipped parsley

In saucepan cook onion in butter or margarine
till tender but not brown. Blend in the celery
soup, clam chowder, water, drained shrimp,
and snipped parsley. Simmer over low heat to
blend flavors, about 5 minutes. Serves 6.

Fix a kettle of hearty Meat and Vegetable Soup when lunch
must be prepared in a jiffy. Convenience foods combine to
make a soup that tastes like it's been simmered for hours.

Ham and Pea Soup

      1 pound split green peas (2 cups)
      1 ham bone
      ½ cup coarsely chopped onion
      ½ cup coarsely chopped carrot
      ½ cup coarsely chopped celery
      2 sprigs parsley
      1 clove garlic, minced
      1 bay leaf
      ¼ teaspoon salt
      ⅛ teaspoon ground thyme
        Dash pepper
      2 13¾-ounce cans chicken
        broth (3½ cups)
      1 cup diced, fully cooked ham

In large kettle combine peas and 5 cups water; bring to boiling. Reduce heat and simmer, covered, 45 minutes. Add ham bone and remaining ingredients except diced ham. Simmer, covered, 1½ hours longer. Remove ham bone and bay leaf. Press vegetables and liquid through a coarse sieve, if desired; return to kettle. Add diced ham and heat to boiling. Serves 8.

Meatball Chowder

      1 beaten egg
      ⅔ cup soft bread crumbs
      ¼ cup finely chopped onion
      ½ teaspoon Worcestershire sauce
      ½ pound ground beef
      2 tablespoons salad oil
      1 beef bouillon cube
      1 cup coarsely chopped carrot
      ½ teaspoon seasoned salt
      1 cup diced, peeled potato
      2 10½-ounce cans condensed
        cream of chicken soup
      2 soup cans milk (2⅔ cups)
      1 16-ounce can cut green beans,
        drained

Combine first 4 ingredients and ¼ teaspoon salt. Add meat; mix well. Shape into 24 meatballs. Brown in oil in large saucepan. Drain off excess fat. Add bouillon cube and 1 cup water; stir to dissolve cube. Add carrots and seasoned salt; cover and cook over low heat 5 minutes. Add potatoes; cook till vegetables are tender, about 10 to 15 minutes. Add soup; blend in milk and beans. Heat through. Serves 8.

Chicken Soups

Use the broth from a stewed chicken, canned chicken broth, or chicken bouillon cubes dissolved in water when the recipe calls for chicken broth—

Easy Chicken-Noodle Soup: Cook 1 cup noodles in 3 cups chicken broth till tender. Serves 4.

Chicken-Rice Soup: Cook ½ cup rice in 3 cups chicken broth till rice is tender. Serves 4.

Chicken-Curry Soup: Mix one 10½-ounce can condensed cream of chicken soup, 1¼ cups milk, and ½ teaspoon curry powder; chill. Add 2 tablespoons snipped parsley. Serves 3 or 4.

Chicken-Mushroom Soup: Combine one 10½-ounce can condensed cream of chicken soup and one 10½-ounce can condensed cream of mushroom soup in a saucepan. Add 1 can water; heat to boiling. Makes 4 servings.

Chili-Frank Soup

      1 cup chopped carrots
      ½ cup chopped celery
      4 frankfurters, sliced
      1 11½-ounce can condensed
        bean with bacon soup
      1 11-ounce can condensed chili
        with beef soup

Cook carrots and celery in 1½ cups water with ¼ teaspoon salt till tender, about 10 to 12 minutes. Add remaining ingredients. Heat through, about 10 minutes. Makes 4 servings.

Devil's Chowder

      1 10½-ounce can condensed
        cream of celery soup
      1 8¾-ounce can cream-style corn
      1 2½-ounce can deviled ham
      1 tablespoon instant minced onion
        Dash paprika
        Dash ground nutmeg
      1 soup can milk

Combine all ingredients except milk. Gradually stir in milk. Cook and stir till heated through. Makes 2 or 3 servings.

For a company luncheon, this not-too-heavy, chilled, Blender Broccoli Soup goes perfectly with dainty, toasty-warm sandwiches.

Blender Broccoli Soup

    1 10-ounce package frozen, chopped
          broccoli, partially thawed
 1½ cups milk
    1 cup light cream
    1 teaspoon instant minced onion
    2 beef bouillon cubes
       Dash ground nutmeg
  ¼ teaspoon salt

Break broccoli in small chunks. Put into blender container with ½ *cup* of the milk. Blend till broccoli is very fine. Add remaining milk, other ingredients, ¼ teaspoon salt, and dash pepper. Blend till smooth, 45 to 60 seconds. Chill. If desired, trim with dairy sour cream and snipped chives. Makes 4 or 5 servings.

❧MENU❧

COMPANY FOR DINNER
Pork Roast
Parslied New Potatoes
Broccoli Spears
Sliced Tomato Salad
Swedish Fruit Soup
Coffee   *Milk*

As a dessert: Serve soup for dessert for an interesting finale to the meal. The most familiar type of dessert soup is the Scandinavian fruit soup made with a blend of dried fruits, delicately spiced and sweetened, then slightly thickened.

Swedish Fruit Soup

    1 11-ounce package mixed
          dried fruits (1¾ cups)
  ½ cup light raisins
    3 to 4 inches stick cinnamon
    1 medium, unpared orange,
          thinly sliced and halved
    1 18-ounce can pineapple juice
  ½ cup currant jelly
  ¼ cup sugar
    2 tablespoons quick-cooking
          tapioca
  ¼ teaspoon salt

In a large saucepan combine mixed dried fruits, raisins, cinnamon, and 4 cups water. Bring to boiling; simmer, uncovered, till fruits are tender, about 30 minutes. Add remaining ingredients. Bring to a boil, cover; cook over low heat 15 minutes longer, stirring occasionally. Remove stick cinnamon. Serve warm or chilled. Makes 8 to 10 servings.

Cherry Soup

    1 16-ounce can pitted dark
          sweet cherries
    1 tablespoon sugar
    2 teaspoons cornstarch
    4 inches stick cinnamon
    1 small piece lemon peel
  ½ cup orange juice
  ⅓ cup dry sherry
       Dairy sour cream

Drain cherries, reserving syrup. Finely chop cherries. Blend syrup with sugar and cornstarch in a saucepan. Add cinnamon, lemon peel, orange juice, and chopped cherries. Cook and stir over medium heat till mixture thickens and bubbles. Cook 1 minute longer. Remove from heat. Remove cinnamon and lemon peel. Stir in sherry. Serve warm or chilled garnished with a dollop of sour cream. Makes 4 servings.

SOUR—**1.** A tart or acid taste. It is one of the basic taste sensations and is associated with the taste of foods such as vinegar or lemon juice. **2.** A mixed, alcoholic beverage having a sour taste.

The ingredients of the beverage include liquor of some type; lemon or lime juice, usually lemon; sugar; and sometimes soda water. These ingredients are shaken with cracked ice, then strained into a sour glass. Generally this drink is garnished with an orange slice and maraschino cherry. The beverages are named after the type of liquor that is used in them, for example, whiskey sour or rum sour.

SOUR CREAM—A creamy, thick dairy product made tangy by the action of a culture on sweet cream. Most of the sour cream available is made from sweet, light cream and is referred to as dairy sour cream in recipes. The milk fat content of the light cream must be at least 18 percent. In many markets, sour half and half (a comparable product with less fat) is available. Imitation sour creams and packaged sour cream sauce mixes are also marketed.

Although sour cream has been used by cooks for centuries, this early product was similar to, but not exactly the same as the dairy product that homemakers can buy today. The first sour cream was probably discovered many centuries ago when the cream skimmed off milk became sour because of the lack of refrigeration. As a result of this discovery, ways were found to quickly use this soured product.

Through the years, people became accustomed to foods prepared with soured cream. They made the cream by setting a container of heavy, sweet cream on the back of the old-fashioned stove until it became thick and had an acid flavor. The exact degree of acidity (sourness) of these early products varied. Sometimes, it was very acid, at other times, it was mild.

With the introduction of milk pasteurization, however, this method could no longer be used, since the pasteurization process kills the bacteria that were originally used to sour the cream. Consequently, scientists had to discover a way to sour pasteurized cream. They did this by inoculating homogenized pasteurized cream with lactic acid culture, then letting it ripen under certain conditions. A constantly flavored sour cream is the result.

Nutritional value: Dairy sour cream is a tasty, stimulating food product that carries the important nutrients of milk. In addition, the milk fat that it contains is easily digested by the body.

Caloriewise, a tablespoon of dairy sour cream adds about 30 calories to the diet. Sour cream made from half and half, a cream with only 10 to 12 percent milk fat, has slightly fewer calories. One tablespoon of this type of sour cream adds about 18 calories to the daily diet.

How to store and use sour cream: Place sour cream purchased from the supermarket refrigerated case in the home refrigerator as soon as possible after purchase. For best quality, use sour cream within three or four days after purchase. Canned imitation sour cream and packaged mixes will keep much longer on the shelf. Once opened, some of these products also need to be kept under refrigeration.

The uses for sour cream are varied. It adds a tangy, gourmet flavor to appetizers, soups, sandwiches, salads, meat dishes, vegetables, baked foods, candies, and desserts. Use it in baking and cooking, or enjoy it as it comes from the carton.

Because of its milk fat content, sour cream adds richness to baked products. In fact, dairy sour cream can replace some of the fat and milk in recipes such as pancakes and biscuits. It also gives distinctive flavor to cakes and cookies.

When cooking with dairy sour cream, remember not to overheat or boil it. If sour cream is cooked at too high a temperature or held over heat too long, even at a low temperature, it will break down, giving a thin, curdled product. When this happens, the appearance will be less appealing, although the flavor will still be satisfactory. If possible, add sour cream at the end of cooking time. Then, just heat the mixture through, but do not boil.

When sour cream is added to canned condensed soups, or if flour is added to the sour cream in a sauce recipe, the sour cream will not separate or curdle.

Sour cream and mayonnaise are blended for the creamy base of Herb-Curry Dip. Crisp, raw vegetables make flavorful dippers.

Sour cream is a perfect ingredient for dips, spreads, salad dressings, frostings, and desserts. It gives tangy flavor to main dishes, such as stroganoff, and it can be incorporated into vegetable or meat sauces. Or, use sour cream alone as a garnish for soup or as a delicious baked potato topper. (See also *Dairy Sour Cream.*)

Herb-Curry Dip

  1 cup mayonnaise
½ cup dairy sour cream
  1 teaspoon mixed herbs, crushed
¼ teaspoon salt
⅛ teaspoon curry powder
  1 tablespoon snipped parsley
  1 tablespoon grated onion
1½ teaspoons lemon juice
½ teaspoon Worcestershire sauce
  2 teaspoons capers, drained

Blend all ingredients. Chill. Serve with carrots and/or celery sticks, and cauliflowerets.

Creamy Onion Dip

1½ cups dairy sour cream
  2 tablespoons dry onion soup mix
½ cup crumbled blue cheese
⅓ cup chopped walnuts

Blend sour cream and onion soup mix. Stir in blue cheese and nuts. Makes 2 cups.

Sour Cream Potato Salad

⅓ cup Italian salad dressing
  7 medium potatoes, cooked in jackets, peeled, and sliced
¾ cup sliced celery
⅓ cup sliced green onion
  4 hard-cooked eggs
  1 cup mayonnaise
½ cup dairy sour cream
1½ teaspoons prepared horseradish mustard
   Salt
   Celery seed

Pour Italian dressing over warm potatoes; chill 2 hours. Add celery and onion. Chop egg whites; add to potatoes. Sieve yolks; mix with mayonnaise, sour cream, and horseradish mustard. Fold into salad. Add salt and celery seed to taste. Chill 2 hours. Makes 8 servings.

Swiss Apple Salad

4 medium unpeeled apples, diced
1 cup diced Swiss cheese
½ cup diced celery
1 cup dairy sour cream
  Dash salt

Combine apples, cheese, celery, sour cream, and salt. Chill thoroughly. Serves 6 to 8.

Avocado-Cream Dressing

Combine 1 medium avocado, peeled and mashed; ½ cup dairy sour cream; 2 tablespoons milk; 2 teaspoons lemon juice; ½ teaspoon salt; ¼ teaspoon dried chervil leaves, crushed; dash onion powder; and 3 drops bottled hot pepper sauce. Chill. Serve over lettuce. Makes 1 cup.

Chicken Liver Stroganoff

  1 cup chopped onion
  2 tablespoons butter or margarine
  ½ pound chicken livers, halved
  1 3-ounce can broiled, sliced
      mushrooms, undrained
  1 tablespoon paprika
  1 cup dairy sour cream
  2 cups hot cooked rice

Cook onion in butter till tender but not brown. Add livers and mushrooms. Stir in paprika, ½ teaspoon salt, and dash pepper. Cover; cook over low heat till livers are tender, 8 to 10 minutes. Stir in sour cream. Heat, *but do not boil.* Serve over hot, cooked rice. Trim with snipped parsley, if desired. Serves 4.

Sour Cream Burgers

Combine 1 cup dairy sour cream, ¼ cup finely chopped onion, 2 teaspoons Worcestershire sauce, 1 teaspoon salt, and dash pepper. Add 2 pounds ground beef; mix well. Shape into 8 patties. Broil 3 inches from heat 6 minutes. Turn, broil 4 to 6 minutes longer. Meanwhile, dissolve 2 beef bouillon cubes in ¼ cup boiling water. Stir in 1 cup dairy sour cream and 2 tablespoons snipped parsley. Heat, *but do not boil.* Place each patty on half of a toasted hamburger bun. Top with cream sauce. Serves 8.

Two-Berry Parfaits

  1 10-ounce package frozen
      raspberries, thawed
  ¼ cup sugar
  2 tablespoons cornstarch
  2 cups fresh strawberries, sliced
  2 teaspoons lemon juice
  1 quart vanilla ice cream
  1 cup dairy sour cream

Drain raspberries; reserve syrup. Add water to syrup to make 1 cup. In saucepan combine sugar and cornstarch; stir in syrup. Add strawberries. Cook and stir over medium-high heat till thickened and bubbly. Stir in raspberries and lemon juice; chill. In parfait glasses layer ice cream, berry sauce, sour cream, and berry sauce. Repeat layers. Serves 6 to 8.

Two-Berry Parfaits combine a ruby raspberry-strawberry sauce, tangy sour cream, and vanilla ice cream in a layered beauty.

Sour Cream-Choco Cake

  ½ cup shortening
  2 cups sifted cake flour
  2 cups sugar
  1 teaspoon baking soda
  ½ cup dairy sour cream
  ½ teaspoon vanilla
  4 1-ounce squares unsweetened
      chocolate, melted and cooled
  2 eggs
      Seven-Minute Frosting
      (See *Frosting*)

Place shortening in large bowl. Sift in flour, sugar, soda, and ½ teaspoon salt. Add sour cream, vanilla, and ⅔ cup water. Mix till flour is moistened. Beat vigorously 2 minutes, scraping bottom and sides of bowl. Add chocolate, eggs, and ⅓ cup water; beat 2 minutes.

Bake in 2 greased and lightly floured 9x1½-inch round cake pans at 350° till cake tests done, about 25 to 30 minutes. Cool 10 minutes; remove from pans. Cool; fill and frost the cake with Seven-Minute Frosting.

Sour Cream Frosting

    1 6-ounce package semisweet
        chocolate pieces
  1/4 cup butter or margarine
  1/2 cup dairy sour cream
    1 teaspoon vanilla
  1/4 teaspoon salt
  2 1/2 to 2 3/4 cups sifted
        confectioners' sugar

Melt semisweet chocolate pieces and butter over *hot, not boiling*, water; remove from hot water and blend in sour cream, vanilla, and salt. Gradually add enough sifted confectioners' sugar for spreading consistency; beat well. Frosts tops and sides of two 9-inch layers or one 10-inch tube cake.

Quick Apricot Pastries

Unroll 1 package refrigerated crescent rolls (8 rolls); pat into bottom of a buttered 13 1/2 x 8 3/4 x 1 3/4-inch baking dish. Spread with 1/2 cup apricot jam. Bake at 425° for 15 minutes. Remove from oven. Reduce heat to 325°. Combine 1 cup dairy sour cream, 1 beaten egg, 1 tablespoon sugar, and 1/2 teaspoon vanilla. Pour evenly over rolls; bake 5 to 6 minutes longer. Serve warm. Makes about 12 pastries.

Old-fashioned Sourdough Bread gets its flavor from the fermented starter batter that is saved from one baking to the next.

SOURDOUGH—Fermented dough used originally instead of yeast for making bread. Early prospectors and cowboy cooks kept a piece of sourdough from every baking to use as a "starter" for leavening the next batch. Not only was it used for bread, but it was also a prime ingredient for flapjacks and biscuits. The word became a nickname for the Alaskan prospector who usually included sourdough in his supplies.

You'll find that making sourdough bread is a relatively slow process, but the distinctive flavor of the bread renders it a big favorite of many people. In some areas of the United States, the starter for sourdough bread is available as also is the baked sourdough bread.

Sourdough Bread

To make Starter Batter: Dissolve 1 package active dry yeast in 1/2 cup warm water. Stir in 2 cups lukewarm water, 2 cups sifted all-purpose flour, 1 tablespoon sugar, and 1 teaspoon salt. Beat till smooth. Let stand, uncovered, at room temperature for 3 to 5 days. Stir 2 or 3 times daily; cover at night. (Starter should have a "yeasty," not sour, smell.) Cover and refrigerate till ready to make bread.

To make bread: In large bowl soften 1 package active dry yeast in 1 1/2 cups warm water (110°). Blend in *1 cup* Starter Batter, 2 teaspoons salt, and 2 teaspoons sugar. Add 3 1/2 cups sifted all-purpose flour. Beat 3 to 4 minutes. Cover; let rise till double, about 1 1/2 hours. Mix 1/2 teaspoon baking soda with 1 1/2 cups sifted all-purpose flour; stir into dough. Add 1/4 to 1/2 cup sifted all-purpose flour to make a stiff dough.

Turn out on lightly floured surface; knead 8 to 10 minutes. Divide dough in half; cover and let rest 10 minutes. Shape in 2 round or oval loaves. Place on lightly greased baking sheets. With sharp knife, make diagonal gashes across top. Let rise till double, about 1 1/2 hours. Bake at 400° for 35 to 40 minutes. Brush tops of loaves with melted butter.

To keep Starter: Add 1/2 cup water, 1/2 cup sifted all-purpose flour, and 1 teaspoon sugar to leftover Starter Batter. Let stand till bubbly and well fermented—at least 1 day. Store in the refrigerator. If not used within 10 days, add 1 teaspoon sugar to the Starter Batter.

SOUR MILK—Milk that has been soured either naturally or artificially. Unpasteurized milk is the only type that will ferment and sour naturally. However, since most of the milk that is sold is pasteurized, a process that kills the natural bacteria that causes milk to sour, naturally sour milk is almost impossible to find. In fact, pasteurized milk has a tendency to spoil instead of becoming sour.

For use in recipes, you can make sour milk very easily. Just add enough fresh milk or diluted evaporated milk to one tablespoon of vinegar or lemon juice to make one measuring cup full. Then, let the mixture stand for about five minutes and use it as the recipe directs.

Buttermilk can be substituted easily for most of the recipes calling for sour milk as an ingredient. Buttermilk is readily available in almost any food market.

Baking soda is used as all or part of the leavening in baked foods made with sour milk. It gives off leavening gas when mixed with the mild acid in the milk. In fact, one-fourth teaspoon baking soda plus one-half cup sour milk has the leavening power equivalent to one teaspoon of baking powder. (See also *Milk.*)

SOUR SALT—Coarse citric acid crystals used in some types of cookery to give the food a pleasantly tart taste.

SOURSOP—A large, pear-shaped tropical fruit with white, slightly acid-tasting pulp and soft prickles on a green skin. This fruit is related to the custard apple. (See also *Custard Apple.*)

SOYBEAN—A pod-bearing, leguminous plant. There are hundreds of varieties of soybeans with at least as many uses, including industrial as well as food products.

The soybean is native to Eastern Asia. Chinese records dating back to 2207 B.C. show that soybeans were among the first crops cultivated. The Chinese considered them to be one of the five sacred grains, along with rice, wheat, barley, and millet, essential to Chinese civilization.

Although there had been earlier experiments with soybeans in America, the varieties introduced by the Perry Expedi-

Noodlelike Spaetzle complements flavorful Seafood Kabobs (see *Kabob* for recipe). Accompany this entree with green beans.

tion on its return from Japan in 1854 launched the crop in the United States. Experimentation has been done since.

Protein, fat, vitamins, and minerals are the major nutrients in soybeans. The protein of the soybean is more complete than most vegetable proteins, and similar to animal protein. The amino acid composition of soybeans is much like that of casein, the protein in milk. Thus, soy products are valuable to people in areas where meat is not easily accessible, and to people on restricted diets. For infants allergic to milk, a soy formula is an alternative.

There are other uses for soybeans. Fresh soybean sprouts are used in Oriental cooking, and on the American table, soybeans are used as a green vegetable. The dried soybeans are baked or boiled much the same as navy beans. Probably the soy product most familiar to American homemakers, is soy sauce although there are many other uses of the vegetable.

In 1911, a Seattle mill first pressed oil from the soybean. Since that time, soybean oil has worked miraculous changes in the food industry by producing shortening, margarine, cooking oil, pastas, ice "cream," whipped toppings, and more.

IRIS (JAMAICA) MADE DRINK COND MILK +

Soy flour or meal is another valuable product that is rich in nutrients. Current research indicates that soy products can provide an effective weapon in the battle against world hunger.

SOY FLOUR—A flour milled from soybeans. It is not a new product since a soy flour was combined with water to make a substitute milk even before the Christian era.

Because soy protein so closely resembles animal protein, products made with soy flour provide an economical meat substitute. Since there is no gluten in this type of flour, it cannot successfully be used alone in baked products.

Products with the appearance and taste of meat are being made from defatted soy flours in a promising development.

SOY SAUCE—A salty, fermented sauce of soybeans, water, and salt. Soy sauce is an essential ingredient in Oriental cookery. It adds both salty flavor as well as its typically brown color and is used in such dishes as chow mein and chop suey.

Japanese call their soy sauce *shoyu*. Flavorwise, it is between the light, and dark Chinese soy sauce. American homemakers can usually find both soy sauce and *shoyu* in their local supermarkets.

Its use is not limited, however, to oriental cooking. Soy sauce has become a popular ingredient in barbecue sauces, other meat dishes, and marinades. And it is an ingredient in the popular teriyaki dishes. (See also *Oriental Cookery*.)

Lamb Chops Oriental

      6 shoulder lamb chops,
         ¾ inch thick
   ½ cup soy sauce
   ½ cup water
      1 clove garlic, minced

Slash fat edges of chops. Place in shallow baking dish. Combine soy sauce, water, and garlic; pour over chops. Cover; refrigerate several hours, turning once. Place the chops on the rack of the broiler pan; broil 3 inches from heat about 10 minutes. Turn chops and broil 5 to 8 minutes longer. Makes 6 servings.

Teriyaki Burgers

Combine 2 beaten eggs; ¼ cup water; 3 tablespoons soy sauce; 1½ cups soft bread crumbs (2 slices); ¼ cup chopped onion; 2 tablespoons sugar; 1 small clove garlic, crushed; and dash ground ginger. Add 1½ pounds ground beef and mix well. Shape the mixture into 6 patties. Broil 4 to 5 inches from heat for 10 minutes, turning once. Makes 6 burgers.

SPAETZLE, SPATZLE *(s̬hpet' sluh, -slē)*—A noodle or dumpling made from batter that is pressed through a colander, and cooked in boiling liquid. Spaetzle originated in Germany but is enjoyed in the cuisines of other countries as an accompaniment to meat dishes or in soups.

Spaetzle

Sift together 2 cups sifted all-purpose flour and 1 teaspoon salt. Add 2 slightly beaten eggs and 1 cup milk; beat well. Place mixture in a coarse-sieved colander. Hold over large kettle of rapidly boiling, salted water. With wooden spoon, press batter through colander. Cook and stir 5 minutes; drain thoroughly. Serve as a meat accompaniment. Makes 5 servings.

Use a wooden spoon to press the Spaetzle batter through a colander into the kettle of boiling water. Drain noodles thoroughly.

SPAGHETTI—Pasta in slender, solid, rod form, or in elbow form. Like the other pastas—macaroni and noodles—spaghetti is made from a flour and wheat dough.

In America, "spaghetti" usually refers to spaghetti and sauce. This is popular family fare because it is filling, low in cost and when purchased ready-prepared (canned or frozen), is a time- and work-saver, too. However, there are many variations on "spaghetti," and given fancy toppings, it becomes a far cry from mother's favorite washday special.

Where spaghetti and other pasta forms originated is a matter for some dispute. Because Marco Polo is a well remembered figure, the story has persisted that he brought spaghetti back to Italy from the Orient. Another group insists that Italy is the cradle of pasta. They cite, among other things, a cook book by an anonymous author which is said to be the first published record of pasta. The publication date of this book predates Polo's trips by several years, so the Italians seem to have a strong case. To promote it, they have established a Spaghetti Museum in Pontedassio near the Italian Riviera.

Another legend claims that a group of invading Mongols brought pasta to Germany in the thirteenth century and from there it found its way to Italy.

While the true birthplace of pasta is not established, its use seems to have spread in the thirteenth century, although ancient documents show its existence in the Orient as early as 5000 B.C.

Whether pasta is native to Italy or not, there is no doubt that pastamaking matured to a fine art as a result of the inventive Italian cooks. The creative upsurge of the Renaissance was reflected in pasta manufacture by the development of myriad pasta shapes and recipes.

Commercial production of pasta was begun in Naples during the Renaissance and by the late fifteenth century, pasta had become the mainstay of the Italian menu. It was during these early periods that cooking itself became highly refined in Italy. Today, Italy is one country that still retains a solid reputation for artful cooking, due in part to its creative development of all types of pasta cookery.

Spaghetti was introduced to the United States by Thomas Jefferson. He brought a spaghetti die back from a trip to Italy in 1786. However, there is a long gap between this date and the actual commercial production of spaghetti in America. This is because the needed wheat variety, durum, was not grown here until many years later. It was first brought to North America in 1853. Then, in 1900, Dr. Mark A. Carleton, a wheat scientist with the United States Department of Agriculture, brought durum varieties from Russia that could successfully be grown in this country.

How spaghetti is made: The flour used in pasta manufacture is usually from durum, a hard, amber-colored spring wheat. The durum flour produces pasta that retains firmness after it is cooked.

For pasta products like spaghetti, durum wheat is milled into a golden, granular product called "semolina." The semolina is mixed with water and kneaded into a soft dough that is forced through a die (pierced metal plate) into long strands. As the spaghetti emerges, a rack moves against it. A knife cuts the strands and these strands move on racks into driers or dehydration chambers. Spaghetti is not baked, but filtered air passes over it until it is dried. After drying, it is cut to exact lengths, weighed, and packaged.

Nutritional value: Children rarely have to be coaxed to finish their spaghetti especially when flavorfully sauced. That is why the nutritional story of spaghetti is so reassuring to mothers. Enriched spaghetti contributes the B vitamins, thiamine, riboflavin, and niacin to the diet, in addition to some iron and protein. Meatballs, which often accompany spaghetti, contribute additional nutrients to the diet.

The calorie news is good, too. A one-cup serving of spaghetti adds up to just about 160 calories. The sauce or meat that usually are served with the pasta will add more calories, but it is the size of the serving that really determines the total calorie tally. In average servings, spaghetti is an aid to weight watchers, as it contributes to a feeling of fullness and lessens the likelihood of overeating.

To avoid breaking up spaghetti, hold handful at one end and dip other end into water. Curl it around in pan as it softens.

Types of spaghetti: While the most familiar spaghetti is the straight, long rod, there are variations. There are even different thicknesses of the long rod which are each separately named—regular spaghetti; somewhat thinner spaghetti, called spaghettini; and nested vermicelli, which looks like a thick skein of delicate strands, or vermicelli in long, straight rods.

Other variations include elbow spaghetti; capellini and fedelini, very thin folded spaghetti; fusilli, which has a zigzag crimp; and tortiglioni, which comes in a spiral shape. Spaghetti à la chitarra is another variety that is named for its resemblance to guitar strings.

The shape has little effect on the flavor of the finished dish, but can add greatly to its eye appeal. Because there are so many interesting possibilities with spaghetti, the adventuresome cook will find it rewarding to experiment with new recipes. If a certain spaghetti variety is called for that the local market can't supply, another spaghetti of similar size usually can be substituted by weight.

How to select and store: The most common spaghetti package sizes are 7, 8, and 16 ounces. When buying, count on eight average or six hearty servings to a pound.

Since spaghetti requires no refrigeration, it is a foresighted homemaker who keeps a good supply on hand. Campers like spaghetti for its ease of storage, too.

Once the package is opened, uncooked spaghetti can be stored in its original package if it closes tightly. Otherwise, it should be transferred to a container that has a tight-fitting lid or cover.

After cooking, store leftover spaghetti in the refrigerator for a day or two. It will keep up to six months in the freezer.

How to prepare spaghetti: A large saucepan and a colander are good basic equipment for all pasta cookery. Also helpful is a slotted spoon to give the cooking pasta an occasional stir, especially at the beginning of the cooking period. It's also a useful piece of equipment to lift out samples for taste testing.

The recommended ratio of water to pasta is four quarts to a pound. Two tablespoons of salt is the right seasoning for this amount. A teaspoon of cooking oil added to the water will reduce splashing when the water boils, and it will prevent the pasta from sticking together.

Children may find it easier to eat the elbow spaghetti that is in shorter lengths. Adults, however, can manage the long strands of spaghetti and often find it a challenge. To keep the strands whole when cooking, hold the spaghetti at one end and immerse the other in the boiling water. As it softens, curl it into the pan until all is covered by the water.

Spaghetti should be cooked, uncovered, until it reaches a stage the Italians call "al dente," which means that it is tender to the tooth. Spaghetti that is too firm or has a starchy flavor is underdone. Taste testing can begin after the spaghetti has boiled about six minutes, but the exact cooking time depends upon the thickness of the product and individual preference. When it is done, spaghetti should be well drained in a colander so that no water is left to thin the sauce.

If spaghetti is to be used in a recipe that calls for further cooking, as in a baked casserole, reduce the cooking time by about one-third. The spaghetti will finish cooking in the oven.

The more varied the sauces that accompany spaghetti, the more interesting its personality becomes. Spaghetti is a natural with ground beef for skillet or casserole type dishes, and it is perfect as a base for other types of meat, such as veal cutlets. Seafood also combines quite well with spaghetti. (See also *Pasta*.)

Clam-Mushroom Spaghetti

      1 6-ounce can tomato paste
    ¼ cup chopped onion
    ¼ cup chopped green pepper
      1 clove garlic, crushed
    ½ to ¾ teaspoon dried basil
         leaves, crushed
    ½ teaspoon dried oregano leaves,
         crushed
    ⅛ teaspoon pepper
      2 7½-ounce cans minced clams
      1 3-ounce can sliced mushrooms
      8 ounces spaghetti, cooked

In saucepan combine first 7 ingredients, ½ teaspoon salt, and 1 cup water. Drain clams and mushrooms; reserve liquids. Add liquids to saucepan; set clams and mushrooms aside. Simmer mixture, uncovered, to desired thickness. Add clams and mushrooms; heat. Serve over drained spaghetti. Serves 4.

Spaghetti Marina

Shrimp and olives add special flavor—

      8 ounces spaghetti
      3 tablespoons butter or margarine
      3 tablespoons all-purpose flour
    ½ teaspoon dried dillweed
   1¾ cups milk
      2 4½-ounce cans shrimp, drained
    ¼ cup sliced, pitted ripe olives
      1 tablespoon snipped parsley
      1 tablespoon lemon juice

Cook spaghetti according to package directions. Drain. In saucepan melt butter; stir in flour, dillweed, and dash salt. Add milk; cook and stir till slightly thickened and bubbly. Add shrimp, olives, parsley, and lemon juice. Heat through. Serve over hot spaghetti. Serves 4 or 5.

Baked Spaghetti

Good to prepare when cooking for a crowd—

    16 ounces spaghetti
      4 pounds ground beef
      2 large onions, chopped (2 cups)
      1 large green pepper, chopped
         (1 cup)
      2 teaspoons salt
      2 10½-ounce cans condensed cream
         of mushroom soup
      4 10½-ounce cans condensed
         tomato soup
      1 quart milk
      1 pound sharp process American
         cheese, shredded (4 cups)

Break spaghetti into 3-inch lengths. Cook in large amount boiling, salted water; drain. In Dutch oven or kettle cook meat, onion, and green pepper until meat is browned. Sprinkle with salt. Gradually stir in soups, milk, and 2 *cups* of the cheese. Divide cooked spaghetti evenly between two 13x9x2-inch baking dishes. Into each pan stir half the soup-meat mixture. Sprinkle the remaining 2 cups cheese atop both. Bake, uncovered, at 350° till hot through, about 1 hour. Makes 20 servings.

All it takes is one large skillet to prepare easy Skillet Spaghetti. The spaghetti cooks till done in the simmering sauce.

Skillet Spaghetti

    1 pound ground beef
    1 6-ounce can tomato paste
    1 18-ounce can tomato juice
1½ to 2 teaspoons chili powder
    1 teaspoon garlic salt
    1 teaspoon salt
    1 teaspoon sugar
    1 teaspoon dried oregano leaves,
        crushed
    2 tablespoons instant minced onion
    7 ounces uncooked spaghetti

In a large skillet break up the ground beef. Add the remaining ingredients except the spaghetti. Stir in 3 cups water. Cover; bring to boiling. Reduce heat; simmer 30 minutes, stirring occasionally. Add the spaghetti; stir to separate strands. Simmer, covered, till spaghetti is tender, about 30 minutes longer, stirring frequently. Pass a shaker of Parmesan cheese, if desired. Makes 4 to 6 servings.

Veal Parmesan with Spaghetti

    6 thin veal cutlets
        (about 1½ pounds)
    2 tablespoons olive oil *or* salad oil
   ½ cup chopped onion
   ¼ cup chopped green pepper
   ⅓ cup dry white wine
    1 16-ounce can tomatoes
    2 8-ounce cans tomato sauce
    1 6-ounce can tomato paste
    1 clove garlic, minced
    1 tablespoon snipped parsley
    1 teaspoon dried oregano leaves,
        crushed
    8 ounces spaghetti
    1 6-ounce package sliced
        mozzarella cheese

Brown the veal cutlets in oil. Remove meat. Add onion and green pepper; cook till tender. Stir in the next 7 ingredients. Add meat. Cover; simmer 30 minutes, stirring occasionally. Cook spaghetti according to package directions; drain. Remove *half* the sauce from meat; stir into spaghetti. Top the cutlets with cheese; cover the pan for 5 minutes. Arrange spaghetti and meat on platter; pass extra sauce and Parmesan cheese, if desired. Makes 6 servings.

Spaghetti Turnover

    1 tablespoon salt
    7 ounces spaghetti
   ½ cup chopped celery
   ¼ cup chopped onion
    1 tablespoon poppy seed
   ½ teaspoon salt
   ¼ teaspoon pepper
   ½ cup light cream
    8 ounces sharp natural Cheddar
        cheese, shredded (2 cups)

Add 1 tablespoon salt to 3 quarts rapidly boiling water. Gradually add spaghetti so that water continues to boil. Cook, uncovered, stirring occasionally until just tender. Drain. Combine spaghetti, celery, onion, poppy seed, ½ teaspoon salt, pepper, and cream.

Lightly grease a large skillet; heat. Spoon *half* the spaghetti mixture into the skillet; top with 1½ *cups* of the Cheddar cheese. Top with remaining spaghetti mixture and sprinkle with remaining cheese. Cover and cook over medium heat, 25 to 30 minutes, running spatula under mixture occasionally to prevent sticking. Unmold onto serving platter. Garnish with parsley, if desired. Makes 6 servings.

Beef and Spaghetti

    1 pound round steak, cut in cubes
    2 tablespoons all-purpose flour
    2 tablespoons shortening
   ½ cup chopped onion
    1 clove garlic, minced
    1 3-ounce can broiled, chopped
        mushrooms
    1 10¾-ounce can condensed
        tomato soup
    1 tablespoon Worcestershire sauce
    3 drops bottled hot pepper sauce
    1 cup dairy sour cream
        Hot cooked spaghetti

Coat meat with flour; brown in hot shortening. Add onion; cook till tender. Add garlic, undrained mushrooms, next 3 ingredients, ½ teaspoon salt, and dash pepper; mix. Cover and simmer till tender, about 1¼ hours; stir occasionally. Stir in sour cream and ¼ cup water; heat, *but do not boil.* Spoon over spaghetti. Pass Parmesan cheese, if desired. Serves 6.

SPANISH COOKERY — The traditional dishes of Spain, which are a blend of the country's history and its natural food resources. Since long before the Christian era, people have invaded, colonized, and captured this land. The new owners influenced the growth of the country. This included planting olive trees and grape vines in the fertile soil, and introducing many new foods from neighboring lands. In turn, when Spain sent her explorers and conquerors, the conquistadores, to the New World, they brought back many strange, new foods. Among them were tomatoes, potatoes, vanilla, and chocolate, all long since blended into the Spanish cuisine.

The fertile land of Spain grows good crops. From the wide variety of foods that grow abundantly, and the fish and shellfish from the seas that surround the peninsula, a recognizable Spanish cuisine developed. As in many countries, there are regional variations in the preparation of national dishes from province to province, partly due to the use of local seasonal foods, and partly due to the ingenuity and taste of those who cook.

Characteristics of Spanish foods: Contrary to popular belief, Spanish food is not pungently hot. Too often it is confused with the Spanish-American cooking that makes generous use of the hot chili peppers. Yet these are practically unkown in Spain. However, garlic, olives, garbanzos (chickpeas), onion, saffron, and olive oil are ingredients that find their way into many of the Spanish dishes.

Fish and shellfish, especially along the coasts of Spain or near the rivers and streams that supply trout and salmon, are interestingly handled by Spanish cooks. Hearty fish soups are included among the seafood dishes prepared there.

Excellent young veal, lamb, pork, and chicken are Spain's principal meats, although good beef is also available. Wild game, such as wild boar and deer, and game birds, including quail, partridge, and pheasant, are also items frequently found in the Spanish cuisine.

Other foods that are served in Spain include fresh vegetables, many of which are used in cooked food mixtures. A simple green salad dressed with olive oil, vinegar, and seasonings is another favorite. Rice grown mainly in the Valencia region of Spain and is used in a variety of dishes with chicken, seafood, or vegetables.

Both dry and sweet sherries are among the popular wines of Spain. Grapes for these wines are grown around Jerez in the southern-most province of Spain, which is considered the home of sherry. Sherry wines are used in preparing a great many dishes and sauces as well as being drunk as a food accompaniment.

The Spanish pattern of meals is simple, but meal hours are a bit startling to many visitors from other countries. Breakfast is a simple meal, usually quite early. The midday meal, around 2 p.m., is the hearty meal of the day, and dinner, really more like supper, is any time after 10 p.m. The long gaps between meals are filled with snacks or tiny meals of sweets or other types of foods. This is when *tapas*, appetizer-like foods, save the day. Many of these are made of seafood, vegetables, and cheese in bite-sized pieces that are just right for nibbling whenever hunger pangs strike any time of the day.

Well-known recipes: Two Spanish soups are unique. One is *sopa de ajo,* a hot garlic soup that is essentially garlic, olive oil, bread, and water, with an egg added at the end. The other distinctive, classic soup is *gazpacho,* a unique salad-soup that is made differently in various provinces. Basic ingredients include tomato, cucumber, garlic, bread, olive oil, and vinegar. The result is a cold, refreshing soup. (See *Gazpacho* for recipe.)

Paella, the Spanish version of pilaf, is another classic dish that was born in Valencia. It is a mixture of chicken, shellfish, meat, vegetables, and rice. This dish, too, varies from region to region, with more or less saffron used in the rice, meat omitted entirely, and the seafood used according to the plentiful supply of seafood on hand. (See *Paella* for recipe.)

Countless dozen of eggs, *huevos,* are cooked according to many traditional and regional ways. If, however, you should see Spanish Omelet on a menu in Spain, don't expect it to be a big, puffy omelet served with a spicy tomato sauce as in America. It is likely to be a thick, hearty omelet with vegetables, such as potatoes and onion, or tomatoes, or seafood that are added to the beaten egg mixture.

Sweets usually accompany coffee or chocolate, sometimes at breakfast, but mostly as a late afternoon snack. *Churros,* made of doughnutlike dough pushed through a pastry tube into deep, hot fat to form circles, or sweet rich rolls are frequently served at breakfast.

Fresh fruits that grow abundantly in Spain are served as desserts, often accompanied by flavored sauces. Included in the wide variety of freshly grown fruits are grapes, oranges, lemons, figs, dates, strawberries, and melons. Other classic desserts include the caramel custard called *flan* (see *Flan* for recipe), and rice pudding with a cinnamon topping.

Spanish Potato Omelet

    2 large potatoes, peeled and finely
        chopped (3 cups)
    ½ cup finely chopped onion
    5 tablespoons olive oil
    6 beaten eggs
    ⅓ cup milk

In a 10-inch skillet cook potatoes and onion in *3 tablespoons* of the olive oil till tender, turning vegetables occasionally. Season with ½ teaspoon salt. Remove from heat.

Combine eggs, milk, ½ teaspoon salt, and dash pepper. Stir in cooked potato mixture. Heat remaining 2 tablespoons olive oil in same skillet. Pour in egg mixture. Cover and cook over low heat till omelet is nearly set, about 10 minutes. Invert omelet by placing plate over skillet and turning all over. Slide the omelet back into the skillet, moist side down. Cook omelet till underside is set, about 1 to 2 minutes. Loosen omelet and slide onto serving plate. Makes 4 servings.

SPANISH CREAM—A delicate molded dessert that is prepared with a soft custard of eggs, milk, and sugar, with gelatin added. The stiffly beaten egg whites are folded into the custard mixture, and as the dessert sets up when chilled in the refrigerator, it separates into two distinct layers, a foamy and a creamy mixture.

SPANISH MACKEREL—A saltwater fat fish that belongs to the mackerel family. The color of this fish is deep blue on the back and silvery below. Along the sides are three rows of gold-colored spots.

The Spanish mackerel is a popular fish along the east coast of the United States and is gaining adherents in other parts of the country. It can be found in the middle Atlantic during the summer months and off the Florida coast during the winter.

Because the scales of this fish are so very thin and fine, it does not have to be skinned or scaled before cooking. Preparation methods for this fat fish include broiling and baking. The fat on the fish keeps it moist during the period of cooking. Oftentimes, it is prepared with a tomato sauce. (See also *Mackerel.*)

SPANISH SAUCE—One of the classic brown sauces that is commonly called Espagnole. (See also *Espagnole Sauce.*)

SPARERIB—A cut of pork from the rib cage of a pig, containing the breastbone, rib bones, and rib cartilage, with a thin covering of meat. Spareribs are not to be confused with back ribs, also referred to as country-style back ribs, which are meatier or less "spare" ribs from the rib area of the loin section. The meat covering the back ribs comes from the loin eye.

Spareribs are available fresh and cured and smoked and should be cooked to the well-done stage by either roasting, braising, or cooking in liquid. Barbecued spareribs are also a popular method of preparation and are delicious cooked over charcoal and basted with a peppery sauce.

Like other cuts of pork, spareribs contribute protein to the diet and are a source of the B vitamins, especially thiamine. The meat from six plain, roasted medium ribs adds 246 calories to the diet. Sauces add a few additional calories, depending on their ingredients. Since there is generally a small amount of meat on spareribs, plan on about 1 to 1½ servings per pound of spareribs. (See also *Pork.*)

Mustard Barbecued Ribs

  1 cup catsup
  ½ cup water
  ⅓ cup red wine vinegar
  ¼ cup salad oil
  2 tablespoons instant minced onion
  1 tablespoon brown sugar
  1 tablespoon Worcestershire sauce
  1 tablespoon whole mustard seed
  2 teaspoons paprika
  1 teaspoon dried oregano leaves,
      crushed
  1 teaspoon chili powder
  ½ teaspoon salt
  ¼ teaspoon ground cloves
  1 bay leaf
  1 clove garlic, minced
  4 pounds pork spareribs

In small saucepan combine all ingredients except spareribs. Simmer, uncovered, 15 to 20 minutes, stirring once or twice. Remove bay leaf. Set sauce aside.

Sprinkle ribs with a little salt. Place ribs, meaty side down, in shallow roasting pan. Roast at 450° for 30 minutes. Remove meat from oven; drain off excess fat. Turn ribs, meaty side up. Reduce oven to 350°. Return ribs to oven; roast 1 hour more. Drain excess fat. Brush sauce over ribs; roast 30 minutes, basting occasionally with sauce. Serves 4 to 6.

Spareribs Cantonese

  4 pounds pork spareribs, cut in
      serving-sized pieces
  ½ cup soy sauce
  1 cup orange marmalade
  ½ teaspoon garlic powder
  ½ teaspoon ground ginger

In a shallow roasting pan place ribs meaty side down. Roast at 450° for 30 minutes. Remove meat from oven; drain off excess fat. Turn ribs meaty side up. Reduce oven temperature to 350°; continue roasting ribs for 1 hour. In a small bowl combine soy sauce, ¾ cup water, orange marmalade, garlic powder, ginger, and dash pepper; blend thoroughly. Pour mixture over the ribs; roast till tender, about 30 minutes longer, basting ribs occasionally with the sauce. Makes 4 to 6 servings.

Mincemeat Spareribs

  4 pounds pork spareribs, cut in
      serving-sized pieces
  1 cup water
    Salt
        .   .   .
  1½ cups prepared mincemeat
  1 10½-ounce can condensed beef
      broth
  2 tablespoons vinegar

Place spareribs, meaty side up, in shallow roasting pan. Add water; sprinkle meat with a little salt. Cover pan with foil. Bake at 350° for 1½ hours; drain. Combine mincemeat, beef broth, and vinegar; pour over ribs in pan. Bake, uncovered, 30 to 45 minutes more, basting occasionally with pan juices. Serves 4 to 6.

Luau Ribs

  2 4½-ounce jars or cans strained
      peaches (baby food)
  ⅓ cup catsup
  ⅓ cup vinegar
  2 tablespoons soy sauce
  ½ cup brown sugar
  1 clove garlic, minced
  2 teaspoons ground ginger
  1 teaspoon salt
    Dash pepper
  4 pounds meaty pork spareribs

Mix together the strained peaches, catsup, vinegar, soy sauce, brown sugar, garlic, ginger, 1 teaspoon salt, and dash pepper. Rub the ribs with salt and pepper. Place the ribs, meaty side up, on a grill. Broil the ribs over *low* coals for about 20 minutes; turn meaty side down and broil till browned, about 10 minutes.

Again turn meaty side up, brush with peach sauce, and broil without turning till meat is well-done, about 30 minutes. Brush frequently with sauce. Makes 4 to 6 servings.

An unusual glaze for spareribs

The topping for Mincemeat Spareribs is → concocted from prepared mincemeat, beef broth, and a hint of vinegar for tartness.

SPARKLING WINE—A wine that is made effervescent by natural means. Traditionally, as in champagne, the carbonation is trapped in the wine bottles when the wine is allowed to ferment a second time. In the newer Charmat process, secondary fermentation occurs in large, sealed tanks. To retain carbonation, the wine is then bottled under pressure. Some of the more popular sparkling wines include champagne, sparkling burgundy, and sparkling rosé. (See also *Wines and Spirits*.)

SPATULA—A utensil with a thin, flexible blade attached to a handle. The blade has no cutting edge. Available in a variety of styles, spatulas are used for spreading, turning, and lifting food.

SPEARMINT—A variety of the herbaceous mint plant used for flavoring food. Spearmint has been used for many centuries and was probably named after the spear- or lance-shaped arrangement of the flowers on the stem. The plant leaves are used to flavor candy, desserts, sauces, jellies, teas, and other beverages. (See also *Mint*.)

SPECULAAS—A spiced cookie that is traditionally served by the Dutch at Christmas. Carved wooden molds are sometimes used for shaping each cookie before baking.

Speculaas

Thoroughly cream ½ cup butter or margarine and 1 cup brown sugar. Add 1 egg and 2 tablespoons milk; beat well. Sift together 2½ cups sifted all-purpose flour, 2 teaspoons baking powder, ½ teaspoon salt, 1 teaspoon ground cinnamon, ½ teaspoon ground cloves, and ½ teaspoon ground nutmeg. Blend into mixture.

Divide dough into thirds; chill.* Roll each portion on floured surface to 9x8-inch rectangle. Cut in twelve 3x2-inch pieces. Place on lightly greased cookie sheet. Sprinkle with ½ cup sliced almonds. Bake at 375° till lightly browned, 10 to 12 minutes. Makes 3 dozen.

*For molded cookies: Press chilled dough into well-floured mold. (Use only one mold at a time.) Remove immediately by turning mold over and tapping on the back. Use a knife point to remove cookie from mold, if necessary.

SPELT—A variety of wheat of economic importance in Europe, but only grown in small quantities in the United States.

SPICE—Any aromatic or fragrant part of a plant used to flavor and season food. Spices may include the berry, root, bark, kernel, fruit, or flower bud from the plant. Although the broad classification of spices encompasses the aromatic plants known as herbs, the following distinction is often used: spices come from tropical plants, while herbs grow in temperate regions.

The history of spices is ancient and filled with endless lore. Prized highly for their medicinal, aromatic, and savory properties, spices triggered explorations to unknown lands and helped shape the economic development of many countries.

Archaeologists believe that primitive man discovered the art of seasoning by accident, probably when he wrapped meat in leaves to keep it relatively free from ashes while it was being cooked over an open fire. It's not too difficult to imagine his astonishment when he unwrapped the meat and tasted the seasoned food.

According to the chiseled stone tablets of the ancient Assyrians, spices were used thousands of years before Christ. The Assyrians claimed that the gods drank sesame seed wine before creating the earth. Other references to spices are found in the *Holy Bible* as well as on pyramid walls.

In ancient times, trade routes were established on land and sea for the purpose of bringing spices back from the Orient to the Western world. Caravans brought pepper and cloves from India, ginger from China, and cinnamon and nutmeg from the Spice Islands. A safe return was not assured, as pirates, robbers, shipwrecks, and storms often were encountered.

Due to the limited supply, spices commanded a high price in the market place, and only the wealthy could afford them. Nevertheless, the uses for spices quickly multiplied. Crowns of bay leaves were awarded to Olympic heroes; spice-scented baths were a luxury enjoyed by the rich; temples were filled with the aroma of incense made from spices; medicinal remedies were prepared from spices; and spice-flavored wines and foods were delicacies.

In the Middle Ages, spices were frequently used as payment for taxes and rent. Pepper was the most valuable of all the spices. Each peppercorn was counted individually, whereas other spices generally were traded in weight measure. For example, one pound of ginger was a fair exchange for one sheep, while one pound of mace was equivalent to three sheep or half a cow. Because of the preciousness of spices, dock guards in London were required to stitch their pockets shut to guard against thievery as spices were unloaded from incoming ships. Despite the risks involved, the spice trade flourished.

As early as 950 B.C., the Arabs controlled the spice routes. They kept other potential spice traders from entering the market by relating tales of piracy and danger which they faced along the spice routes. The Arabs were successful in keeping the source of the spices a secret from European traders for some time.

The travels of Marco Polo, which began around 1271, revealed the source of many spices, and European merchants quickly realized they could secure the valuable spices by sea. Competition for control of the routes increased as England, Spain, Portugal, and Holland raced to the Orient to bring back the valuable merchandise.

The quest for spices resulted in the discovery of new lands. Columbus's famous voyage in search of a new route to the Orient, led him to the discovery of America, and other countries also sent out expeditions to find new trade routes. Although many of the ventures ended unsuccessfully, the search for spices continued.

During the 1500s, the English concentrated on finding trade routes to the North, since the Spaniards held the routes to the west and the Portuguese controlled the eastward routes. Although the English were unsuccessful in reaching the spice countries by traveling north, they made important and strategic navigational discoveries. In doing so, they established themselves as a mighty sea power by the end of the sixteenth century.

The following century, the Dutch gained control of the Portuguese-held spice ports in the Indies and established the Dutch East Indies. The Dutch stranglehold was

Whole cloves and bay leaf season Spicy Chops and Cabbage. To complete this skillet meal, add diced apple for color and flavor.

so powerful that they often burned or destroyed excess spices to keep the prices high. They continued their monopoly of the spice trade for almost 200 years. However, by 1799, English sea victories resulted in the liquidation of the monopoly.

The British were helped greatly by the French, for while the French government did little to promote the search for spices, French sea captains discovered southern routes and the spice-rich islands of the Atlantic. Although the French were unable to establish a monopoly along the southern routes, their efforts did aid the fall of the Dutch spice monopoly.

At about the same time, American sea captains entered the market by sailing from Salem, Massachusetts, to Sumatra and back. For about 100 years, American vessels returned loaded with black pepper.

Today, the spice trade is still a very prosperous business, although the means of securing these aromatic plants is no longer the mission of danger and mystery it was centuries ago. Most spices are now readily available at a reasonable cost.

Almost every country in the world produces some spice; however, the tropical spices are still obtained in greatest quantity from the original spice-rich countries in the East. Some of the spices supplied by countries in the Americas include ginger and allspice from Jamaica, nutmeg from Grenada, sesame seed from Nicaragua and Salvador, and fenugreek seed from Argentina. Spices produced in the United States are sesame seed, laurel, basil, tarragon, mustard, chili powder, paprika, and red pepper. Since the supply of American-grown spices is small, it is necessary to import a major portion of all spices used in the United States.

Classification of spices: There are various methods for classifying spices. If grouped according to properties, spices are divided into three categories—stimulating condiments (black pepper, capsicum peppers, garlic, horseradish, and mustard); aromatic spices (anise, cardamon, cinnamon, cloves, and ginger); and sweet herbs (basil, chervil, fennel, parsley, and sage).

Spices are often arranged according to the plant families to which they belong. Some of the larger families include the *Libiatae*, or mint family; the *Umbelliferae*, or parsley family; the *Compositae*, or aster family; and the *Liliaceae*, or lily family.

It is also possible to classify the great number of spices according to the plant part from which they are refined. For example, the plant parts and their respective spices include the dried flower bud (cloves); the fruit (allspice, black pepper, nutmeg, and vanilla); the underground root (ginger, horseradish, and turmeric); the bark (cinnamon); and the seed or seed-like structures (anise, caraway, cardamom, coriander, dill, poppy, and sesame).

Forms of spices: Most spices are imported in whole form and are checked by government inspectors before they go to a grinding company. Some of the more popular spices marketed in whole form include allspice, cinnamon, cloves, ginger, black pepper, red pepper, and saffron.

Many spices are also sold in ground form. Those available in most supermarkets include allspice, cardamom, celery seed, cinnamon, cloves, coriander, cumin, ginger, mace, mustard, nutmeg, paprika, black pepper, red pepper, white pepper,

saffron, turmeric, and some sweet herbs. Since food manufacturers often prefer a finer or coarser grind than that used in the home, spice processors offer many grinds.

Spice blends are prepared from a mixture of herbs and spices and are sometimes preferred by the homemaker for cooking purposes. Popular spice blends include apple pie spice, cinnamon sugar, barbecue spice, chili powder, curry powder, herb seasoning, Italian seasoning, mixed pickling spice, poultry seasoning, pumpkin pie spice, seafood seasoning, seasoned or flavored salt, and shrimp spice.

How to store: Spices maintain their flavor longer when stored in a cool, dry place. Avoid keeping spices in warm areas of the kitchen. Also, store spices in a tightly covered container. Exposure to air increases flavor loss. Generally, whole spices have a longer storage life than ground spices. In areas subject to prolonged hot temperatures, spices such as paprika, crushed red pepper, cayenne, chili powder, and aromatic seeds are best stored in the refrigerator.

To determine the freshness of a spice, note the color and flavor. When fresh, most spices have a bright, rich color and a readily apparent aroma when the container is opened. If either color or aroma appears weak, replace the spice.

How to use: Whole spices are ideal for seasoning hot beverages, soups, stews, and other foods that have long, slow cooking, as the flavor of the spice is released slowly with moist heat. To use, place whole spices in a cheesecloth bag for easy removal. If whole spices are added to an uncooked marinade, let the marinade stand several hours, as more time is needed to extract the flavor in a cold mixture.

Ground spices, which provide a more instant flavor, are excellent used in baked products, salads, desserts, casseroles, and other short-cooking or unbaked foods. Since the flavor of the ground spice is released quickly, add the spice near the end of the cooking period unless the cooking time is short. Ground spices, such as cinnamon or nutmeg, also are attractive when they are sprinkled over a dessert or salad as a garnish. (See also *Herb.*)

Seasoning guide for spices

Allspice	Nutmeg
Baked ham	Bananas
Beef stew	Beef
Cake	Chicken Soup
Cookies	Creamed vegetables
Meat loaf	Custard
Pot roast	Doughnuts
Pumpkin pie	Eggnog
Shellfish	Fish
Tomato sauce	Pears
Vegetable soup	Rice pudding
Cinnamon	**Paprika**
Apples	Chicken
Cake	Chili
Cookies	Cream sauce
Hot cereal	Eggs
Prune butter	Fish
Pudding	Potatoes
Spiced fruit	Veal
Cloves	**Pepper—Black**
Chocolate pudding	Barbecue sauce
Fruitcake	Gravy
Fruit pastries	Stew
Ham	Vegetable soup
Roast pork	**Pepper—Red**
Spiced fruit	Cheese dishes
Stew	Chowder
Ginger	Cream soup
Carrots	Deviled ham
Chicken	Eggs
Cookies	Pasta
Fruit pastries	Seafood
Marmalade	Stew
Pears	**Pepper—White**
Pot roast	Chicken
Pudding	Cream soup
Spice cake	Fish
Stew	Ham
Sweet potatoes	Mayonnaise
Mace	Poultry
Cherry pie	**Saffron**
Chocolate desserts	Bread
Creamed eggs	Cake
Cream sauce	Rice
Fish sauce	Tea
Fruit cobbler	**Turmeric**
Meat stuffing	Creamed eggs
Oyster stew	Fish
Pound cake	Pickles
Welsh rabbit	Relishes

Spicy Chops and Cabbage

4 pork loin chops
2 tablespoons water
½ teaspoon salt
2 whole cloves
½ small bay leaf
1 medium he⸳⸳⸳⸳⸳⸳⸳⸳⸳arsely
   shred⸳⸳
1½ cur⸳⸳⸳⸳⸳⸳⸳⸳apple
¼ ⸳⸳⸳⸳⸳⸳⸳⸳u onion
¼ cup⸳⸳⸳ar
1½ teaspoons all-purpose flour
½ teaspoon salt
2 tablespoons vinegar
2 tablespoons water

Trim fat from chops. In skillet cook trimmings till small amount of fat accumulates; discard trimmings. Brown chops in accumulated fat. Add 2 tablespoons water, salt, cloves, and bay leaf; cover and simmer for 30 minutes.

Remove chops from skillet; discard cloves and bay leaf. Add cabbage, apple, and onion. Combine sugar, flour, and ½ teaspoon salt. Stir in vinegar and 2 tablespoons water. Pour over cabbage, stirring to mix. Cover and simmer for 5 minutes. Return pork chops to skillet; cover and cook till chops and cabbage are tender, 20 minutes longer. Makes 4 servings.

Gingered Ham Slice

1 fully cooked center cut ham
   slice, 1 inch thick
    • • •
½ cup ginger ale
½ cup orange juice
¼ cup brown sugar
1 tablespoon salad oil
1½ teaspoons wine vinegar
1 teaspoon dry mustard
¼ teaspoon ground ginger
⅛ teaspoon ground cloves

Slash fat edge of ham. Combine ginger ale and remaining ingredients; in shallow dish pour mixture over ham. Refrigerate overnight or let stand at room temperature 2 hours, spooning marinade over ham several times. Broil ham slice over *low* coals about 15 minutes on each side; brush often with marinade. To serve, spoon marinade over ham. Serves 5 or 6.

Polynesian Pork Steaks, reminiscent of other island specialties, simmer slowly in a tangy sauce made with ginger and coconut.

Polynesian Pork Steaks

         6 pork arm or blade steaks
         2 tablespoons salad oil
         1 4¾-ounce jar strained
            plums (baby food)
       ¼ cup flaked coconut
         1 tablespoon vinegar
         1 tablespoon salad oil
         2 teaspoons soy sauce
       ½ teaspoon ground ginger
       ½ teaspoon grated lemon peel

In skillet brown steaks in salad oil. Sprinkle with salt. Combine remaining ingredients, 2 tablespoons water, ½ teaspoon salt, and dash pepper; pour around steaks. Cover; simmer till tender, 35 to 40 minutes. Remove steaks to platter; spoon sauce over. Serves 6.

Spicy Fruit Dressing

In mixing bowl combine 1 cup dairy sour cream, ½ cup apple cider *or* apple juice, ½ cup salad oil, ½ teaspoon ground cinnamon, ¼ teaspoon ground nutmeg, and dash salt; beat with rotary beater till smooth. Chill thoroughly. Serve with fruit salads. Makes 2 cups.

Cran-Cheese Squares

         1 3-ounce package orange-
            pineapple-flavored gelatin
         1 cup orange juice
       ½ cup whipping cream
         1 3-ounce package cream cheese,
            softened
       ¼ cup chopped pecans
                  • • •
         1 envelope unflavored gelatin
            (1 tablespoon)
         1 16-ounce can whole cranberry
            sauce
         2 tablespoons lemon juice
       ¼ teaspoon ground allspice
       ⅛ teaspoon ground nutmeg
         1 cup orange sections
         1 7-ounce bottle ginger ale,
            chilled (about 1 cup)

Dissolve orange-pineapple-flavored gelatin in 1 cup boiling water; stir in orange juice. Chill till partially set. Whip cream. Blend a little whipped cream into cream cheese; fold in remaining whipped cream. Add nuts; fold cream mixture into gelatin. Pour into 9x9x2-inch pan; chill till *almost* firm.

Soften unflavored gelatin in ¼ cup cold water; stir over low heat till dissolved. Combine cranberry sauce, lemon juice, allspice, nutmeg, and orange sections; stir in gelatin. Slowly pour ginger ale down side of bowl; stir gently to mix. Pour slowly over cheese layer. Chill till firm. To serve, cut into squares. Makes 9 servings.

Spiced Peaches

         5 cups sugar
         2 cups water
         1 cup vinegar
       12 inches stick cinnamon, broken
         2 teaspoons whole cloves
            Small peaches, peeled

Combine sugar, water, vinegar, cinnamon, and cloves; heat to boiling. Into syrup drop enough peaches to fill 2 or 3 pints. Heat mixture about 5 minutes. Pack fruit in hot pint jars; add syrup to within ½ inch of top. Adjust lids. Process in boiling water bath for 20 minutes (count time after water returns to boil). Seven pounds fresh peaches yields 9 pints fruit.

Spicy Coconut Chiffon Pie

    1 cup flaked coconut
    1 teaspoon ground cinnamon
    ¼ teaspoon ground ginger
    ⅛ teaspoon ground mace
    1 envelope unflavored gelatin
    ½ cup sugar
 1¼ cups milk
    4 beaten egg yolks
    1 teaspoon vanilla
    ¼ teaspoon cream of tartar
    4 egg whites
    ½ cup whipping cream
    1 baked 9-inch pastry shell
        cooled (See *Pastry*)

Mix first 4 ingredients; spread in shallow pan. Toast at 350° till coconut is brown, about 8 minutes; stir occasionally. In saucepan combine gelatin, sugar, and ¼ teaspoon salt. Slowly stir in milk. Add egg yolks. Cook and stir over low heat till mixture thickens. Stir in vanilla. Cool thoroughly.

In large mixer bowl add cream of tartar to egg whites; beat till stiff but not dry. Whip cream. Fold egg whites and whipped cream into yolk mixture. Chill till partially set. Pile *half* of the chiffon mixture in pastry shell. Sprinkle *half* of the coconut over filling. Repeat layers; chill. To serve, garnish with additional whipped cream, if desired.

Spice-Nut Cake

Sift together 2 cups sifted all-purpose flour, 1 cup granulated sugar, 1 teaspoon baking powder, 1 teaspoon salt, ¾ teaspoon *each* baking soda, ground cloves, and ground cinnamon. Add ⅔ cup shortening, ¾ cup brown sugar, and 1 cup buttermilk *or* sour milk.

Mix till all flour is moistened. Beat 2 minutes at medium speed on electric mixer. Add 3 eggs; beat 2 minutes more. Stir in ½ cup finely chopped walnuts. Pour into 2 greased and lightly floured 9x1½-inch round pans. Bake at 350° till done, 30 to 35 minutes. Cool 10 minutes; remove from pans. Cool completely.

Frost with *Maple Fluff Frosting:* In 1-quart saucepan boil 1 cup maple-flavored syrup over medium heat for 5 minutes. Gradually pour hot syrup over 3 stiffly beaten egg whites, beating constantly till frosting forms soft peaks.

Spicy Prune Cake

 1½ cups sifted all-purpose flour
    ¾ cup granulated sugar
    ¼ cup brown sugar
    1 teaspoon baking powder
    ½ teaspoon baking soda
    ½ teaspoon ground cinnamon
    ¼ teaspoon salt
    ¼ teaspoon ground ginger
    ½ cup cold water
    ½ cup salad oil
    1 4¾-ounce jar strained
        prunes (baby food)
    1 egg
    1 teaspoon vanilla
    ½ cup chopped walnuts
            • • •
    ½ cup sifted confectioners' sugar
    ⅛ teaspoon ground cinnamon
    1 tablespoon light cream

In mixer bowl sift together flour, granulated sugar, brown sugar, baking powder, baking soda, ½ teaspoon cinnamon, salt, and ginger. Add water and next 4 ingredients. Blend; beat 1 minute at medium speed of electric mixer.

Turn into greased and floured 9x9x2-inch baking pan. Sprinkle nuts over batter. Bake at 350° for 30 minutes; cool cake in pan. Mix remaining ingredients. Drizzle over cake.

Sprinkle chopped nuts over Spicy Prune Cake batter before baking. When cool, drizzle nut-topped cake with confectioners' icing.

SPIDER — An old-time name for a heavy, three-legged iron pot or pan that was set over fireplace coals for cooking.

SPINACH — An annual, dark green, leafy vegetable that is eaten raw or cooked.

Although most spinach culinary history has been lost, its origin has been pinpointed to southwestern Asia. Spinach plants existed in this area many centuries ago, but how cultivation and use spread is unclear. Some historians believe that spinach was used by the Chinese prior to its introduction to Greece, Italy, and Spain, while others disagree.

How spinach is produced: Spinach plants have a short-term growth cycle that necessitates specific climate and soil conditions for optimum leaf development. As the plants take only eight weeks to mature, the seeds often are sown between the rows of slower-growing crops. The plants require cool weather and rich, sandy, well-watered, well-limed soil. Spinach is planted in the South during the winter and in other regions in the spring and fall.

Nutritional value: One serving of cooked spinach (½ cup) provides only 21 calories. This portion also adds outstanding amounts of vitamins and minerals to the diet. It is an excellent source of vitamin A, iron, and B vitamin riboflavin, and, if raw or properly cooked, vitamin C. Niacin is present in moderate amounts.

Types of spinach: There are fewer spinach varieties used for commercial production than for some other vegetables. The two most important types are the Broad Flanders and the New Zealand spinach.

How to select and store: Choose spinach leaves that are large and fresh-looking, and have good green color. Avoid leaves with wilted or yellow areas. Since fresh spinach shrinks when it is cooked, count on one pound of the fresh leaves yielding about 1½ cups cooked. Frozen or canned spinach is available also.

Even the freshest spinach maintains its quality for only a few days, so, for best storage results, wrap or cover the leaves, and place them in the vegetable crisper. Add crushed ice to the spinach package to help hold the leaves at peak quality.

How to prepare: Spinach lovers attest to the fact that proper washing and cooking are essential to remove sand. Because spinach grows low to the ground, the leaves often contain small amounts of sand. To remove it, place a bunch of leaves in a pan of lukewarm water. After a few minutes, lift them out. Drain the leaves and discard the now-sandy water. Repeat several times more until no sand appears in the bottom of the pan. This warm water method more easily removes the sand than would washing each leaf under cold water.

The flavor of spinach is best retained when the leaves are cooked only in the water that clings to the washed leaves. Reduce the heat when the steam begins to form, and cook spinach, covered, for three to five minutes. Turn leaves often with a fork. For optimum nutritional value, use a small amount of water while cooking.

How to serve: Whether fresh, frozen, or canned, whole leaves or chopped, spinach is an attractive vegetable when properly cooked. In salads, uncooked fresh spinach is used for color and flavor or as a substitute for lettuce.

Spinach combines well with a host of seasonings and foods. Allspice, basil, cinnamon, dill, marjoram, mint, nutmeg, oregano, rosemary, or sesame seed is used with spinach in the cooking liquid, or for salads, in the salad dressing. Hard-cooked egg, chopped or sliced, is a popular addition to raw or cooked spinach. Creamy sauces are used as toppings or in casseroles. Among these, any dish with Florentine in the title is sure to contain spinach. (See also *Vegetable.*)

Spinach-Avocado Bowl

Place 10 ounces fresh spinach, torn in bite-sized pieces, in salad bowl. Arrange 2 medium avocados, peeled and sliced; ½ pound bacon, crisp-cooked, drained, and crumbled; and ½ cup chopped peanuts over spinach. Serve with Russian-style salad dressing. Serves 8 to 10.

The flavor essence and fine texture of fresh spinach—Popeye's favorite vegetable—is preserved when served uncooked in salads or when cooked in the water that clings to the leaves.

Orange-Spinach Toss

    4 cups fresh spinach, torn in
        bite-sized pieces
    3 oranges, peeled and sectioned
    4 slices bacon, crisp-cooked,
        drained, and crumbled
  ½ cup chopped peanuts
    1 envelope French-style salad
        dressing mix

In a salad bowl combine spinach, orange sections, bacon, and peanuts. Prepare French-style salad dressing mix according to package directions. Pour desired amount over spinach mixture. Toss lightly to coat. Makes 4 servings.

Spinach-Lettuce Toss

    5 slices bacon
    3 cups torn leaf lettuce
    3 cups torn, fresh spinach
  ¼ cup diced celery
    2 tablespoons crumbled blue cheese
    1 tablespoon chopped green onion
  ¼ cup vinegar
    2 tablespoons sugar
  ½ teaspoon Worcestershire sauce

Cook bacon till crisp. Drain; reserving drippings. Crumble bacon; combine with next 5 ingredients. To drippings, add remaining ingredients; bring to a boil. Toss with salad. Serves 6.

Wilted Spinach Salad

        1 pound fresh spinach
     ½ cup sliced green onion
        Dash freshly ground pepper
                • • •
        5 slices bacon, diced
        2 tablespoons wine vinegar
        1 tablespoon lemon juice
        1 teaspoon sugar
     ½ teaspoon salt
        1 hard-cooked egg, coarsely
            chopped

Wash the spinach, discarding the stems. Pat dry on paper toweling; tear in bite-sized pieces into a salad bowl. Add the sliced green onion. Sprinkle with pepper. Chill.

At serving time, slowly fry bacon in deep chafing dish or electric skillet till crisp-cooked. Add vinegar, lemon juice, sugar, and salt. Gradually add spinach, tossing just till the leaves are coated and wilted slightly. Sprinkle the salad with chopped egg. Serve immediately. Makes 4 to 6 servings.

Tuna-Spinach Toss

        2 cups torn spinach
        1 cup torn lettuce
     ½ small red onion, thinly sliced
            and separated into rings
            (about ½ cup)
        1 6½- or 7-ounce can tuna,
            drained and flaked
        4 ounces Swiss cheese, cut
            into narrow 2-inch strips
            (about 1 cup)
                • • •
     ¼ cup olive *or* salad oil
        1 tablespoon vinegar
        1 tablespoon lemon juice
     ½ teaspoon salt
     ¼ teaspoon dried tarragon
            leaves, crushed

Toss spinach and lettuce in large salad bowl. Place onion rings around sides of bowl. Heap tuna in center; surround with cheese. Combine olive oil, vinegar, lemon juice, salt, tarragon, and dash pepper in screw-top jar; shake well. Just before serving, toss dressing mixture with salad. Makes 4 servings.

Tangy Spinach Toss

        2 tablespoons sliced green
            onion
     ¼ cup butter or margarine
        2 tablespoons all-purpose flour
     ¼ teaspoon salt
        1 cup water
        2 tablespoons lemon juice
        1 tablespoon prepared horseradish
     ½ teaspoon Worcestershire sauce
                • • •
        2 hard-cooked eggs
        1 pound fresh spinach, torn
            in bite-sized pieces
        Paprika

Cook onion in butter about 1 minute; blend in flour and salt. Add water, lemon juice, horseradish, and Worcestershire sauce; cook and stir till mixture boils.

Dice *one* egg; add to dressing. Pour dressing over spinach in salad bowl; toss lightly. Slice remaining egg for garnish; sprinkle with paprika. Serve at once. Serves 6 to 8.

Spinach Surprise

        1 pound fresh spinach
        2 tablespoons butter or margarine
     ¼ cup light cream
     ½ tablespoon prepared horseradish
        Hard-cooked egg slices

Cook spinach; drain and chop. Add butter, cream, and horseradish. Heat through. Season to taste with salt and pepper. Garnish with hard-cooked egg slices. Makes 3 or 4 servings.

Chinese Spinach

        1 pound fresh spinach
        2 tablespoons salad oil
        1 tablespoon soy sauce

Wash and pat dry the spinach leaves. Remove stems and cut into 1-inch pieces; tear leaves into bite-sized pieces. Heat salad oil and soy sauce in skillet; add spinach. Cover and cook just till wilted, about 1 minute. Uncover; cook and toss till spinach is crisp-tender and well-coated, about 2 minutes. Makes 4 servings.

For Tangy Spinach Toss, a new version of salad dressing coats fresh spinach leaves. Minus oil or mayonnaise, the thickened mixture blends lemon juice, horseradish, and Worcestershire.

Spinach Supreme

  2 **10-ounce packages frozen chopped spinach**
1½ **cups milk**
  2 **slightly beaten eggs**
  1 **1¾-ounce envelope dry cream of leek soup mix**

Cook spinach according to package directions; drain thoroughly. Combine milk and eggs; gradually stir into the soup mix. Add spinach and mix well. Turn into a 10x6x1½-inch baking dish. Bake at 350° until the edges of the casserole are set, but center is still creamy, about 30 minutes. Serves 6 to 8.

Spinach-Potato Bake

1 **10¼-ounce can frozen condensed cream of potato soup, thawed *or* 1 10½-ounce can condensed cream of potato soup**
1 **10-ounce package frozen chopped spinach, thawed**
2 **beaten eggs**
1 **teaspoon instant minced onion Dash salt**

Combine all ingredients and dash pepper, mixing well. Turn into lightly greased 10x6x1½-inch baking dish. Bake, uncovered, at 350° for 30 minutes. Makes 4 to 6 servings.

Spinach Elegante

    2 10-ounce packages frozen
        chopped spinach
    3 slices bacon, crisp-cooked,
        drained, and crumbled
    1 6-ounce can sliced mushrooms,
        drained (1 cup)
    ¼ teaspoon dried marjoram
        leaves, crushed
    1 cup dairy sour cream
    ½ cup shredded sharp process
        American cheese

Cook spinach according to package directions. Drain well; spread on bottom of a 10x6x1½-inch baking dish. Arrange bacon and mushrooms over. Sprinkle with dash pepper and marjoram. Bake at 325° for 15 minutes. Cover with sour cream and cheese. Heat in oven till cheese melts, about 5 minutes. Serves 6.

Spinach Delight

    2 10-ounce packages frozen chopped
        spinach, cooked and drained
    4 slices bacon, crisp-cooked
        drained, and crumbled
    1 5-ounce can water chestnuts,
        drained and sliced
    1 10-ounce package frozen Welsh
        rarebit, thawed (about 1 cup)
    1 cup canned French-fried onions

Place the cooked spinach in a 10x6x1½-inch baking dish. Top with bacon and water chestnuts. Spread Welsh rarebit evenly over top. Garnish with the canned French-fried onions. Bake at 350° till heated through, about 20 to 25 minutes. Makes 6 to 8 servings.

Épinards à la Crème (Creamed Spinach)

Chop and drain 1 pound fresh cooked spinach, Add ¼ cup medium white sauce (see *White Sauce*), ½ teaspoon salt, dash pepper, dash Worcestershire sauce, and dash bottled hot pepper sauce. Mix thoroughly. Spread into an 8-inch pie plate. Top with ¼ cup hollandaise sauce (see *Hollandaise Sauce*). Brown lightly at 425° for 15 minutes. Makes 4 servings.

Shrimp à la Rockefeller

    ¼ cup butter or margarine
    1 teaspoon celery seed
    1 teaspoon Worcestershire sauce
    1 cup chopped lettuce
    ¼ cup chopped green onion
    1 small clove garlic, minced
    2 10-ounce packages frozen chopped
        spinach, thawed and drained
    1 cup light cream
    1 beaten egg
    8 ounces cleaned, cooked shrimp
    2 tablespoons butter, melted
    ¼ cup fine dry bread crumbs
    ¼ cup grated Parmesan cheese

In medium saucepan combine ¼ cup butter, celery seed, Worcestershire sauce, and ½ teaspoon salt. Stir in lettuce, green onion, and garlic; simmer, covered, 2 to 3 minutes. Add the spinach, cream, and beaten egg. Cook and stir till mixture begins to simmer. Divide *half* the shrimp among four individual casseroles or 8-ounce baking shells. Add hot spinach mixture. Top with remaining shrimp. Combine 2 tablespoons melted butter, bread crumbs, and cheese. Sprinkle evenly over the casseroles. Bake at 375° just till hot, about 15 minutes. Makes 4 servings.

Spinach-Carrot Custard

    ¼ cup butter or margarine
    ¼ cup all-purpose flour
    1½ cups milk
    1 tablespoon instant minced onion
    2 slightly beaten eggs
    1½ cups shredded carrots, cooked
        and drained
    1 10-ounce package frozen chopped
        spinach, cooked and drained

In saucepan melt butter; blend in flour. Add milk, onion, and ½ teaspoon salt. Cook and stir till mixture thickens and bubbles. Remove from heat. Stir small amount of hot sauce into eggs. Return to hot mixture and cook till blended, stirring constantly. Add carrots and spinach. Pour into eight 5-ounce custard cups. Bake at 325° till knife inserted halfway between center and edge comes out clean, about 20 to 25 minutes. Makes 8 servings.

SPINACH NOODLE—A type of pasta, also known as a green noodle, that gets its characteristic color and flavor from the finely chopped spinach that is added to the basic dough. When making spinach noodles at home, use an electric blender to chop the spinach, if possible. Commercially made spinach noodles in one or more of the classic shapes are found in Italian food stores and some supermarkets.

SPINY LOBSTER—Another name for the crayfish or rock lobster. (See *Crayfish, Lobster* for additional information.)

SPIRIT—A highly alcoholic liquid that is made by distilling the fermented juice of foods such as grains, sugars, fruits, and vegetables. Brandy, gin, rum, vodka, whiskey, and liqueurs are among spirits used both as beverages and as recipe ingredients. (See also *Wines and Spirits*.)

SPIT—A large skewer or turning rod on which food is balanced for rotisserie cooking. (See also *Rotisserie*.)

SPLIT—1. To cut a food into two parts or to divide a food into its natural parts by applying pressure or a sharp point to a seam or natural line of division. 2. An ice cream sundae that derives its name from the fruit cut in half lengthwise and arranged on the bottom of the dessert dish. 3. The name given to the small beverage bottle that contains about six ounces.

Chickens are split lengthwise for broiling or grilling. English muffins are split with a fork before toasting, and peas that did not separate during drying are split mechanically to make split peas.

For dessert splits, several scoops of ice cream, either vanilla or assorted flavors, are placed in a row on top of the fruit. Sundae toppings are spooned over ice cream and fruit, and the dessert is capped with whipped cream, chopped nuts, and a cherry. Bananas are popular for splits because the long strips of fruit are attractive and the flavor is delicious with many flavors of ice cream and toppings.

The split bottle is mainly used for wine, especially champagne, and holds about one-quarter the amount of a regular bottle.

SPLIT PEA—Dry peas, either green or yellow, from which the thin skins have been removed, allowing the seeds to split apart at the natural breaking point. Some of the splitting takes place while the peas are drying; the balance, during processing.

Soaking split peas before cooking is necessary only if you wish to retain the shape in a finished dish such as when baking them like dry beans with pork. First, add split peas to boiling water; boil two minutes. Remove from heat; cover and let soak for a half hour. (See also *Pea*.)

Split Pea Soup

> 1 pound green or yellow split
>   peas (2¼ cups)
> 2 quarts cold water
> 1 meaty ham bone (1½ pounds)
> 1½ cups sliced onion
> 1 teaspoon salt
> ½ teaspoon pepper
> ¼ teaspoon dried marjoram
>   leaves, crushed
>
> • • •
>
> 1 cup diced carrots
> 1 cup diced celery

In a large saucepan cover split peas with the 2 quarts cold water. Add ham bone, sliced onion, salt, pepper, and marjoram. Bring mixture to boiling; cover, reduce heat, and simmer (*don't boil*) 1½ hours. Stir soup mixture occasionally. Remove ham bone from soup; cut off meat and dice. Return meat to soup; add diced carrots and celery. Cook slowly, uncovered, 30 to 40 minutes. Serves 6 to 8.

SPONGE—1. A light, frothy dessert that gains its lightness and porous texture from the air incorporated into it by folding in beaten egg whites or gelatin, which is whipped when partially set.

2. Yeast bread dough after the first stage of rising in the "sponge" method of breadmaking. A batter of yeast, liquid, and some of the flour, allowed to rise until bubbly, resembles a sponge. Then, the remaining ingredients are added and breadmaking proceeds as usual. (See *Bread, Dessert* for additional information.)

SPONGE CAKE—A moist, yellow cake containing egg yolks that is traditionally made without shortening and which gets most of its volume from the air trapped in the egg whites folded into the batter.

In years past, before home freezers made freezing egg yolks practical, homemakers baked the egg yolk version of sponge cake as a companion to an angel food cake that was made from the egg whites. Today, most sponge cake recipes call for whole eggs, but occasionally you will find a recipe that uses more egg yolks.

When mixing a sponge cake, beat the egg yolks and the egg whites separately. First, beat the yolks and a liquid, such as fruit juice like orange or pineapple juice, until thick and lemon-colored. Then add flour and part of the sugar to the yolk mixture. Next, beat together the whites, cream of tartar, if used, and the remaining sugar. Finally, gently fold the batter into the egg whites, retaining as much air as possible. The cake is customarily baked in an ungreased tube cake pan.

Orange Sponge Cake

  1⅓ cups sifted cake flour
  ⅓ cup sugar
  6 egg yolks
  1 tablespoon grated orange peel
  ½ cup orange juice
  ⅔ cup sugar
  ¼ teaspoon salt
  6 egg whites
  1 teaspoon cream of tartar
  ½ cup sugar

Combine sifted cake flour and the ⅓ cup sugar. Set aside. Beat egg yolks till thick and lemon-colored. Add the grated orange peel and orange juice; beat till very thick. Gradually add the ⅔ cup sugar and salt, beating constantly. Sift flour mixture over egg yolk mixture, a little at a time, folding just till blended. Wash beaters. Beat egg whites with cream of tartar till soft peaks form. Gradually add remaining ½ cup sugar, beating till stiff peaks form. Thoroughly but gently fold yolk mixture into whites. Bake the cake in an *ungreased* 10-inch tube pan at 325° about 55 minutes. Invert cake in pan; cool.

Almond Brittle Torte

  1½ cups sifted all-purpose flour
  ¾ cup sugar
  8 egg yolks
  ¼ cup cold water
  1 tablespoon lemon juice
  1 teaspoon vanilla
  8 egg whites
  1 teaspoon cream of tartar
  1 teaspoon salt
  • • •
  ¾ cup sugar
  ½ teaspoon instant coffee powder
  2 tablespoons light corn syrup
  2 tablespoons water
  1½ teaspoons *sifted* baking soda
  • • •
  2 cups whipping cream
  1 tablespoon sugar
  2 teaspoons vanilla
  ½ cup toasted almond halves

To make sponge cake: Sift flour and ¾ cup sugar into mixing bowl. Make well in center; add egg yolks, ¼ cup water, lemon juice, and 1 teaspoon vanilla. Beat till batter is smooth.

Beat egg whites with cream of tartar and salt till very soft peaks form; add ¾ cup sugar gradually, two tablespoons at a time. Continue beating till stiff peaks form. Fold egg yolk batter gently into egg white meringue.

Pour batter into an *ungreased* 10-inch tube pan. Carefully cut through batter, going around the tube 5 or 6 times with knife to break large air bubbles. Bake at 350° till top springs back when touched lightly, about 50 to 55 minutes. Invert pan; cool.

To make almond brittle topping: While cake bakes, mix ¾ cup sugar, coffee powder, corn syrup, and 2 tablespoons water in a saucepan. Cook to soft-crack stage (285° to 290°). Remove from heat; add soda at once. Stir vigorously, but only till mixture blends and pulls away from pan. Pour into buttered 8x8x2-inch pan. *Do not spread or stir.* Cool. Tap bottom of pan to remove candy. Crush into coarse crumbs.

To assemble torte: Remove cake from pan and split crosswise in 4 equal layers. Whip cream with 1 tablespoon sugar and 2 teaspoons vanilla; spread *half* between cake layers and the remainder over top and sides. Sprinkle surface with candy crumbs. Trim with almond halves by inserting them porcupine-style all over cake.

Sponge cakemaking tip

Remember to wash beaters and bowl used for egg yolks before using them to whip whites. Any trace of fat from the yolks will prevent the egg whites from whipping properly.

Numerous serving possibilities are yours with a sponge cake. Dust it with confectioners' sugar, or frost it, top it with ice cream and sweetened fruit, or use it as the basis for elegant desserts such as an Almond Brittle Torte.

By varying the ingredients or mixing techniques, you can produce many cake versions of excellent volume and flavor.

Although originally sponge cakes did not contain leavening other than the air whipped into the egg whites today, baking powder is commonly used to ensure good volume in the finished cake. Likewise, foam cakes by definition do not contain shortening, but there are delicious versions of sponge cake that count small amounts of butter—for flavor and tenderness—among their list of ingredients.

Not all sponge cakes are the tall, tube cakes. For example, the practical and versatile Hot Milk Sponge Cake is baked in a square pan or a single-layer cake pan. Other variations include ladyfingers—which are actually miniature sponge cakes baked in special pans—and jelly rolls, which are made from sponge cake batter baked in large, flat pans. (See also *Cake.*)

Create a luscious dessert by spreading whipped cream atop and between slices of golden sponge cake. Crushed candy and almonds add the finishing touches to Almond Brittle Torte.

Pineapple Fluff Cake

6 egg yolks
½ cup pineapple juice
1 tablespoon lemon juice
1½ cups sifted cake flour
1 teaspoon baking powder
¾ cup sugar
6 egg whites
¼ teaspoon salt
¾ cup sugar

Beat egg yolks till thick and lemon-colored. Add pineapple and lemon juices; beat till well combined. Sift cake flour, baking powder, and ¾ cup sugar together twice. Add to egg yolk mixture. Wash the beaters.

Beat egg whites with salt till soft peaks form; gradually add remaining ¾ cup sugar, beating till stiff peaks form. Fold batter into egg whites. Bake in *ungreased* 10-inch tube pan at 325° about 1 hour. Invert; cool.

Hot Milk Sponge Cake

1 cup sifted all-purpose flour
1 teaspoon baking powder
¼ teaspoon salt
½ cup milk
2 tablespoons butter
2 eggs
1 cup sugar
1 teaspoon vanilla

Sift together flour, baking powder, and salt. Heat milk and butter till butter melts; keep hot. Beat eggs till thick and lemon-colored, 3 minutes on high speed of electric mixer. Gradually add sugar, beating constantly at medium speed for 4 to 5 minutes. Add sifted dry ingredients to egg mixture; stir just till blended. Slowly stir in hot milk mixture and vanilla; blend well. Turn into greased and floured 9x9x2-inch baking pan. Bake at 350° for 25 to 30 minutes. Do not invert. Cool in pan.

SPOON—**1.** A wooden, metal, or plastic implement consisting of a small, shallow bowl with a handle, used for cooking or eating. It is useful for stirring, creaming, and transferring foods. **2.** The act of transferring a mixture using a spoon.

SPOON BREAD—A baked cornmeal mixture the consistency of porridge. Spoon bread, a popular dish in the South, is served warm topped with butter in place of rice or potatoes with the main course.

Spoon Bread

1 cup cornmeal
3 cups milk
1 teaspoon salt
1 teaspoon baking powder
2 tablespoons salad oil
3 well-beaten egg yolks
3 stiffly beaten egg whites

Cook cornmeal and *2 cups* of the milk till the consistency of mush; remove from heat. Add salt, baking bowder, oil, and remaining milk. Add well-beaten yolks; fold in stiffly beaten egg whites. Bake in a greased 2-quart casserole at 325° about 1 hour. Makes 6 servings.

SPRAT—A small, saltwater fish related to the herring. Sprats are also called brisling and are used as sardines. They live along the coasts of Europe and grow to a maximum of five inches in length.

Sprats are sold fresh, canned, pickled, and smoked. (See *Herring, Sardine* for additional information.)

SPREAD—**1.** Any food or mixture of foods that is soft enough to be distributed over the surface of a food such as bread or crackers with a knife or spatula. **2.** To distribute butter, frosting, filling, or mixture over the surface of a food.

Spreadable mixtures take many forms. Butter, margarine, peanut butter, and jam are popular spreads for bread. So are soft cheeses, deviled ham, seafood mixtures, and many sandwich fillings or canapé toppings. Appetizer spreads are sometimes packed into a small, buttered bowl or mold. When chilled, the mixture sets up enough to retain the shape of the mold but stays soft enough so that guests can spread it easily on crisp crackers or toast rounds. Smoothing a frosting over top and sides of a cake and buttering bread or toast are examples of spreading techniques.

Clam Spread

A peppy seafood appetizer spread flecked with bits of chopped, unpeeled cucumber—

1 7½-ounce can minced clams
1 clove garlic
1 8-ounce package cream cheese, softened
1 teaspoon lemon juice
1 teaspoon Worcestershire sauce
¼ teaspoon salt
Dash pepper
½ cup finely chopped, unpeeled cucumber
Snipped parsley

Drain clams, reserving 1 tablespoon liquid. Rub mixing bowl with cut clove of garlic. In bowl blend clams, clam liquid, and next 6 ingredients. Chill. Turn into a serving bowl; sprinkle with parsley. Makes 1½ cups.

Crab and Cheese Spread

1 6-ounce package smoky cheese spread
1 3-ounce can deviled crab spread
¼ cup chopped pimiento-stuffed green olives
2 teaspoons milk

Combine all ingredients in a bowl. Blend thoroughly with electric mixer. Spread mixture on melba toast or unsalted crackers, or stuff mixture into celery sections. Makes 1¼ cups.

Zesty Chicken Spread

1 5-ounce can chicken spread
2 tablespoons mayonnaise or salad dressing
1½ teaspoons prepared horseradish
¾ teaspoon Worcestershire sauce
¼ teaspoon dry mustard
¼ cup chopped almonds, toasted
1 tablespoon milk

Blend all ingredients. Chill. Thin with additional milk, if desired. Spread on crackers or party rye bread slices. Garnish with crisp bacon, if desired. Makes ¾ cup spread.

Ham Salad Sandwich Spread

A blender-quick way to use leftover ham—

Put ½ cup mayonnaise; 1 large sweet pickle; 1 small stalk celery, sliced; and ½ teaspoon prepared mustard in blender. Blend till pickle and celery are chopped. Add 1½ cups cubed, fully cooked ham, ½ cup at a time. Blend after each addition to chop ham. Chill. Makes 1⅔ cups.

Olive-Cheese Ball

1 8-ounce package cream cheese, softened
4 ounces blue cheese
¼ cup butter, softened
½ cup chopped, pitted, ripe olives well drained
1 tablespoon snipped chives
¼ cup chopped walnuts

Cream together cheeses and butter. Stir in olives and chives. Chill slightly. Form into ball. Chill thoroughly. Press nuts into ball. Trim with parsley, if desired. Makes 2½ cups.

SPRIG—In cooking, a small shoot or leafy twig of fresh herb or plant used in a bouquet garni or to decorate food. Mint and parsley sprigs are the most familiar examples. (See also *Bouquet Garni.*)

An Olive-Cheese Ball is one of the best cracker spreads ever. Flavor and spreadability come from blue and cream cheeses.

SPRINGERLE *(shpring' uhr lē)* — A thick, hard, anise-flavored cookie with a raised design made by pressing rolled dough with a carved block or rolling pin. The cookies are a German Christmas tradition.

The carved blocks or rolling pins used for making the cookies may have simple or intricate patterns, depending on the skills of the craftsman. Trees, people, stylized flowers, or Christmas designs are popular patterns. Many old, beautifully carved molds hold places of honor in museum collections of cooking utensils.

Because of the square corners on the molds, the finished cookies are square or rectangular in shape. A sharp knife is used to cut the cookies apart before baking. Baking time is watched carefully so that the cookies are not brown when done, but emerge from the oven a delicate yellow color. (See also *Christmas.*)

Springerle

> 4 eggs
> 1 pound sifted confectioners' sugar (about 4 cups)
> 20 drops anise oil
> 4 cups sifted all-purpose flour
> 1 teaspoon baking soda
> Crushed aniseed

With electric mixer, beat eggs till light. Gradually add sugar; continue beating on high speed till mixture is like soft meringue, 15 minutes. Add anise oil. Sift together flour and soda; blend into mixture at low speed. Cover bowl with foil; let stand 15 minutes.

Divide dough in thirds. On lightly floured surface, roll each piece in an 8-inch square, a little more than ¼ inch thick. Let stand 1 minute. Lightly dust springerle rolling pin or mold with flour; roll or press hard enough to make a clear design. With sharp knife, cut cookies apart. Place on floured surface; cover with a towel and let stand overnight.

Grease cookie sheets and sprinkle with 1½ to 2 teaspoons crushed aniseed. Brush excess flour from cookies; with finger, rub underside of each cookie very lightly with cold water and place on cookie sheets. Bake at 300° till light straw color, about 20 minutes. Makes 6 dozen cookies. Store in airtight container.

Beautiful, hand-carved blocks are used to imprint the design on Springerle, an anise-flavored Christmas cookie from Germany.

Springerle can also be imprinted by using a specially carved rolling pin on which the designs are marked off into squares. After rolling the pin over the dough, use a sharp knife to separate the cookies.

SPRINGFORM PAN—A straight-sided, round baking pan in two sections held together with a spring latch. When food is to be removed, the latch is opened and the sides lifted off leaving the food on the bottom section. A springform pan is used for cheesecakes and other desserts that would not lift out intact from a standard pan. This Strawberry-Rhubarb Cheesecake uses a springform pan to advantage.

Strawberry-Rhubarb Cheesecake

  1½ cups zwieback crumbs
  ⅓ cup sugar
  ¾ teaspoon ground cinnamon
  6 tablespoons butter, melted
  3 well-beaten eggs
  2 8-ounce packages cream
      cheese, softened
  1 cup sugar
  2 teaspoons vanilla
  ½ teaspoon ground nutmeg
  ¼ teaspoon salt
  3 cups dairy sour cream
  1 cup fresh rhubarb, cut in 1-inch
      pieces (¼ pound)
  ⅓ cup sugar
  1 tablespoon cornstarch
      Dash salt
      Red food coloring
  2 cups fresh strawberries, halved

Unlatch the clamps on a springform pan to release the sides before lifting the top section away from cheesecake or dessert.

Combine first 4 ingredients. Mix till crumbly; press onto bottom and about 1½ inches up sides of buttered 9-inch springform pan. Chill.

Combine next 6 ingredients; beat smooth. Blend in sour cream. Pour into crust. Bake at 375° just till set, about 40 to 45 minutes. Filling will be soft. Cool to room temperature.

In small saucepan combine rhubarb, ⅓ cup sugar, and ½ cup water. Bring to boiling; reduce heat. Simmer, uncovered, till almost tender, about 1 minute, being careful not to break up rhubarb. Remove from heat. Drain, reserving syrup. Add water if necessary to make ¾ cup. Mix cornstarch, dash salt, and 2 tablespoons cold water; add to syrup mixture. Cook and stir till thickened and bubbly; cook 1 minute more. Remove from heat; stir in 7 or 8 drops food coloring. Cool to room temperature. Arrange strawberries and rhubarb on cheesecake; spoon glaze over. Chill. Serves 12.

SPRINKLE—To scatter drops of liquid, crumbs, seasonings, or fine particles of one food lightly over another food.

SPRING LAMB—A designation for a lamb marketed during spring, summer, and early fall. The term, also known as genuine spring lamb, is used to distinguish this year's lambs from last year's.

Spring lamb is tender meat that is prized for its delicate flavor. Most shoulder, leg, and rib cuts can be cooked by dry heat in an oven, a broiler, or on an outdoor grill. Sometimes, however, very lean chops or cubed lamb are braised. (See also *Lamb*.)

Lamb Chops Supreme

In large skillet slowly brown 6 shoulder or sirloin lamb chops, ½ inch thick, in small amount of hot shortening. Season with salt and pepper. Drain off fat. Add one 10½-ounce can condensed consommé; ½ cup chopped celery; ½ cup sliced green onion with tops; and ½ teaspoon dried thyme leaves, crushed. Cover; simmer till meat is tender, about 40 to 45 minutes.

Stack chops to one side. Drain one 3-ounce can broiled, chopped mushrooms, reserving liquid. Blend liquid into 3 tablespoons all-purpose flour. Gradually stir flour mixture into consommé in skillet; cook and stir till thickened and bubbly. Add mushrooms and 1 tablespoon dried parsley flakes; heat through. Serves 6.

SPRITZ, SPRITS — A rich, Scandinavian butter cookie that is shaped by forcing soft dough through a cookie press. Sometimes, the dough for spritz cookies is tinted or the cookies are sprinkled with colored sugars before they are baked.

Although not difficult to use, a cookie press takes patience and practice. Be sure to follow the press manufacturer's directions carefully. It is important that the disk is placed in the press so that the cutting edge will be against the dough, thus, releasing the cookie easily after pressing. Another hint that works with many types of cookie presses is to give the handle a reverse half turn after pressing each of the cookies onto the cookie sheet.

The cookie press comes equipped with several disks, each producing a different design. The designs usually include a ribbon, Christmas tree, star, or perhaps a camel. Rings and wreaths can be made by pressing the dough in a long, slender ribbon, cutting the ribbon into four-inch strips and shaping easily into a circle.

Spritz

    1½ **cups butter or margarine**
     1 **cup sugar**
     1 **egg**
     1 **teaspoon vanilla**
    ½ **teaspoon almond extract**
     4 **cups sifted all-purpose flour**
     1 **teaspoon baking powder**

Thoroughly cream butter and sugar. Add egg, vanilla, and almond extract; beat well. Sift together flour and baking powder; add gradually to creamed mixture, mixing to smooth dough. Do not chill the dough.

Force dough through cookie press onto *ungreased* cookie sheet. Bake at 400° about 8 minutes; cool. Makes 6 dozen cookies.

For perfectly shaped spritz cookies

Be sure to let the cookie sheet cool between batches of cookies. Dough pressed onto a hot cookie sheet will melt out of shape.

SPUMONI, SPUMONE *(spuh mō' nē)* — A multilayered Italian ice cream This rainbow-hued frozen dessert is composed of strips of ice cream of various flavors and colors packed into a mold. Pieces of nuts or fruits may be incorporated into one or more of the layers. At serving time, the ice cream is unmolded and sliced across the layers so that each serving contains a strip of each color.

The basic ice cream mixture is rich. Each layer contributes its own flavor and color to a beautiful and delectable dessert. While there is a certain degree of latitude in the number of layers, a creamy, chocolate, a green, and a pink layer are fairly typical. The creamy layer is often flavored with rum, which gives spumoni an almost eggnog quality. The chocolate layer may be ice cream or a smooth chocolaty-flavored whipped cream mixture.

The green layer gets its characteristic flavor from finely chopped pistachio nuts. Even when almonds are substituted, the layer is still tinted green. The pink layer derives its color and flavor from the fruit, often strawberries or raspberries, used to prepare it. The color can be deepened, if desired, by adding a few drops of red food coloring before piling into the mold.

Commercially made spumoni is frequently packed in rectangular cartons, which make the frozen dessert easy to slice. However, when preparing spumoni at home, you can create a more spectacular effect by using a two-quart metal or heatproof glass mixing bowl for the mold. Attractive, wedge-shaped portions show off the colored layers to the best advantage.

Although spumoni is a time-consuming dessert to prepare because time must be allowed for each layer to freezer before the next one is added, the finished mold is a work of art and well worth every minute spent. (See *Ice Cream, Italian Cookery* for additional information.)

An Italian spectacular

Gather compliments galore with colorful→ Italian Spumoni. Trim the elegant ice cream mold with tinted whipped cream.

Italian Spumoni

1½ pints French vanilla ice cream
1 teaspoon rum flavoring
6 candied *or* maraschino cherries

1½ pints French vanilla ice cream
½ teaspoon almond flavoring
Few drops green food coloring
⅓ cup finely chopped, unblanched
   almond *or* pistachio nuts

¾ cup whipping cream
⅓ cup instant cocoa powder mix

• • •

1 10-ounce package frozen red
   raspberries, thawed
¾ cup whipping cream
⅓ cup sifted confectioners' sugar
Few drops red food coloring

To make eggnog layer: For mold, chill a 2-quart metal or glass bowl in the freezer. In another mixing bowl stir in 1½ pints ice cream just to soften; stir in rum flavoring. Refreeze only till workable. With chilled spoon, spread quickly in layer over bottom and sides of the *previously chilled* bowl, being sure ice cream comes all the way to top. (If ice cream tends to slip, refreeze in bowl till workable.) Circle cherries in bottom of bowl. Freeze till firm.

To make pistachio layer: Stir remaining 1½ pints ice cream just to soften; stir in almond flavoring, green food coloring, and nuts. Refreeze only till workable. Quickly spread over inside of first layer. Freeze till firm.

To make chocolate layer: Combine ¾ cup whipping cream and cocoa; whip till peaks hold. Quickly spread over pistachio layer. Return to freezer; freeze till firm.

To make raspberry layer: Drain berries (do not use syrup); sieve berries. Mix together ½ *cup* of the whipping cream, confectioners' sugar, and dash salt; whip to soft peaks. Fold in sieved berries. (Add a few drops red food coloring, if needed.) Pile into center of mold; smooth top. Cover the mold tightly with foil. Freeze 6 hours or overnight.

To serve: Whip remaining cream; tint pink. Peel off foil. Invert on *chilled* plate. To loosen, rub bowl with towel wrung out in hot water; lift off bowl. Trim with pink-tinted whipped cream piped on with pastry tube. Add frosted grapes, if desired. Cut spumoni in small wedges. Makes 12 to 16 servings.

How to pack spumoni

Stir vanilla ice cream to soften. Blend in flavoring. Spread ice cream up sides of large mixing bowl or mold. Freeze firm.

Working quickly, spread pistachio layer inside mold. Freeze. Repeat with other layers, freezing mold after each addition.

Freeze Spumoni firm—six hours or overnight. To serve, invert mold on *chilled* platter and use a hot towel to loosen ice cream.

SPROUT, SPROUTS — 1. The edible shoot of certain plants. 2. With "s" added, a colloquial word for brussels sprouts that is occasionally applied also to bean sprouts. (See *Bean Sprouts, Brussels Sprouts* for additional information.)

SPUN SUGAR — Sugar syrup, plain or colored, that is boiled to the long-thread stage then quickly drawn, a little at a time, into long threads. The hot syrup is dropped in a thin stream from a special implement, back and forth between two bars. Strands harden quickly but can be bunched and shaped into nests or rosettes, which are often used to hold ice cream or as decorations for fancy desserts.

SQUAB — A young pigeon, not more than four weeks old, weighing about one pound. Although squab are difficult to locate, ready-to-cook birds are marketed frozen. If there is a hunter in your family, you may have wild squab to enjoy.

Through the centuries, these young pigeons have been on the menu for gigantic feasts and humbler family fare alike. They were roasted for diners' pleasure at Roman banquets, and, as cooking became more sophisticated over the years, they were sauced or stuffed with forcemeat before being presented at the tables. Cooks doing their marketing in London in 1272 found pigeons selling three for a penny.

In America, during colonial times and in the movement of pioneers westward, pigeons were among the native food supply. During migration of the birds, rural families, city dwellers, and travelers ate the tender meat daily in some form. The passenger pigeon was one of the major species used for food. The supply seemed inexhaustible at that time, but, this was not the case. By 1914 the species was extinct.

Today, squab, though not so plentiful, is nonetheless delicious when available and cooked properly. Because the meat is tender, the birds can be fried or roasted on a spit. Stuffing and roasting is another popular method of preparation. Since there is little internal fat in the young squab, it is delicious cut up and cooked in a seasoned sauce, which preserves juiciness and adds flavor. (See also *Game*.)

Savory Squab

4 12- to 14-ounce ready-to-cook squab, split lengthwise
2 tablespoons butter or margarine
1 tablespoon finely chopped onion
1½ teaspoons chicken-flavored gravy base
¼ cup dry sherry
2 teaspoons cornstarch

Brown squab in butter in large skillet about 10 minutes. Add onion, gravy base, ½ cup water, and dash pepper; bring to boiling. Simmer, covered, till tender, about 30 minutes. Remove squab to warm serving platter. Skim fat from sauce. Combine wine and cornstarch; blend with mixture in skillet. Cook and stir until mixture thickens and bubbles. Serve sauce over squab. Makes 4 servings.

Squab on a Spit

2 12- to 14-ounce ready-to-cook squab
¼ cup currant jelly
1 teaspoon prepared mustard

Mount squab on spit. Attach spit to rotisserie in broiler and broil for 45 minutes. Brush occasionally with Currant Glaze the last 15 minutes of cooking time. Makes 2 servings.

Currant Glaze: Combine currant jelly and mustard in small saucepan; heat, stirring until jelly melts and sauce is heated.

Sweet-Sour Squab

4 12- to 14-ounce ready-to-cook squab, split in quarters
¼ cup butter or margarine
¼ cup sliced green onions
¼ cup tarragon vinegar
1 tablespoon sugar
¼ teaspoon salt

Brown squab on all sides in butter in large skillet. Add onion and cook until tender but not brown. Combine vinegar, sugar, and salt; add to skillet. Cover and simmer until tender, about 30 to 35 minutes. Remove squab to platter and serve. Makes 4 servings.

SQUASH

*Shapely, colorful, and nutritious, these vegetables
add seasonal splendor to a meal.*

Many foods commonly cooked in America today are descendants of the American Indian dishes. Squash is just one of these foods. The Indians named squash *askuta-squash*, which means "eating raw or uncooked." Although this may be the manner in which they used squash, our tastes have developed a preference for it cooked.

Squash, along with muskmelons, watermelons, cucumbers, and pumpkins, belongs to the gourd family. The plants of this family are all vine-growing and are characterized by large leaves and tendrils that attach to other objects for support.

This vegetable is classified into two main groups—summer and winter squash —according to how fast the squash grows and at what stage it is harvested. Within these groups, there are numerous varieties that differ from one another in size, shape, color, and texture. Some are about the size of a cucumber; others, as big as a watermelon. The varietal names are often indicative of their shape—acorn, turban, and crookneck, for example. Skin colors are light to dark green and yellow to bright orange. One variety of squash even has a blue cast. Textures vary from crisp and moist to soft and dry.

Like tomatoes and kidney beans, squash are native to the Western Hemisphere. They have been utilized and cultivated by Indians for centuries—first by the South American and later by Central and North American tribes. The earliest cultivators

Squash in profusion

← From the arrival of summer to the passing of autumn, there's an array of fresh squash varieties harvested to suit every taste.

raised squash primarily for the edible seeds since it was the seeds rather than the pulp that made up the largest portion of these early squash varieties. During the settlement of Virginia, Capt. John Smith found the Indians raising and eating a squash variety that they called *macocks*. Not until the latter part of the 1500s, however, did European explorers take squash back to their homelands. In areas such as Italy, squash became so popular that these people developed several varieties of their own, such as zucchini. In northern Europe, squash plants did not thrive as well as they did in the south.

How squash are produced: In the United States, squash are grown both commercially and in home gardens. In colder regions, the plants must be cultivated as annuals since they are quite susceptible to freezing temperatures, while in areas where warm temperatures remain year round, squash are perennials. They prefer light, sandy, yet fairly rich soil.

Squash seeds are planted in "hills." (These are not mounds as the name implies, but depressed areas where water collects during a rainfall.) To get a head start on the growing season in the north, plants are sometimes started indoors a few weeks before the last winter frost. Some other varieties are seeded outdoors and mature in a short growing season.

Squash harvest time depends on the variety of squash. Summer squash are picked a few days after they develop so that the rinds and seeds are still tender. Winter squash varieties are allowed to fully mature on the vines and are picked before the first frost of winter. Even though the rinds are hard, winter squash must be picked carefully to avoid bruises.

Summer squash

These quick-growing vegetables are so soft-shelled and seeded that they can be eaten shell and all. Choose one of the many varieties to highlight your meals.

Nutritional value: Summer squash have a higher percentage of water than do their winter relatives. One-half cup of cooked summer squash adds only 15 calories to a meal while providing a fair amount of vitamin A and the B vitamin niacin. Moderate amounts of vitamin C are present too.

Types of summer squash: Because the shape, size, and color of each variety is so diverse, squash are easy to identify. A description of the summer squash most frequently used follows:

Chayote is pear-shaped and about acorn squash size. The rind is soft and pale green; the inner flesh is tinged with green, too. This variety has a single, large seed that is soft enough to eat.

Crookneck has a curved or straight neck and a bulging base. The yellow rind is bumpy; the pulp is yellow and grainy.

Cymling, Scallop, or Pattypan develops into a scallop-edge disk. The smooth or slightly rough skin is green when young but increasingly whitens as it matures. The interior flesh is green-tinged. There is also a yellow form.

Italian or Zucchini, first cultivated in Italy, is shaped like a straight cylinder that graduates to a slightly larger size at the blossom end. The skin is dark green and is speckled with pale yellow, stripelike markings. The greenish-white flesh is very fine.

Squash seeds as food

Although South Americans relish the taste of squash as much as North Americans, they also make good use of the seeds. Sometimes the seeds are roasted and eaten like peanuts. Or, the shelled seeds are ground for use in sauces. Squash seeds ground to a paste and sweetened are even the basic ingredient for specially molded and decorated confections.

How to select and store: Although fresh summer squash are available during a major portion of the year in some localities, the peak crops are marketed during the summer. Some summer varieties are also available in the frozen state.

In selecting summer squash, the more immature the squash, the better. Choose squash that are heavy for their size, firm well-formed, and glossy. The rinds should be fresh-looking according to the variety. Avoid hard and dull-rinded squash.

Because of their immaturity, summer squash do not keep well. Refrigerate them in the vegetable crisper for short periods only. For best flavor and texture, use summer squash as soon as possible.

How to prepare: Because the rinds and seeds of summer squash are tender they are not removed when cooked. To prepare the squash for eating, wash but do not peel. Cut off the stem and blossom ends.

The squash may be left whole or be halved, sliced, or cubed as desired. (Cut Chayote squash right through the seed.)

The texture of summer squash is best when slightly crisp so that the pieces retain their shape. For slices and cubes, cook, covered, in a small amount of boiling, salted water for 8 to 15 minutes.

How to use: For lightly seasoned summer squash, salt, pepper, a dash sugar, and butter are usually added to the cooking liquid. If you wish, simply stir-fry squash slices in sizzling seasoned butter. Other flavorings used to enhance the delicateness of summer squash include beef or chicken bouillon cubes, Parmesan cheese, basil, bay leaf, mace, marjoram, mustard, and rosemary. Vegetable combinations using summer squash are popular, too—tomatoes, onion, and green pepper are typical ingredients used with summer squash.

Whole or halved summer squash perform a dual role as vegetable and serving dish when filled with a savory stuffing. Try different stuffing mixtures based on another vegetable, meat, or bread.

Summer squash need not always be cooked before eating. Marinate uncooked slices in a piquant salad dressing, or use the raw pieces in a lettuce or meat salad.

Savory Vegetable Trio

  ½ pound fresh green beans, cut up
  ½ cup chopped onion
  ¼ cup snipped parsley
   1 teaspoon salt
  ¼ teaspoon dried thyme leaves,
      crushed
  ¼ teaspoon ground sage
  ⅛ teaspoon pepper
   2 cups cubed yellow summer squash
   3 large tomatoes, peeled and
      cut in wedges
   2 tablespoons butter or margarine

In saucepan combine beans, onion, parsley, salt, thyme, sage, pepper, and ½ cup water. Bring to boiling. Cover; reduce heat and simmer 10 minutes. Add squash; simmer, covered, till vegetables are tender, about 10 minutes more. Drain. Add tomatoes and butter; cover and heat through. Makes 6 servings.

Summer Squash Skillet

  ½ cup chopped onion
  ½ cup chopped green pepper
   2 tablespoons butter or margarine
   1 tablespoon sugar
   1 teaspoon all-purpose flour
   1 teaspoon salt
  ¼ teaspoon pepper
   2 cups cubed pattypan squash
      (about ¾ pound)
   3 medium tomatoes, peeled and
      cut in wedges

Cook onion and green pepper in butter till tender; stir in sugar, flour, salt, and pepper. Add squash and tomatoes. Cook over low heat just till vegetables are tender. Serves 4 to 6.

Zucchini squash has become one of the most popular of the summer squash varieties. A crisp texture and mild flavor are its decidedly appealing characteristics. Coupled with zippy cheeses or with fresh vegetables such as tomatoes and mushrooms, a pleasing texture and color contrast is achieved. Add zucchini slices to scrambled eggs, then sprinkle with Parmesan cheese for a delicious and easy supper.

Zucchini Sweet–Sour Medley

   2 tablespoons salad oil
   4 teaspoons cornstarch
   1 tablespoon sugar
   1 tablespoon instant minced onion
   2 teaspoons prepared mustard
  ¾ teaspoon salt
  ½ teaspoon garlic salt
    Dash pepper

      •   •   •

  ½ cup water
  ¼ cup vinegar
   4 cups bias-sliced zucchini
      squash (3 or 4 zucchini)
   1 cup bias-sliced celery

      •   •   •

   2 tomatoes, quartered

In a medium skillet stir together salad oil, cornstarch, sugar, instant minced onion, prepared mustard, salt, garlic salt, and pepper. Add water and vinegar to seasoning mixture; cook and stir till mixture thickens and bubbles.

    Add zucchini and celery; cook, covered, till vegetables are crisp-tender, about 7 to 8 minutes. Stir occasionally. Add tomatoes and cook the mixture, covered, till heated through, 2 to 3 minutes more. Makes 6 servings.

Brown sugar-glazed apples spiced with ginger are mounded in acorn squash halves to give Apple-Filled Squash their golden glow.

Skillet Squash

2 medium zucchini squash
1 medium onion
2 teaspoons butter or margarine
½ teaspoon salt
   Dash coarsely ground pepper

. . .

1 medium tomato, cut in wedges
1 2-ounce can sliced mushrooms,
   drained

Scrub squash in cold water; cut off ends. Cut into thin, crosswise slices (about 2 cups). Thinly slice onion and separate into rings. Melt the 2 teaspoons butter in a 12-inch skillet; add salt and pepper. Cook onion in butter till crisp-tender. Add the squash.

Cover and cook 6 minutes, stirring occasionally. Add tomato and mushrooms. Continue cooking, covered, till tomato and mushrooms are heated through and squash is crisp-tender, about 4 minutes. Remove to serving bowl with slotted spoon. Makes 6 servings.

Saucy Zucchini

Has a cheese and buttered crumb topping—

1 pound zucchini squash, thinly
   sliced (about 4 cups)
2 medium onions, thinly sliced
   (about 1 cup)
2 tablespoons butter or margarine
2 tablespoons all-purpose flour
1 teaspoon salt
   Dash pepper
1 cup milk

. . .

2 ounces sharp process American
   cheese, shredded (½ cup)
½ cup buttered bread crumbs

Cook zucchini and onion in small amount boiling water till tender. In a saucepan melt butter; blend in flour, salt, and pepper. Add the milk all at once; cook, stirring constantly, until mixture thickens and bubbles. Combine the sauce with the cooked vegetables.

Place the mixture in a 10x6x1¾-inch baking dish. Top with shredded cheese and then with buttered crumbs. Bake at 350° for about 25 minutes. Makes 4 to 6 servings.

Zucchini Florentine

Sliced squash bakes in a well-seasoned custard—

6 small zucchini squash, cut
   in ¼-inch slices
2 tablespoons butter or margarine

. . .

1 cup evaporated milk
3 slightly beaten eggs
1 teaspoon salt
¼ teaspoon garlic salt
¼ teaspoon pepper

. . .

¼ teaspoon paprika

Place zucchini in a 1½-quart casserole; dot with butter. Bake at 400° till zucchini is partially cooked but still crisp, about 15 minutes. Combine milk, eggs, salt, garlic salt, and pepper; pour over zucchini. Sprinkle with paprika. Set casserole in a shallow pan, filling pan to 1 inch with hot water.

Bake at 350° till a knife inserted halfway between center and edge comes out clean, about 40 minutes. Makes 6 servings.

Cheese-Sauced Zucchini Fritters

A deluxe side dish—

1½ cups sifted all-purpose flour
 2 teaspoons baking powder
 ¾ teaspoon salt
 1 cup milk
 1 beaten egg
 1 cup finely chopped zucchini
    squash
    Cheese Sauce

Stir together flour, baking powder, and salt. Combine milk, egg, and zucchini; add to dry ingredients and mix just till moistened. Drop from tablespoon into deep, hot fat (375°). Fry, a few at a time, for 3 or 4 minutes; drain. Spoon Cheese Sauce over. Makes 24 fritters.

Cheese Sauce: Melt 2 tablespoons butter or margarine; blend in 2 tablespoons all-purpose flour, ¼ teaspoon salt, and dash pepper. Add 1¼ cups milk all at once. Cook and stir till thickened and bubbly. Add ½ cup shredded sharp process American cheese and ½ cup shredded process Swiss cheese; stir till melted.

Zucchini, Chinese-Style

    2 slices bacon
    3 medium zucchini squash,
        scored and sliced diagonally
 1/4 cup chicken broth

      • • •

    2 teaspoons cornstarch
 1/2 teaspoon salt
    2 teaspoons cold water

Cook bacon till crisp; remove from skillet. Add sliced zucchini to bacon drippings in skillet; toss to coat. Pour chicken broth over zucchini. Cover and steam till squash is almost tender, about 4 to 5 minutes.

Blend cornstarch and salt with cold water; stir into zucchini mixture. Cook, stirring constantly, till mixture bubbles. Turn into serving dish; garnish with crisp-cooked, crumbled bacon. Makes 4 or 5 servings.

Zucchini with Walnuts

    1 pound zucchini squash, cut in
        1/2-inch slices
 1/3 cup sliced green onion
    2 tablespoons butter or margarine
    2 tablespoons dry sherry
 1/2 teaspoon salt
 1/4 cup walnut halves

In medium saucepan combine zucchini slices, green onion, and butter. Cook, uncovered, over low heat for 5 minutes. Stir in sherry and salt; cover and cook over low heat till vegetables are tender, 5 minutes more. Stir in walnuts; serve immediately. Serves 5 or 6.

Zucchini Supreme

    4 cups sliced zucchini squash
    1 medium onion, thinly sliced
        and separated into rings
    3 medium tomatoes, peeled and
        sliced
 1/2 cup chopped green pepper
    1 8-ounce package sliced process
        American cheese
    3 cups 1/2-inch caraway rye
        bread cubes
 1/4 cup butter or margarine, melted

Alternate layers of zucchini, onion, tomato, and green pepper in 13 1/2 x 8 3/4 x 1 3/4 -inch baking dish; season. Cut cheese slices in half diagonally; place atop casserole. Sprinkle with bread cubes; drizzle with butter.

Cover and bake at 350° for 45 minutes; uncover and bake till tender, about 15 minutes longer. Makes 8 to 10 servings.

Garden Vegetable Bowl

 1/4 cup butter or margarine
    4 cups sliced zucchini squash
        (about 1 pound)
 1 1/2 cups cut fresh, frozen, *or* drained,
        canned whole kernel corn
 1/2 cup chopped onion
 1/3 cup chopped green pepper

      • • •

 1/2 teaspoon salt
    1 tablespoon fresh, snipped dill
        or 1 teaspoon dried dillweed

Melt butter in skillet; add zucchini, corn, onion, and green pepper. Sprinkle with salt. Cover and cook, stirring occasionally, till vegetables are tender, about 10 to 12 minutes. Sprinkle with dill. Serves 4 to 6.

For a menu change-of-pace, substitute Nutmeg Whipped Squash for the mashed potatoes. (See *Acorn Squash* for recipe.)

Thinly slice zucchini teams up with tomato wedges and sliced mushrooms in a simple version of buttery Skillet Squash.

Steak and Zucchini Supper

        1 **pound round steak, cut in thin strips**
        1 **tablespoon salad oil**
        1 **10½-ounce can mushroom gravy**
    ½ **cup water**
    ½ **envelope spaghetti sauce mix with mushrooms (about 2 tablespoons)**
        3 **to 4 medium zucchini squash, cut in 1½-inch slices**
        Hot cooked noodles *or* rice

In a skillet quickly brown steak strips in hot salad oil. Add gravy, water, and spaghetti sauce mix; stir till well combined. Cover; cook over low heat for about 20 minutes, stirring occasionally. Add zucchini slices. Cover and continue cooking till zucchini is crisp-tender, about 10 to 12 minutes. Serve over noodles or rice. Makes 4 servings.

Winter squash

These are the late-harvested varieties most closely associated with the bounty of fall and Thanksgiving celebrations. The fully mature squash have hard rinds and seeds, neither of which is usually eaten.

Nutritional value: The long growing season of winter squash enables many nutrients to build up in this vegetable. Winter squash contain more calories than do summer squash (63 calories for one-half cup baked squash). The vibrant yellow color of the pulp is indicative of its excellent contribution of vitamin A. Winter squash is considered also to be a fair source of the B vitamin riboflavin.

Types of winter squash: The list of popular winter squash varieties is even more lengthy than the summer ones. These, too, are diverse in appearance and taste.

Acorn, also called Des Moines, or Table Queen, is one of the most popular of all squash varieties. It is easily identified by its acorn shape. Acorn squash usually varies from five to eight inches in length. The thin, smooth rind is a shiny deep green, parts of which change to orange and dull green in prolonged storage. The pale orange flesh turns to a brilliant yellow when cooked and is very tender, fairly dry, and sometimes fibrous.

Banana is elongated just as its name implies. This large squash often weighs as much as 12 pounds. The olive gray or creamy pink rind is fairly smooth and moderately thick. The light orange flesh is moderately dry and fine-textured.

Butternut may be 9 to 12 inches long with a cylindrical shape that is enlarged at the bottom third. The seed cavity is in this bulbous portion. The exterior is a light creamy brown or dark yellow, while the interior is orange and fine-textured.

Delicata or Sweet Potato is small like an acorn squash but oblong in shape. The thin rind is light yellow with green striping. The orange-colored pulp becomes tender and dry upon cooking.

Delicious is a top-shaped squash with the stem at the large end. It varies in length from 8 to 12 inches and in diameter from 8 to 10 inches. The slightly warted and ridged rind is dark green or bright orange-red, depending on the strain, and has stripes at the blossom end. The flesh is thick, yellow, and dry.

Hubbard has a globe shape and a fairly thick, tapered neck. The blossom end has a smaller taper. The bumpy, ridged rind may be dark bronze-green, blue-gray, or orange-red in color. The thick orange-yellow flesh is deliciously sweet.

Turban is turban-shaped at the blossom end. This large squash is 8 to 10 inches long and 12 to 15 inches in diameter. The extremely hard rind is thick and very warted. Probably the most colorful of squashes, its turban is blue and its base is a bright red-orange. The bright orange flesh cooks to a sweet, dry, and often fibrous product.

How to select and store: Select winter squash that are heavy for their size, have hard rinds, and good coloring and shaping for the variety. Rinds that are soft or tender are immature and lack flavor and texture. Peak harvesting seasons are in the fall, but packages of frozen winter squash are available all year long.

Winter squash are more stable to store than summer squash. If handled carefully to prevent bruising, they can be kept many months in a cool, dry place. Any cuts or bruises result in rapid decay.

How to prepare: Winter squash are usually washed, halved, and seeds and strings are removed before further treatment, although small varieties can be baked whole.

Small varieties, such as acorn squash, are left whole or are cut in halves or rings. Bake them in a shallow pan at 350°, cut sides down, for 35 to 40 minutes. Turn cut sides up and bake 20 to 25 minutes more. Cover the pan with foil the first half hour of baking to speed the cooking process. These squash may also be peeled, cubed, and cooked in a small amount of boiling, salted water. Cover and cook the squash till tender, about 15 minutes.

Large squash are either cut in serving-sized pieces or are peeled and cubed. Serving-sized pieces may be placed on a baking sheet, covered with foil, and baked at 350°. Hubbard squash requires about 1¼ hours of baking. When cooked, covered, in boiling, salted water, cubed squash should be done in 15 minutes.

How to use: Most squash lovers enjoy this vegetable in pieces or mashed. When left in a serving-sized piece, winter squash can be filled with a meat stuffing for a main dish. Simply fill the cavity with butter and brown sugar or honey, and it becomes a side dish.

Mashed squash can be dressed up with butter, pineapple, marshmallows, nuts, or raisins. Try allspice, basil, chives, cinnamon, ginger, or oregano for seasoning. (See also *Vegetable*.)

Apple-Filled Squash

      3 **acorn squash**
      2 **tablespoons butter or margarine, melted**
      1 **18-ounce can pie-sliced apples**
    ¾ **cup brown sugar**
      1 **teaspoon lemon juice**
    ¼ **teaspoon ground ginger**
      3 **tablespoons butter or margarine**

Halve squash lengthwise; remove seeds. Brush with melted butter and sprinkle with a little salt. Place, cut side down, in large baking dish. Bake at 350° for 35 minutes. Combine apples, brown sugar, lemon juice, and ginger.

Turn squash, cut side up, in baking dish. Fill centers with apple mixture. Dot with butter. Continue baking till squash is tender, 25 minutes more. If desired, sprinkle with ground cinnamon before serving. Serves 6.

Saucy Dilled Butternut

      4 **cups peeled, cubed butternut squash (about 1½ pounds)**
      2 **tablespoons sliced green onion with tops**
      1 **tablespoon butter or margarine**
    ½ **cup dairy sour cream**
      2 **tablespoons milk**
    ½ **teaspoon salt**
      Dash pepper
    ½ **teaspoon dried dillweed**

In saucepan cook squash in boiling, salted water till tender, about 10 minutes; drain well. Cook green onion in butter till tender. Blend in sour cream, milk, salt, and pepper. Heat, *but do not boil.* Arrange squash on serving plate; top with sour cream mixture. Sprinkle with dillweed. Makes 4 to 6 servings.

Squash Delight

2 medium acorn squash
½ cup diced, fully cooked ham
2 tablespoons chopped green pepper
2 tablespoons chopped celery
2 tablespoons butter or margarine
1½ tablespoons all-purpose flour
¾ cup milk
2 tablespoons sliced pimiento-stuffed green olives
2 hard-cooked eggs, chopped
½ teaspoon salt
Dash pepper
1 tablespoon butter or margarine, melted
⅓ cup fine dry bread crumbs

Cut squash in half; remove seeds. Bake, cut side down, in shallow pan at 350° for 35 to 45 minutes. Cook ham, green pepper, and celery in 2 tablespoons butter till tender.

Blend in flour; add milk all at once. Cook, stirring constantly, until mixture thickens and bubbles. Add olives, hard-cooked eggs, salt, and pepper. Spoon mixture into cavities of squash. Combine 1 tablespoon butter and bread crumbs; sprinkle over top. Bake at 350° for 15 minutes more. Makes 4 servings.

Squash Chips

Acorn squash
Salt
Ground ginger

Peel and seed squash. Slice tissue paper-thin as for potato chips. Soak in ice water for 1 hour. Drain and pat dry. Fry in deep, hot fat (360°) until brown. Drain on paper toweling; sprinkle squash with salt and ginger.

Delicata Bake

Quarter 2 delicata squash; seed. Bake in shallow pan at 350° till almost tender, about 40 minutes. Form 1 pound bulk pork sausage into 24 balls; brown in skillet. Drain.

Mix one 17-ounce can applesauce and 1 teaspoon ground cinnamon. Season squash with salt and pepper. Top squash with applesauce, then sausage. Bake 20 minutes more. Serves 8.

Squash Soufflé

Careful timing from oven to table is important—

3 pounds hubbard squash
1 cup milk
2 tablespoons butter or margarine
1 cup coarsely crushed, rich, round crackers (about 20 crackers)
2 tablespoons finely chopped, canned pimiento
1 teaspoon salt
1 teaspoon grated onion
Dash pepper
Dash ground nutmeg
2 well-beaten eggs

Cut unpeeled squash into 3- to 4-inch squares. In a saucepan cook the squash, uncovered, in a small amount of boiling, salted water till tender, about 20 to 25 minutes. Remove pulp and mash (about 2 cups); discard rind.

In large saucepan heat together milk and butter over low heat till butter melts. Add ¾ *cup* of the cracker crumbs; mix well. Add squash, pimiento, salt, onion, pepper, and nutmeg. Stir in eggs. Pour into 1-quart casserole; top with remaining ¼ cup crumbs. Bake at 350° till knife inserted just off-center comes out clean, about 1 hour. Garnish with additional pimiento strips, if desired. Serves 4 to 6.

Golden Squash Soup

Gives an autumn meal a different twist—

¼ cup chopped onion
2 tablespoons butter or margarine
2 tablespoons all-purpose flour
½ teaspoon salt
Dash pepper
Dash ground nutmeg
2 cups milk
1 cup chicken broth
1 cup cooked, mashed winter squash
2 tablespoons snipped parsley

Cook onion in butter till tender but not brown. Blend in flour, salt, pepper, and nutmeg. Stir in remaining ingredients; cook and stir till mixture comes to boiling. Serve at once; garnish with parsley sprigs and a sprinkle of nutmeg, if desired. Serves 3 or 4.